MOUNTAIN HEROES
PORTRAITS OF ADVENTURE

MOUNTAIN HEROES
PORTRAITS OF ADVENTURE

For Millie,

Good luck with your DofE...

HUW LEWIS-JONES

CONWAY

Published in association with
POLARWORLD

First published in Great Britain in 2011 by Conway, an imprint of Anova Books Company Ltd, 10 Southcombe Street, London W14 ORA, in association with Polarworld.

Designed by Liz House.
Volume and art direction by Huw Lewis-Jones.
Printed and bound by 1010 Printing International Ltd, China

Every effort has been made to seek permission to reproduce those images for which Conway and Polarworld do not hold the copyright. We are grateful to individuals who have assisted in this. Any omissions are entirely unintentional and corrections should be addressed to the Publisher.

FRONT COVER: Climbers make their final progress on the summit mushroom of Nevado Chopicalqui (6,350m), Cordillera Blanca, Peru, 2009. Although not technically demanding, the peak offers many aspiring mountaineers their first taste of an expedition at high altitude. Cover shot created by rising star of adventure and mountain photography, French alpinist Alexandre Buisse.

FRONT MONTAGE, pp. 6-7.
Top left to bottom right: Early alpinists pose on the challenging granite ridge of the Dent du Requin, 'the Shark's Tooth', now one of the most popular of the Chamonix Aiguilles; Kurt Diemberger on the summit of Shartse on its first ascent in 1974, photographed by his companion Hermann Warth; A party traverse a wild snow cornice on the Grand Combin, a rare glass lantern slide by the Abraham Brothers; Temba Sherpa below the summit of Baruntse Peak, 2009; Everest veteran Tom Hornbein at home in Colorado, 2011; 'Sun and Wind' by Polish mountaineer-photographer Bogdan Jankowski; Alex Lowe leads some tricking aid climbing, shot by Gordon Wiltsie, Great Sail Peak, Baffin Island, 1998; Glen Denny with camera on the Mazatlan Ledge, the second exploration ascent of the North American Wall on El Capitan, shot by his companion Tom Frost, 1964; 'Ladies and their Guides', the Mer de Glace, Mont Blanc, by Charnaux Frères, 1886; Dougal Haston tackles Everest's Hillary Step, thick with monsoon snow, during his successful summit attempt with Doug Scott, 1975; Doug Tompkins puts up a new route on Mount Fitzroy in 1968 – accompanied by Yvon Chouinard and photographer Chris Jones – and he would soon make his company The North Face world famous; Denis Urubko and Simone Moro take in the first rays of sun at 7,600m on the first winter ascent of Gasherbrum II, 2011; Hard British climber Ben Moon, by Nigel Millard, 2011; Everest Expedition team member steps across a crevasse in the East Rongbuk Glacier, by W.R. Smyth-Windham, 1936; Jamling, son of Sherpa Tenzing Norgay, as an eight-year-old boy at the Himalayan Mountaineering Institute camp, 1973; Hildegard Diemberger, daughter of renowned mountaineer Kurt, a respected researcher of Tibetan culture, Cambridge, 2011.

REAR MONTAGE, pp. 286-87.
Top left to bottom right: Famed for his mountain élan and technical expertise, Italian-born alpinist Walter Bonatti adjusts his snow goggles; Himalayan pioneer, American George Lowe, 'still at it' at the age of sixty-six, Eldorado Canyon, 2011; Pierre Mazeaud makes his way toward the summit of Everest during the first French ascent, 1978; The mountains of Baruntse reflected in the glasses of Australian mountaineer Robert Rich, 2009; Corey Rich on photo assignment for The North Face, shot by Todd Offenbacher, Cordillera Blanca, Peru, 2004; A young Galen Rowell, before he picked up a camera to become one of the most celebrated outdoor photographers of his generation, by Glen Denny, Yosemite, 1964; Inspiring young German photographer-alpinist Thomas Senf on the summit of Mount Ulvetanna, Queen Maud Land, by Alexander Ruchkin, 2010; A young Quechua girl in the Santa Cruz Valley of the Cordillera Blanca, Peru weaves a spell on Cory Richards; Famed mountain photographer Ed Cooper climbing the Angel Crack, Tumwater Canyon, in the spring of 1960; Ed Webster enjoying morning tea at 7,500m on the Kangshung Face of Everest, during its first ascent to the South Col, by Stephen Venables, 1988; Heinrich Harrer cooks during the first ascent of the Eiger North Face, 1938; Ski-alpinists Tomas Olsson and Tormod Granheim moving together on the Cosmiques Ridge, Chamonix; Ecologist Adam Watson gives a wry smile, Cairngorms, 2011; 'Hot Snow', skier Rudi Gertsch by Bruno Engler, Mount Norquay, 1966; Leo Houlding suffers as he tries to sleep during his ascent of Mount Asgard, Baffin Island, by Alastair Lee, 2009; Sherpa guide, by Cory Richards, 2009.

REAR PAGE: A high-altitude Khumbu porter greets photographer Claudia Lopez, Baruntse base camp, Nepal, 2009.

ISBN: 9781844861392

polarworld

www.anovabooks.com
www.conwaypublishing.com
www.polarworld.co.uk

PREVIOUS PAGE: Cory Richards 'after the avalanche' and lucky to be alive, Gasherbrum II, 2011. He describes the scene: 'I was still partially buried. My main camera had been torn from my grasp, so I was left with a little point-and-shoot. My face was cold, but the tears were very warm, an emphatic assurance that I was not dead. The sound of the shutter brought me back to life, speeding warp-speed through a tunnel of emotion. I was lucky to be there at the surface – not buried 100m deep in a tomb of snow'.

RIGHT: A group of early alpinists clamber to the summit of a glacial serac, French Alps, 1890.

CONTENTS

LEFT: Mountain guide Rick Potter leads his partner Martina Palm up the Aiguilles Marbrées, Mont Blanc massif, before the lens of respected alpine photographer John Norris.

FOLLOWING PAGE: Steve House free-climbing the Italian Route on the South-West Face of Taulliraju (5,830m) in the heart of Peru's Cordillera Blanca, photographed by his partner Marko Prezelj in 2005. Marko and Steve bivied in an ice cave under the pillar cornice, before pushing for the summit ridge, castellated in towers of wind-sculpted snow. When the great French climber Lionel Terray conquered the summit for the first time in 1956 he wrote, 'never, perhaps, in the whole history of mountaineering, has the ascent of a peak been such sheer hard work'.

FACING THE SUMMIT

Mountains and the journeys we make in them help clean the mind and replenish the soul. The mountains become your friends, your companions through life, constant and yet still demanding your attention. Your eyes are always lifted to the horizon, remembering previous freedoms or scouring for new routes. Memories are made of challenges overcome, storms survived, sunlight celebrated and companions recalled. In the mountains, we have truly found life.

JOHN MCCARTHY, 2011

When I think of mountaineering with four cylinders of oxygen on one's back and a mask over one's face – well, it loses its charm.

GEORGE MALLORY, in a letter to a friend, 1922

Whatever you can do, or dream you can do, begin it.
Boldness has genius, power, and magic in it!

WILLIAM H. MURRAY, 1951

FOREWORD
FACING THE SUMMIT
SIR CHRIS BONINGTON

We gazed across a frozen lake up a wide valley cloaked in snow. Our objective lay ten miles off in the distance. Black rocky crags and ramparts of ice shrouded in clouds. It was magnificent, frightening and beautiful. To two sixteen year olds, in the real mountains for the first time, it was our own Mount Everest. We were as excited and as full of awe as I'm sure George Mallory and his compatriots must have been on that first recce in 1921.

This was our first glimpse of Snowdon after hitchhiking from our homes in London hoping to climb it. We had bought hobnailed army boots and cut down old school macs. It turned out to be one of the hardest winters in years. Having hitched a lift to Pen y Pass, we followed some people who looked like *real* climbers up a snow-covered track, to be swept in an avalanche when about half way up. Fortunately we weren't hurt, though did retreat. Anton hitched home soon afterwards, but I was captivated by everything that had happened that day. I stayed on at the Capel Curig Youth Hostel and ventured out again onto the hills. That night I listened to the talk of climbers and walkers. I was enthralled and my misadventure sewed the seeds of a passion that has filled my life ever since.

On getting home I found a friend of the family who took me climbing at Harrison Rocks, a little sandstone outcrop to the south of London. I discovered that it came easily to me, and I also found that it gave me a sense of euphoria that I had never before experienced. I went on to climb in Wales and Scotland in my holidays, meeting up with people who knew as little as I did. We had our adventures and narrow scrapes, every climb giving a sense of discovery. I was serving an apprenticeship that was to stand me in good stead in later years, first in the Alps and then on the Greater Ranges. What I gained from it has remained much the same through all these years and I suspect is similar to that experienced by many of my fellow climbers.

It starts with the sheer joy of physical expression of using one's agility and strength to achieve an objective, the same experienced by any athlete, but added to this, is the thrill of risk – of staking one's life on one's judgment and ability. We are doing this in the midst

'Mutual Assistance', gentlemanly climbing on the Matterhorn, from an original glass lantern slide from Edward Whymper's personal set for his lecture *My Scrambles Amongst the Alps*, 1893.

of magnificent wild scenery and that sense of wonder will never leave us. Exploration is also an important element, both of the geographical sense – be it a new route on a Lakeland crag or the way up an unclimbed Himalayan peak – or in the *exploration* of the self, in stretching limits or getting a deeper level of self awareness. There are friendships developed and made that much stronger because of the intensity of the

The greatest joy in climbing is to be in charge of one's own destiny, to be out in front, making the decisions, balancing risk.

experience and the level of trust placed in each other. Finally, there is that element of competition; to be the first to put up a route or reach a summit, to enjoy the approval, even respect, of our peers and perhaps the general public. Most of us have that competitive edge, some to a much greater degree than others and the secret is to keep it in balance.

People have climbed and travelled in the mountains since earliest times – a Bronze Age hunter left his spear on the summit of the Riffelhorn (2,928m) – but these early ventures were no higher than necessary for hunting game or perhaps crystals. Mountain passes provided routes for migration, trade or invasion. Summits had been reached for both aesthetic and scientific reasons. Hadrian climbed or perhaps was carried up Mount Etna in the second century AD to see the sun rise, the Romantic poets wandered the hills of the Lake District in the late eighteenth century, whilst man of science Saussure offered a reward for the first man to reach the summit of Mont Blanc for the sake of research. It was won by Paccard, a Chamonix doctor, and the crystal hunter Balmat. The prize might have provided a catalyst but I suspect the of thrill of exploration, the stimulus of risk combined with competition to be the first were also factors.

It was only in the nineteenth century that mountaineering became a sport for its own sake with a code of practice and structure of its own. It started with a small group of individuals from the United Kingdom with the money and leisure to spend comparatively long periods peak bagging in the Alps. They employed local guides from the start but the relationship tended to be one of partnership on the mountain though the social divides were observed in the valley. It was well named the Golden Age – it was one of exciting exploration and discovery as progressively harder peaks were climbed and techniques evolved. You

started your walk to the climb from the valley, there were no mountain huts, and gear and clothing were rudimentary. The first climbing club to be founded was The Alpine Club in London in 1857.

The way people climbed and the rules they set themselves evolved, often with fierce controversy, from the very beginning. It was essentially the same human drive that has influenced mankind's evolution over the centuries – the spirit of adventure and innovation often in conflict with institutional conservatism. One of the first arguments was over the use of guides. The greatest joy in climbing is to be in charge of one's own destiny, to be out in front, making the decisions, balancing risk. In taking on a guide, one is delegating or at least abrogating that process to another. Alfred Mummery, for example, was one of the most important innovative climbers of the late nineteenth century. He started his climbing with guides but was frustrated by its limitations and began climbing guideless, making a series of technically challenging new routes. He lost his life in 1895 in an attempt that was years ahead of its time, on Nanga Parbat one of the steeper and more difficult 8,000m peaks in the Himalaya.

Meanwhile, climbing was spreading across Europe. Climbers from Germany and the Austrian Empire, with the dramatic rock peaks of the Austrian Alps and Dolomites on their doorsteps, were developing techniques using pitons to climb their steep limestone walls. A great divide in ethics developed between the British who practised their rock climbing skills on the relatively small crags of the United Kingdom, rejecting the use of artificial aids and the Central and Eastern Europeans who used pitons. Ironically, one of the greatest free climbers of all time was Paul Preuss – a Munich-based climber of the early twentieth century – who eschewed the use of artificial aids except in emergencies. In a way, it was the conflict between the pragmatic and the idealistic, with the ideal being to stretch human ability to its limit, to approach the mountains with the minimum force and to leave the minimum trace of one's progress. In this respect, the ultimate is to climb solo without the use of any artificial aids – Paul Preuss did exactly that.

In the period between the two World Wars, climbing developed in two separate ways – the British taking a strong ethical stance against the use of artificial aids whilst in Germany, Austria and Italy climbing standards rocketed with all the big North Walls of the Alps falling to different teams with the use of some artificial aids, but also being climbed in a bold and daring manner.

RIGHT: A climber inches his way up the formidable West Face of Yosemite's Leaning Tower, 1965. The photograph is by Glen Denny, who with Warren Harding completed the impressive first ascent in October 1961. Harding's route roused the ire of the campfire critics, on just how many bolts are justified to summit a route. Harding maintained that he was free to choose his own manner of climbing, and 'everyone else can go to hell'. Nonetheless, the ascent of the overhanging West Face was big news, attracting wide television coverage, as climbing entered the media mainstream. Royal Robbins, arch critic of Harding, made the second ascent, solo, some eighteen months later. Maybe it was something of a statement, but it was also a brilliant undertaking.

Often these climbs, sometimes unreasonably, were castigated by members of the British climbing establishment as reckless and politically motivated. At the same time climbers were venturing into the

We were climbing to the limit over a long period of time exposed to both objective dangers and climbing mistakes – I lost all too many friends on these expeditions over the years.

Himalayas to try the highest peaks. Here you could see the development of the siege-style approach using high-altitude porters, set camps and fixed ropes but at the same time a lightweight approach was being developed, led by Eric Shipton and Bill Tilman, though both were prepared to compromise when it came to Everest.

The end of the Second World War saw a social revolution making it much easier for working-class lads, in the Northern Industrial cities of the United Kingdom, to get on the crags. There was a bit more money, the five-day week and a changed perception of what could be achieved. Joe Brown and Don Whillans, young plumbers from Salford, were at the forefront, starting on the gritstone crags on their doorsteps, venturing further afield to Snowdonia, the Lakes and the Scottish Highlands. Soon, they moved on to the Alps to establish new routes, embracing British free climbing ethics but using the much-maligned piton where necessary. They both went on to the Himalaya; Joe making the first ascent of Kangchenjunga with George Band, a representative of the Oxbridge old-school, which was also adapting to modern climbing methods, whilst Don went to Tirich Mir with Wilfrid Noyce, a summit deep in the Hindu Kush. He would turn his considerable skills to the South Face of Annapurna, making the first ascent with Dougal Haston, and two attempts on the South West Face of Everest.

This was the mountaineering world that I stumbled into. As a rock climber I repeated some of the Brown-Whillans routes in Snowdonia, and then, on venturing into the Alps with Hamish MacInnes, at the time one of the leading all round mountaineers in Scotland, kicked off with an abortive attempt on the North Wall of the Eiger. We went on to make the first British ascent of the South West Pillar of the Dru, where we inadvertently met up with Whillans – the start of another fruitful climbing partnership that led to our first ascent of the Central Pillar of Frêney.

In this respect I had the privilege of taking part in an exciting era of British climbing in the Alps and then the Himalayas, when the world's leading alpinists were taking techniques refined in the Alps to climbing technically challenging big walls and faces on 8,000 peaks. The stories of the heroism, and tragedy, of many of these innovative mountain men are sewn throughout this book. In this, I must commend our editor Huw Lewis-Jones in bringing this project to life; his skill and gentle hand has created for us a vibrant and meaningful vision of man and the mountains – a photographic tribute to our shared love of these wild places, and our admiration for those who look upwards to the hills.

In the early 1970s, the South Face of Annapurna and then the South West Face of Everest became the leading objects of my ambition and attention. They were both hugely challenging climbing problems and ones of logistics and planning as well. At that time, I could not conceive of using 'alpine-style' tactics – of packing a rucksack at the bottom of one of these huge faces and keeping going till we reached the top – though on Annapurna there are now several routes that have yielded to these tactics. It's all part of a natural and healthy evolution. I found an intellectual fascination in the intricate planning and execution of our expeditions to these big Himalayan Faces, of helping a large team of climbers who are strong individualists to work together for a common end, to sustain the flow of supplies from camp to camp, of reacting to the inevitable crises that dictated changes of plan. But there was a human cost as well. We were climbing to the limit over a long period of time exposed to both objective dangers and climbing mistakes – I lost all too many friends on these expeditions over the years. It is something we can't really justify but just accept that the fascination of climbing and stretching the limits is so great that it is something we can't give up. It is a pleasure to see familiar faces, of friends gone but not forgotten, within the pages here.

As we were tackling these big routes, others were developing alpine-style techniques on the 8,000 peaks. Reinhold Messner was at the forefront of this revolution, making the first ascent of a new route, on Gasherbrum I with Peter Habeler in 1975 and then in 1979 reaching the summit of Everest without supplementary oxygen as part of a conventional expedition. Having made a new route climbing solo up the Diamir Face of Nanga Parbat that same year, he made the first and only genuine solo ascent of Everest, climbing it from the North during the monsoon when he was the only person on the mountain. He went on to be the first man to climb all fourteen 8,000 peaks.

Today, climbing has spread into many different strands. On rock, 'trad' climbing, as it has always been pursued in the United Kingdom, has become more sophisticated with complex camming devices and wedges replacing the inserted chock stones of my youth, but the principle remains the same – you place rather than hammer in your protection and the second removes it and little trace is left of your passing. Sport climbing on the Continent with pre-placed bolts was a natural evolution from the use of pitons that had always been present. It enabled climbers to reduce the risk level to a minimum to enable them to stretch their gymnastic ability to the limit. There is room for both approaches but it seems a pity to see routes up lines abounding in cracks and natural placements, protected by regular bolts placed neatly at two-metre intervals. Today there is a healthy move on the Continent to get back into trad climbing with its stimulus of calculated risk and art of placing protection. Climbers like Leo Houlding on the cutting edge are exploring new limits, speed climbing, BASE-jumping from the top of their climbs and taking solo routes to ever more extreme limits.

In the Great Ranges, with the growth of commercial expeditions, there is a focus on Everest and the 8,000 giants, with fixed ropes being run out to the summits and comparatively inexperienced climbers being guided, sometimes hauled, to the top. The media have always been attracted to easily measured superlatives – the quickest, oldest, youngest and so on – and it is these expeditions that tend get into the papers and on television. At the same time, however, the leading

ABOVE: The ice-axe of Andrew Irvine who, with Mallory, went missing on Everest in 1924. It was recovered in 1933. His body has never been found. Noel Odell had been watching their progress high on the North Ridge rock-steps that fateful day, 8 June 1924, before 'the whole fascinating vision vanished, enveloped in cloud'.

LEFT: A Sherpa ferries gear up a rope ladder in the Khumbu Icefall, 1953 Everest Expedition, by Alfred Gregory.

OVERLEAF: Packing case from the 1922 Everest Expedition, which gathered in Darjeeling before the long trek overland through Tibet. It look some four hundred yaks and a team of fifty porters to carry all their loads to base camp in the Rongbuk Valley.

Climbers who ascended the Riffelberg in August 1894, a party that included the renowned mountain guides Christian Klucker and Ulrich Almer.

Chris Bonington nears the West Summit of Shivling (6,501m), during its first ascent, 1983.

Klucker Damion V. Almer My Gerald Joseph Gentinetta

Photo Howard Barrell

The Rijiel about Cp 5 (August. 1894)

reaching its base we realized it was too steep, too big and that we probably had neither the ability, gear, nor neck to try it. On our way back to our base camp some five miles away we passed below another peak called Shivling. Its west summit hadn't been climbed and it looked challenging but feasible. We decided to go for it.

That night we walked up the moraine above us to try and make out a route through the crumbling walls that formed the mountain's outer defenses. We spied an avalanche chute leading up to a sheer icefall but there seemed to be a small gully that escaped from beneath it. We set out the next morning with fifteen-kilo sacks, and yes, the gully did enable us to escape the avalanche chute, get a safe bivouac site and reach a higher glacier basin where we had another bivouac. From there we were able to reach a shapely rock ridge leading to the summit some 1,000m above. Two more bivouacs, and some hard and interesting climbing, took us to the crest of the ridge just below the top. As darkness fell, the clouds boiled up around us, giving the threat of a change in the weather, but during the night it had cleared, offering us at first light magical views of the surrounding mountains stretched below us.

climbers from around the world, frequently ignored by the media, are tackling ever harder, longer and more committed routes on the world's most remote mountains.

I have always been fascinated by the unknown, finding ways up unclimbed peaks. This is what I have been doing for much of the time since leading my big expeditions. Perhaps my most memorable and enjoyable experience was in 1983, with a long-term climbing mate of mine, Jim Fotheringham. We had set out to make the first ascent of the huge West Face of Kedarnath Dome in the Garhwal Himalaya. On

One last bivouac, a rope-length's climb to a perfect, pointed snow summit with room for only one person at a time and then a scary retreat down the other side, for we reckoned the way we had come up was too dangerous to descend. Six days of wonderful climbing, with the outcome always uncertain, spontaneous action, feeling the rock with our hands, good times with a good mate, and all of this among magnificent mountains. To me, this is what climbing is all about.

Cumbria, 2011

THE MOUNT EVEREST
EXPEDITION
DARJEELING

MOUNTAINS IN AN UNCERTAIN WORLD

Something hidden. Go and find it. Go and look behind the Ranges –
Something lost behind the Ranges. Lost and waiting for you. Go!

RUDYARD KIPLING, *The Explorer,* **1898**

I will lift up mine eyes unto the hills, From whence cometh my help.

Psalm **121:1**

Everything tests man, say the Gods,
So that he, robustly nurtured, learns to give thanks for all,
And understands the freedom,
To set out where he will.   **FRIEDRICH HÖLDERLIN, 1826**

COMMENTARY

MOUNTAINS IN AN UNCERTAIN WORLD

JACK D. IVES AND BRUNO MESSERLI

Daunting rock pinnacles, knife-edged arêtes, cascading glaciers, and explosive avalanches of blinding snow – and a team of grim-faced climbers risking everything to bag another summit – this is perhaps the conventional image conjured up by the word *mountains.* It is a vignette that might recall upper sections of the Alps, the Andes, or the Himalaya. But these lofty regions represent only a small fraction of our total mountain terrain. Sadly, images of the heroic age are now too often supplanted by the reality of warfare in the mountains, abused natural resources, impoverishment of mountain peoples, and the environmental and economic disruption caused by climate change.

Mountains are found on every continent, from the equator to as close to the poles as land exists. As a single great ecosystem, they encompass the most extensive known array of landforms, climates, flora, and fauna, as well as human cultures. From a geological point of view they comprise the most complex and dynamic of the Earth's underlying structures that are still in the process of formation as the numerous volcanoes and frequent earthquakes testify.

No surprise then, that it is hard to limit the mountains to simple definition. Ask the people of northern England and Wales – perhaps shepherds at high pasture in the Lake District, or farmers at work in the shadow of Snowdonia's imposing crags – and they would all affirm that they live among mountains, yet altitudes there barely exceed 1,000m. Peasants of southern Peru or Tibetan nomads likewise would be classed as mountain people; their local surroundings exceed 4,000m and yet may be as flat as the prairies of central Canada. The well known German mountain geographer of the twentieth century, Carl Troll, described the highest parts of equatorial Indonesia, for example, as 'high mountains without a high-mountain landscape' – unlike the remote, challenging, conventionally 'mountainous' *Hochgebirge* of popular imagination. It's clear that the diversity of the mountain world defies easy categorization.

PREVIOUS PAGE: The Cosmiques Ridge and the sprawling North Face of Mont Blanc du Tacul (4,248m), Chamonix, captured by rising star of French mountain photography Alexandre Buisse, 2008.

LEFT: Marko Prezelj's companions descending from the Aiguille du Midi after several days of climbing, and fresh snow, in the French Alps, 2009.

ABOVE: Professors
Jack D. Ives and Bruno
Messerli, renowned
mountain advocates and
educators. Portraits by
celebrated German-
Canadian photographer
Hans-Ludwig Blohm
and German alpinist
Thomas Senf.

ABOVE RIGHT: Nightfall
above Everest base
camp, by Cory Richards,
2009.

Academics today take a pragmatic approach to the problems of definition. It is broadly accepted that mountains occupy more than a fifth of the world's land surface, and that they provide the direct support-base for more than a tenth of humanity. When natural resources, including water, minerals, forests, grazing land, and hydro-power are considered, more than half of humankind depends to some degree on the largesse of the mountains. To this must be added their pivotal role as repositories of cultural and biological diversity, their value as amenity and tourism assets, and their lamentable implication in a panoply of natural and human catastrophes.

We no longer have the luxury of viewing mountains simply as spectacular scenery or as goals to be attained by strenuous physical effort. They are certainly special regions, but they are places where communities live and have lived for centuries, and where environmental sustainability is a matter of survival not just to those who live there but to the many millions more for whom they are just a hazy blue line on the horizon.

In the far distant past when the first societies were evolving, mountains were the object of veneration, inspiration, and even fear; they had a profound influence on the emergence of many religions, including those that survive today. This spiritual approach to mountains fortunately persists and has been examined by Edwin Bernbaum in his outstanding work *Sacred Mountains of the World*, where he argues for its essential relevance in any effort to achieve environmental stability.

With the dawn of the eighteenth-century European Enlightenment, fear began to ebb and the quest for inspiration led to the 'Golden Age' of alpinism,

landscape art, poetry, and the privileged tourism of the era. The identification of end points, or turning points, in the development of alpinism is highly subjective, but must include Alfred Wills's ascent of the Wetterhorn in 1854 and Edward Whymper's ascent of the Matterhorn in 1865, the Aiguille du Grépon, first climbed in 1881 by Mummery, Bergener, and Venetz; the Austrian-German assault of Eiger's *Nordwand* in 1938; Maurice Herzog and Louis Lachenal's gruelling adventure on Annapurna in 1950, the first successful attempt on an 8,000m peak; or John Hunt's triumphant expedition in 1953 which put Edmund Hillary and Tenzing Norgay on the summit of Mount Everest. Mountaineering extended beyond the Alps to high mountains throughout the world, and remains a vital source of character formation, challenge, and creative thought.

Today most people maintain that mountain peaks are never *conquered* – because (to paraphrase George Mallory's quip), they are still *there*, unfazed and unaccommodating. We may climb, we may litter, but we always leave. It is perhaps symbolic that Hillary rated as his proudest accomplishment the building of schools and hospitals in the Khumbu. Nevertheless, electrifying feats of mountaineering still unfold, as many of the portraits in this volume testify.

Tourism ushered in a new engagement between humans and mountains. It began in the Alps as an elitist diversion at the height of the British Empire and, with the rapid increase in accessibility during the twentieth century, merged into mass tourism and trekking all over the world. In the early years following the second world war this rapid growth of tourism was greeted

with great anticipation as one likely solution to world poverty, particularly among mountain communities. That optimism has faded and the impacts have had mixed results at best. Nevertheless, the increased contact with hitherto isolated subsistent people has introduced a sharper awareness of alternatives to the frantic pace of life in the 'outer' world – an interest in regions characterized by the ingenuity, courage, persistence, and dignity of mountain dwellers from whom we all have much to learn.

Exploration and scientific research unfolded as another dimension in our awareness of mountains, also linked chronologically to the development of alpinism and nineteenth-century tourism in the Alps. The close association of mountaineering and research is exemplified by many of the early scholars, some included in this book: Horace-Bénédict de Saussure, Sveinn Pálsson, Alexander von Humboldt, Jean Louis Agassiz, John Tyndall, among others. Much of this early scientific development was motivated by intellectual curiosity, which certainly needs no justification, although imperial and national overtones were to emerge. Nevertheless, glaciology and tectonic geology unfold as vital academic disciplines.

In recent years, while tourism and adventure among the high places have continued to flourish, a new approach defines the ambitions of those working hard to protect and preserve our mountain world. It might now be characterized, rather prosaically, as 'applied research'.

In the late 1960s concerns about environmental deterioration were beginning to surface from within various international agencies and non-governmental organizations. World-wide collaboration began to appear, especially following the 1972 Stockholm Conference on the Human Environment. A flashpoint was reached with the International Geographical Union's 1968 decision to recognize Carl Troll's contributions to mountain geography; he was granted his 'personal' Commission on High-Altitude Geoecology. The United Nations Educational, Scientific, and Cultural Organization (UNESCO) quickly perceived the utility of Troll's IGU

In recent years, while tourism and adventure among the high places have continued to flourish, a new approach defines the ambitions of those working hard to protect and preserve our mountain world.

commission for the development of its own mountain project within the new Man and the Biosphere (MAB) Programme; MAB Project 6 was launched in 1973 as a 'study of the impact of human activities on mountain ecosystems'. The IGU commission's name was subsequently changed to 'Mountain Geoecology' and many of its objectives were incorporated into the newly created United Nations University project: 'Highland-Lowland Interactive Systems' in 1978.

The quarterly journal *Mountain Research and Development* was founded in 1981 by the International Mountain Society. Its mission statement emphasizes the progression from purely academic mountain research into the international political arena as 'applied mountain geoecology'. It called upon all of us, 'to strive for a better

ABOVE: Temba Sherpa, below the summit of Nepal's Baruntse Peak (7,168m), and one of the expedition's porters back at base camp, by Columbian mountaineer-creative, the lovely Claudia Lopez, 2009.

OVERLEAF: Rewarded with clear weather after a winter ascent, Stephan Siegrist and Ann Eylin Sigg approach the summit of the Eiger, 2010.

balance between mountain environment, development of resources, and the well-being of mountain peoples'. Today, this message is more important than ever.

The few of us involved at the onset of the current mountain political agenda felt we were voices crying in the wilderness. As the movement for appropriate development gained strength, however, it soon faced a quandary. At the beginning of the 1970s the

Mountains, the world over, endure in all their stark beauty and mystery. Lifting their summits to the sky, they inspire and challenge us…

world's news media were suddenly inflamed with alarmist reports relating primarily to the Himalaya. The mountain paradigm of the day quickly became entrenched. There was an insistence that rapid population growth amongst 'ignorant' Himalayan farmers was leading to massive deforestation and construction of unstable agricultural terraces on steep slopes. It was assumed that monsoon downpours were washing away these foolhardy constructions and were causing countless landslides and catastrophic flooding and siltation across Gangetic India and Bangladesh.

In 1979 it was even predicted that all accessible forest cover in Nepal would be eliminated by the year 2000. We termed this, for convenience, the 'Theory of Himalayan Environmental Degradation' and devoted all available research capacity to determine the facts, eventually exposing its projections to exaggeration and misguided emotion.

The combined activities of the United Nations University, IGU, and the International Mountain Society led to close contact with Maurice Strong who, in 1990, was appointed Secretary-General of the United Nations Conference on Environment and Development (UNCED), more popularly known as the Earth Summit that convened in Rio de Janeiro in 1992. Together with the ardent support of Jean-François Giovannini and the Swiss Development Cooporation, the efforts of the now rapidly growing group of concerned scholars successfully stage-managed the insertion of the 'mountain chapter' into AGENDA 21 of the Rio Earth Summit.

Following Rio, 'mountain well-being' moved from the back stage of world political and environmental attention to front and centre. This climaxed at the United Nations headquarters in New York on 11 December 2001 when the International Year of Mountains was launched. Under the adept leadership of the UN Food and Agricultural Organization (FAO), the designated lead agency for the mountain chapter, mountain environmental and development problems began to receive widespread attention. Many NGOs

were set up, with Bern University becoming a major focal point, and now 11 December is celebrated each year as the 'Day of the Mountains'. Although progress has slowed down in many regions, the twentieth anniversary of the Rio Summit in 2012 offers an opportune juncture to regenerate momentum. This is the time for the world mountaineering community to come together as advocates and ambassadors for the mountains we all love – the mountains we all *need*.

The reality of climate change is now undeniable – the Earth *is* warming and the leading indicators have been decisively manifested in the mountains and the polar regions. However, the urge to exaggerate and over-dramatise, to cry death and destruction, remains a serious problem that hampers effective progress and understanding. The Himalaya, once again, feature prominently in the press, specifically regarding the contention that large numbers of melt-water lakes are forming on the surfaces and in front of retreating Himalayan glaciers and will inevitably burst, bringing death and destruction to hundreds of millions downstream. To this has been added the threat of the Ganges withering to a mere seasonal stream. Lack of good data is one of the primary constraints on proper evaluation.

Mountains are among the least known and least understood areas of the world. Unreasonable and unsupportable statements propagated by the world-wide news media are dangerous, yet complacency about the shared dangers and threats and the very real pressures that our mountain world faces must be avoided.

Our near-total lack of hydro-climatological information from vast glacierized regions such as the Himalaya and Andes needs to be corrected so that real evaluations can be made from a reliable database. The countries concerned and the relevant international agencies are beginning to move ahead to fill this need. The first tasks, however, must be to reduce the burden of conflict and to facilitate the involvement of mountain people in the management of their local resources and in development of relations with society at large. The ongoing problems of poverty and warfare are so formidable that they cannot be solved in the short term. But we must pursue them relentlessly; we must have *hope*.

We know, in the words of a former mayor of Narvik, that 'the mountains wait'. Theodor Broch was writing of the invasion of his town in 1940. The spiritual presence of the mountains of Arctic Norway inspired the local people to withstand five years of horror during the second world war. Mountains, the world over, endure in all their stark beauty and mystery. Lifting their summits to the sky, they inspire and challenge us, prompting our determination and fortifying the courage of the generations who will follow us.

Ottawa and Bern, 2011

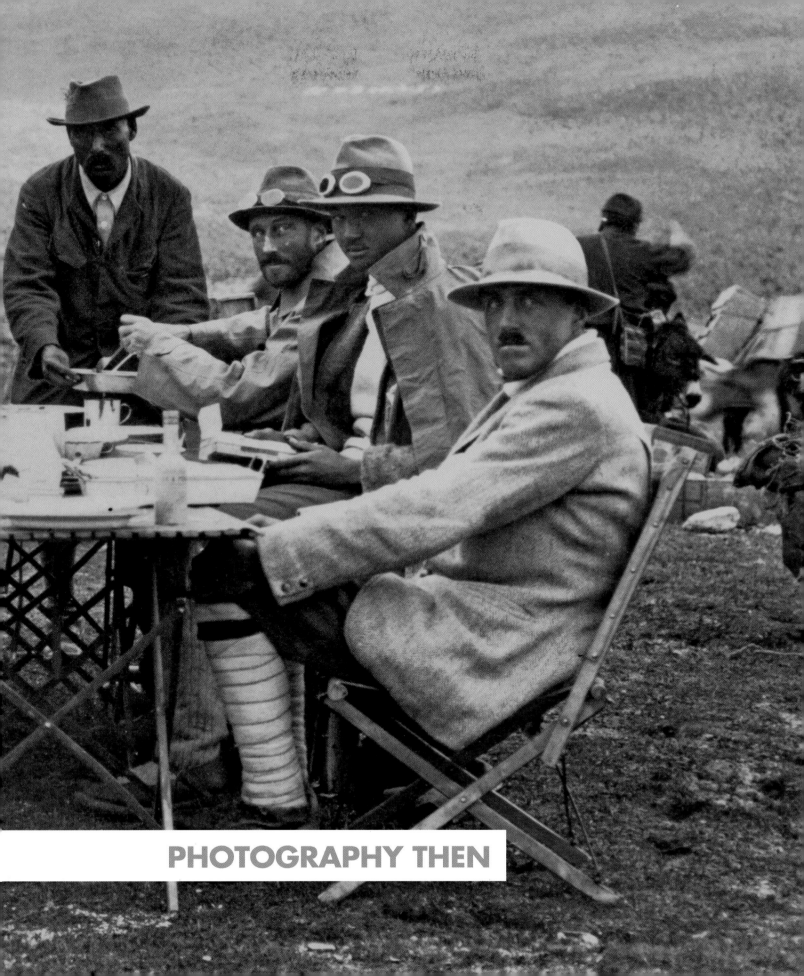

Great things are done when men and mountains meet;
This is not done by jostling in the street.

WILLIAM BLAKE, *a poem in his notebook*, **1808**

There is a region of heart's desire
        free for the hand that wills;
land of the shadow and haunted spire,
land of the silvery glacier fire,
land of the cloud and the starry choir,
        magical land of hills;
loud with the crying winds and streams,
thronged with the fancies and fears of dreams.

GEOFFREY WINTHROP YOUNG, 1927

The authentic Englishman is one whose delight is to wander all day, amongst rocks and snow; and to come as near breaking his neck as his conscience will allow.

SIR LESLIE STEPHEN, 1871

ESSAY

PHOTOGRAPHY THEN
HUW LEWIS-JONES

Often it is best to begin in the most obvious place. It is 29 May 1953. Two figures stagger up a final crest of snow, before, at long last there is nothing left to climb. 'The whole world stretched out below us', Edmund Hillary would later describe. He carries his camera inside his shirt to keep it warm. He reaches for it and cranks out some frames before he is happy with the result. His partner Tenzing Norgay lifts his ice-axe to the sky; on its shaft the flags of Britain, Nepal, the United Nations and India whip in the breeze, flying in the thin air at the highest spot on earth. These friends are the first men ever to reach this sacred place. They savour the moment.

They would soon descend 'to earth, to fame, adulation, and the tumultuous press of the crowds', but for this glorious hour no one in the world – not even their fellow expedition climbers – knew precisely where they were. In a gesture of private joy, Tenzing places a packet of biscuits, a toy cat, a pencil and a handful of lollies into a hole in the snow as a gift to the Gods who live on the summit. Hillary meanwhile wheels around taking a series of shots in all directions, proof of their position, higher than all others. Vast mountains appear to kneel far below them; great ranges march off into the distance. Without photos, he had been told, would anyone have believed it?

It makes sense to start our photographic journey at the very top, though its not all downhill from here. The first reports of the ascent arrived in London to coincide with the coronation of Queen Elizabeth II and news of this grand exploit acted as a tonic, to an empire in decline. From newspaper souvenirs to cinema screens, motivational posters and porcelain mugs, t-shirts and tea towels, to billboards and banknotes, this photograph has travelled widely, taking on a life of its own. Exemplifying the spirit of success and achievement, is has become an icon. It is certainly the most famous mountain portrait of them all and perhaps one of the definitive images of the twentieth century.

A leader in *The Guardian* on 3 June 1953 described the ascent as a 'timely and brilliant jewel in the Queen's diadem', but was unsure that it would have a lasting value. 'Everest is in its nature a terminal

PREVIOUS PAGE: The 1922 Everest team at a breakfast stop en route for Tibet's Rongbuk Glacier. Seated, left to right, Wakefield, Morris, General Bruce, Karma Paul, Geoffrey Bruce, an unnamed gurkha, and Norton. This splendid shot is by pioneering photographer Captain John Noel.

LEFT: Tenzing Norgay on the summit of Mount Everest at 11.30am on 29 May 1953. Tenzing waves his ice-axe on which are hung the flags of Britain, Nepal, the United Nations and India, a photograph by his companion Edmund Hillary.

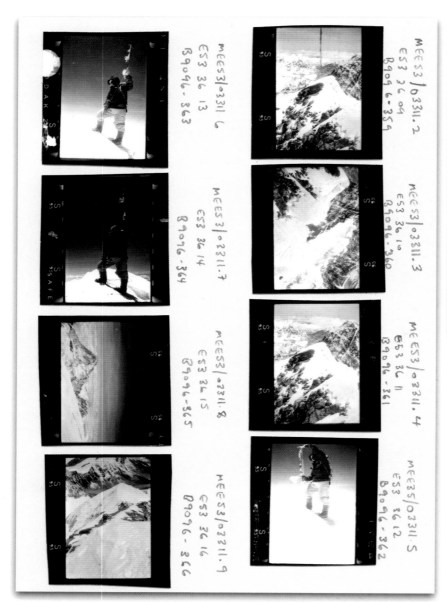

The Himalayan Mountain. Mount Everest from Phalot. India Tibet.

point; it is like one of those great peaks that stand aside from the main chain of the range. It is doubtful whether anyone will ever try to climb it again now that it has been done'. How wrong they were. Since that glorious day in May, many thousands of eager people have hauled themselves up its flanks, some via technical ridges and towering faces, the majority plodding up the route that Hillary and his companions pioneered, doomed always to follow in another man's tracks. In one 1993 expedition forty people reached the peak in the course of a day, more than did so during the first twenty years after the 1953 success. 'They might as well have provided a bus', Hillary said at the time.

Our highest summit is still revered and treasured in its way, but the mountain has been littered with garbage and despoiled by crowded routes, competition and controversy. It has also seen more than the necessary share of death and disaster. Men have now photographed, filmed, blogged and broadcasted from its sacred snows. They have jumped off, skied down, slept, urinated, argued, embraced, fought and fallen from our highest place. You can stream live footage via satellite into the homes of your audience. All are changed by the experience, but not all deal with their fame with the grace that many of the greats in this book have shown. The highest mountain does not always make the humble man.

Let's descend to the era in which photography was born and also describe the modest goals of this project. Clearly, photos go on many journeys and they tell a story that so often words cannot. And yet, they don't provide the whole story. They reminisce and enshrine, inflate and obscure. Climbing, too, attracts as much admiration as it does exasperation. Edward Strutt, for example, wasn't alone in being unimpressed by attempts to climb the great Alpine North Face, the *Eigerwand*. He cut to the chase: 'It's an obsession for the mentally deranged'. Mountains have the power to change a man, though not always for the better. 'I know of one upright young man, a tee-total churchgoer', Walt Unsworth once described, 'whom climbing turned into a foul-mouthed fornicating shod'.

This book is a visual tribute to men and women who have been inspired by the mountains to acts of madness, fortitude, and frequent brilliance. We greet visionaries, maniacs, abominable mountain men, good and bad fathers, restless sons, bold daughters, forgiving wives. We include some twelve former Presidents of the Alpine Club, from Sir Leslie Stephen through to our contributors Bonington, Scott and

Venables. Some, like Martin Conway and John Hunt, would be knighted for their contributions to the mountains, yet there are also men here who shied away from the limelight, preferring the solace of the wilderness to the sound of applause.

Success on Everest sparked a new golden age of high-altitude mountaineering. Of the fourteen mountains above 8,000m, only Annapurna had been scaled when Hillary and Tenzing made their photos that day. Just five weeks later, the world's ninth highest peak, Nanga Parbat, was summitted and by the end of the decade only Shishapangma, which lay off-limits in Chinese Tibet, remained unconquered. It was an age of new heroes, just as that great wave of activity in the Alps during the late-nineteenth century had spawned a generation of climbers fit for public consumption. Celebrated at lectures, scrutinised like film-stars yet much praised in print, these mountain men found themselves embraced by a frenzy of interest and condemnation. Most wished they could escape back to the silence of the hills, and many did just that. Some did not return.

This book brings forward the voices and the visions of many of these adventurous souls. But, what makes a hero, who decides, and do people really want to be held up in this way? With renown comes responsibility, limitation, expectation, and competition too. The very notion of heroism in the hills is an awkward one, and such a 'cheapening grandness' seems to go against a sensitive approach. When so many great climbs were attempted out of jingoism or personal egotism, there are still others who have become climbers purely for the physical and mental challenge. 'Heroes are in the eye of the beholder', the admirable Tom Hornbein tells me. 'You have yours, I have mine. Many we share'. Clearly, there are the special few whose courage and whose selfless deeds are worthy of real praise, but more often than not men, and increasingly women, are climbing high for all sorts of personal reasons. Many of these desires, hidden in the deeper recesses, are not as saintly as one might wish for. Heroes are the stuff of dreams, their peaks ever brilliant but elusive and the summit is a lonely place. Hillary frequently put his own celebrity into perspective: 'If someone wants to believe I am a heroic figure, fine, but for me, I did a reasonable job at the time. I didn't get carried away then, and I never have'.

There are also too many talented mountain photographers to feature in this book. Time and space force my hand. Never aiming to be definitive, this is just a celebratory collection of interesting lives, remarkable climbs, inspirational expeditions, and simple joys. Vittorio Sella, arguably the greatest mountain photographer of all time, is not here. But, of course, a great many catalogues and exhibitions have been created about him, and he was not particularly interested in photographing people.

This book is not just an album of figures who have climbed to the top, but also those people who have shown innovation and humanity on their way to the summits.

They provided scale, but more often than not, Sella felt they got in the way. The mountain faces were the true objects of his love and scrutiny. His first photographs of the Aletsch Glacier or the series made after his celebrated first winter ascent of the Matterhorn in 1882, are so breathtaking in their clarity and composition that they are surpassed by little in modern photography.

The omission of a figure like Sella may be read as one thread of ambition for a project like this. Though we have started in the most obvious of places, we do not always take the familiar route. True there are a great many famous names in this book, but I have always tried to include a range of talents and experiences, whilst also searching for new ways to look at those men we know much about. This book is avowedly not just about Everest. Though the mountain is, quite naturally, the biggest and best to most minds, there are wide ranges of achievement elsewhere to enjoy. This book is not just an album of figures who have climbed to the top, but also those people who have shown innovation and humanity on their way to the summits. Not the who but rather the *how*; those who capture something of the spirit of the mountains as they enter them, and those who leave the hills as quietly as they came.

Inclusion does not imply a hierarchy; there are rogues as well as legends here. This gallery does not seek to answer the frustrating and frequent question – why climb? – but rather we try to show some of the joy and the challenge that the mountains offer us all, if we are willing to seek it out. Those that keep having to ask the question *why* may never quite get it. For the rest of us, no justification is required.

LEFT: Rare contact prints from Hillary's summit camera film, the first views from the highest point on the planet, 1953. They stayed on the top of the world for half an hour or so whilst Hillary, as proof of their success, took a series of shots over the mountains that stretched out far below them.

Probably the earliest surviving photograph of Everest, a half-plate print, looking across the foothills from Phalut, 1875.

OVERLEAF: A selection of French and Swiss Alpine mountain guides – photographs that served both as proofs of identity and credentials for future work, and as keepsakes of happy climbs for clients who wished to paste their faces into albums back at home. Among this rogues gallery we can see, clockwise from top left: Anton Ranch, Christian Barandun, Balthasar Thom, and Joseph Hohler. These unpublished images, among many others, have recently been discovered in the rich but neglected photographic archives of The Alpine Club, London.

I've been fortunate to trust in the guidance and judgement of celebrated men like Bonington, Scott, Venables, and so too George Band and Kurt Diemberger, among many others, who have offered their thoughts as my wanderings among historic and modern mountains progressed. All were encouraging, participating freely in that spirit of fellowship, something so integral to happiness in the hills and which always offers a satisfying reward. If this book is measured a success, it will be that people enjoy its rich photography and pause awhile on the writings. Something may resonate. Inspired perhaps to step outdoors, the book flung aside, maybe the reader will head off to see something of these beautiful mountains with their own eyes. To my mind, this book will then have more than a reason enough.

WITH ICE-AXE AND CAMERA

Walter Parry Haskett Smith balances precariously on the Napes Needle, a pinnacle on Great Gable in the English Lake District. It is late June 1886. He has just climbed up alone, without any protective devices at all – rejecting the ropes, spikes, and ladders used by inferior scramblers. This is frequently mentioned as the first day of rock-climbing as we know it, liberated in independence from 'mountain bagging'. It was achieved for the athletic pleasure of a route on difficult rock for its own sake, rather than something to endure on the way to a lofty summit. He wriggled his way back down the crack, down another block, to place both feet on solid ground. There was no photographer there that day to validate the ascent with an image. But Haskett Smith didn't need a picture to prove it to his friends. He looked up to the top with satisfaction to see his white handkerchief where he had left it, fluttering in the breeze.

Increasingly, small groups of young chaps would meet in the Lakes during the holiday weekends. Wearing their oldest suits and heavy country boots, tied to each other with a length of hemp rope, they set off to discover just how far they dared venture in this brave new vertical world. It was something of a matter of luck that two of the best early climbers – George and Ashley Abraham – were also professional photographers, 'the Keswick Brothers'. They started climbing in the early 1890s, teaming up with the leading 'tiger' of the day Owen Glynne Jones, and rarely going on the crag without their camera and glass-

plates. Jones' exuberant style did much to popularize this emerging sport. They toured together all over Britain – to North Wales, the Highlands of Scotland and the Isle of Skye. They also ventured with Jones to the Swiss Alps where they made a number of stirring first ascents in the summer of 1899. They were all planning a trip to the Himalayas at Christmas. The brothers had to return home to business, so later in August Jones set out with his guides to try the Ferpècle Arête of the Dent Blanche. One of his companions slipped during the climb, dragging Jones down with him to their deaths.

Though not adventurous at first, the technique of photography – born in a French attic in 1826, improved in Parisian and London studios, and eventually offered onto the street – would soon reach great heights. By 1833, when photographic pioneer Henry Talbot experienced the frustrations of trying to draw the Alpine horizon from the shore of Lake Como, mountains had already begun to be rehabilitated from regions of despair and fear into monuments of beauty and delight. He returned from his honeymoon and set about experimenting with a variety of apparatus, determined to find a way of fixing an image on paper. When he finally announced his success to a London audience in 1839, his positive/negative process was still rudimentary. Yet within a few years he was able to demonstrate his invention's viability by means of the world's first photographically illustrated book, *The Pencil of Nature*, published in parts beginning in 1844. In less than a decade, Talbot would bring about a wholly new way of creating pictures, perfecting both the chemical and optical aspects of the process, and enabling the medium to create complex images for use of the botanist, the historian, the artist and the traveller.

Mountains appeared in photographs from the very first moment the technology appeared. The sublime majesty, and static immovability of the lofty mountain, ensured it crept into most early photographs of the 1850s and it was not long before peaks and crags became the main subjects of photographs in their own right. Large-scale tourism, made possible by huge advances in transport in continental Europe, would develop rapidly over the following decades and it was inevitable that views of, and from, the mountains would become a staple of photography, as ubiquitous then as the mountain postcard is today – brightly-coloured in their serried ranks, in the racks outside the shops at Alpine tourist traps.

German photographer Friedrich von Martens was appointed to take photographs on a French government expedition to the Alps in 1844 and he would go on

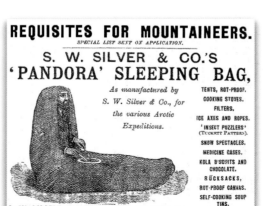

to create stunning panoramas over the following decades. French geologist Aimé Civiale created equally spectacular panoramas in the Pyrenees and the Austrian Alps. His camera gear weighed over 500 pounds, and needed twenty-five mules to carry it. Georges and Pierre Tairraz's photographic expeditions along the glaciers of Mont Blanc provided images perfect for the omnibuses of tourists arriving in Chamonix with money in their pockets and friends to impress at home. British photographers abroad tried their hand at the new art too. It is claimed that John Ruskin produced the first 'sun portrait of the Matterhorn' experimenting with his daguerreotype above Zermatt sometime in 1849, but nothing survives. William England struggled up the Mer de Glace in the 1860s, yet produced some marvellous

Whymper's Scrambles Amongst the Alps inspired a generation… A great number of hardy souls climbed from their armchairs to follow his example.

wet-collodion negatives. Edward Whymper perfected the dry-plate process at high altitude in 1880 during one of his ascents of the volcano Chimborazo. He also used his own photographs as the basis for fine engravings in his books, or as bright new magic lantern slides for his sell-out lecture tours.

Claude-Marie Ferrier made his money from stereoscopic Alpine views, and countless others followed. Wealthy manufacturer and amateur glaciologist, Daniel Dollfus-Ausset funded Louis and Auguste Bisson, fashionable Parisian studio photographers, to make a series of expeditions to the Alps. On 24 July 1861 and 13 May 1862 Auguste braved

severe difficulties – including the freezing of the collodion on his plates – to capture some of the first views from the summit of Mont Blanc. The results were spectacular, although commercial sales failed to clear the brothers' debts and they went bankrupt.

Photographers ranged more widely as the century progressed. Surveyor and explorer John Frémont was the first to bring a daguerreotype kit into the Rocky Mountains in the 1840s, though he may just as well have carried a boulder in his knapsack. He was completely inept at the technique and over the course of three expeditions produced not a single useful image. With greater success, San Francisco-based Carleton Watkins risked his life to capture spectacular mountain views in Yosemite and Yellowstone, creating exceptionally clear mammoth-plate photographs for tourists, railway and mining companies, until his eyesight failed in 1892. In the great earthquake of 1906, fire consumed his studio and its contents. Some of the most detailed views of the great mountains were lost forever. Yet, there were others to follow him.

Mountain explorer and aviator Brad Washburn's luminous aerial photographs of uncharted wildernesses in Alaska and Canada's Yukon, along with his stunning maps of the Grand Canyon and Everest itself, have rarely been bettered. Armed with his gigantic Fairchild F-8 camera, his portraits of the most forbidding of peaks and their challenging North Faces have been compared to the work of his lifelong friend Ansel Adams, a man who also gave the mountains a new life through the majesty of his photographic art. Leigh Ortenburger's panoramas of the upper Quebrada Alpamayo, shot with his trusty Linhof Technika III from high camps, still sparkle with timeless clarity. One could list countless others. Byron Harmon's images would shape the way the Canadian Rockies were imagined. With goldline rope, leather boots, and cameras that weighed as much as a 100 pounds, the twin brothers Bob and Ira Spring ably captured the beauty of the mountains of the Pacific Northwest during a 'classic age' of American mountaineering.

Photographs were gradually presented in new ways. From the society soirée of the early years, through illustrated books, to blockbuster photographic touring exhibitions, the remote mountains touched audiences at home. Whymper's *Scrambles Amongst the Alps* inspired a generation to value the challenge and wonder of the mountains. A great number of hardy souls climbed from their armchairs to follow his example. Others were satisfied enough to make

The figures should look in the new slide not blacker than here. The ice should be brought out rather more than here.

their ascents by attending one of his lectures and thus the genre of travel writing and mountain adventure was born. Choosing two influential illustrated books from this period, I pick H.B. George's *The Oberland and its Glaciers* and C.D. Cunningham's fashionably groundbreaking *Pioneers of the Alps*. George's *Oberland* appeared in 1866, recounting his summer explorations 'with ice-axe and camera'. It was likely the first book dedicated to the mountain photograph. London photographer Ernest Edwards of Baker Street actually created the images, but in time George had perfected his own equipment, not least when the invention of dry plate revolutionized the logistics of alpine work. His camera was miniature for those days, a small box about four inches square, with his axe cleverly rigged up as a tripod.

Cunningham's 1887 tome, now highly prized among collectors, was the first publication to devote its pages to the art of the mountain portrait; it is the original collection of 'Mountain Faces'. Epic climbs, and equally prodigious beards, was the order of the day and a number of those trusty Swiss mountain guides are featured here. The man behind the camera was Captain William Abney, who took his armoury over to Zermatt and Chamonix for the summer to aim his new thirteen-inch lens at the 'craggy and bronzed complexions of a succession of rugged fellows'. Even the legendary guide Melchior Anderegg was pressed into service, helping round up his naturally modest

companions, to have their faces recorded for posterity. After an hour's instruction, it is said Melchior became something of an expert himself and thereafter 'a beam of sunlight was an object worthy of all his respect'.

Other names are long forgotten but were important at time. I think of Sydney Spencer or that mountaineering botanist and prodigious author Frank Smythe. Or, recall enterprising Swiss climber Jules Beck, who from 1866 began making regular excursions in the Alps. Such were the difficulties faced and the lengthy exposure times needed, he rarely managed more than a dozen shots a day. Fabric designer turned topographic-photographic pioneer, Adolphe Braun also travel widely, from the mountainsides to the newly opened Suez Canal. Or William Donkin, photographic mountaineer of the moment, with a gallery on the Strand and a string of expeditions under his belt. He was lost, camera in hand, in an avalanche in the Central Caucasus in 1888.

Since the 1850s, when Everest was first identified as the tallest peak in the world, climbers of all nationalities vied to reach it. The RGS and the Alpine Club formed a joint committee in 1920 called the Mount Everest Committee (MEC), which in turn became the Joint Himalayan Committee after the end of the Second World War. The objective of the MEC was twofold: to reach the summit of Everest, and to research its distinctive environment. Between 1921 and 1953, the MEC sent out nine expeditions to research and climb Everest, a mountain which at that time was in one of

LEFT: Advertising the 'Requisites for Mountaineers': the snazzy Pandora Arctic sleeping bag of 1894; the new Kodak camera of 1893 tried and tested by Peary in Greenland, and (page 34) Rev. H.B. George's miniature camera and ice-axe tripod adaptor, bespoke engineered by Murray and Heath in 1869.

ABOVE: Edward Whymper wrote instructions across his photographs for his engravers and glass lantern slide makers. This image was intended for a series of new slides on 'Climbing Techniques' to be used within his *Scrambles* lectures of the 1890s. Three men are seen first descending a deep crevasse – 'if this part could be a little darker, I should be glad' – and the same men later pose for this ice traverse – 'the figures should look in the new slide not blacker than here. The ice should be brought out rather more than here'.

019417   019418   019419   019420

GA-9   GA-10   GA-11   GA-12

019425   019426   019427   019428   019429

GA-17   GA-18   GA-19   GA-20   GA-21

019436   019437   019438   019439   019440

copy
neg
D2386

GA-28   GA-29   GA-30   GA-31   GA-32

019447   019448   019449   019450   019451

GB-39   GB-40   GB-41   GB-42   GB-43

019458   019459   019460   019461   019462

GB-50   GB-51   GB-52   GB-53   GB-54

the most inaccessible places on earth. The North Pole and South Pole had both been reached successfully before any Westerner had set a foot on Everest's flanks.

Far from the Himalaya, at both the London headquarters of the Royal Geographical Society and the Alpine Club can be found the footprints of that ambition. In slide drawers, acid-free envelopes, filing cabinets and velvet-lined boxes, in piles that aspire to reach the ceiling, are the maps, letters, and photographs that open a window on this world. The pictures one can uncover in these archives are in many parts arresting, mundane, intriguing, tedious and dusty, yet at times also astonishingly beautiful. This is the particular test of the researcher's patience.

THE GREATER RANGES

Mountain landscapes are now so integral to our ideas of splendor and refuge, we can feel a deep connection despite their being so remote. They are places to awaken the soul. The magic of seeing Everest for the first time at close quarters can be felt in the words of George Mallory in 1921: 'Mountain shapes are often fantastic seen through a mist: these were like the wildest creations of a dream ... gradually, very gradually, we saw the great mountainsides and glaciers and ridges, now one fragment, now another, through the floating rifts, until, far higher in the sky than imagination dared to suggest, a prodigious white fang – an excrescence from the jaw of the world – the summit of Everest appeared'.

Photography has long been an important component of mountain expeditions. Today it would be hard to imagine an expedition without a camera, though of course many people are willing to leave camera, and mobile, at home and head out beyond reception – to escape these trappings of modern life for a moment. Since the birth of photography, explorers have understood the value of good imagery, to sustain an image of their adventures, in their own minds as much as for their audiences. Exploration is often defined by the success of the storytelling.

Consider intrepid Captain John Noel, who as a young man disguised himself as a native to foray illicitly into Tibet, approaching closer than any white man to the flanks of the great mountain. When he returned to duty two months overdue from leave, the explanation he offered his colonel was that his calendar had been swept away by a river. The colonel

gently advised him to take two calendars next time. For the 1922 Everest expedition Noel was appointed official photographer, though it was by no means a popular idea. George Mallory, for one, aired the view that he 'did not wish to be an actor on a film'. Nor did the film of the expedition – lacking the drama of a successful summit bid – receive much critical acclaim. George Bernard Shaw joked that it had all the appearance of 'a picnic in Connemara surprised by a snowstorm'. Nonetheless, it eventually drew a handsome profit, running for ten weeks at London's Philharmonic Hall, and ensuring Noel's chance to film the next Everest attempt in 1924.

This expedition turned out to be one of the 'great heroic sagas' of mountaineering history, which still draws massive interest to this day. 'St Noel of the Cameras' – as his leader Charles Bruce was wont to call him – spent long periods at high altitude and developed thousands of feet of film in tough conditions. Noel even brought some 25,000 cigarettes with him to keep his photographic porters happy while he aimed for the perfect pictures to do the mountain justice: 'to dabble fatuously in trivialities in the face of Everest's grandeur would be sacrilege', he later wrote. His work was indeed a triumph. He captured the mood of events too with what now seems a chilling immediacy. Even Mallory's last note, written before he and Irvine disappeared from view, was addressed to Noel – and recorded on celluloid. Whether or not Mallory reached the summit is still debated. Several expeditions in recent years have hunted for his elusive pocket camera and film, hoping they would hold some proof of what happened to the pair. A photograph could be the crucial evidence; there is yet the faint possibility of seeing the summit through Mallory's eyes, before tragedy engulfed him.

On returning to London, Noel's film, much of it hand-tinted, was a huge commercial success. It had drama, mystery and not to forget – again a Noel touch – a group of Tibetan monks who joined the tour. The Dalai Lama was said to be furious, in his own unassuming way, and ensured that there were no further British expeditions through Tibet for almost a decade. Noel retired to live on Romney Marsh. Even into his nineties, in the 1980s, he was still going regularly to Kodak House in London, showing his work of half a century before, and now being fêted by the younger mountaineering generations. He planned, too, to return to Everest, but it was just the flickering embers of an obsession. His photographs of Everest's golden age nonetheless live on.

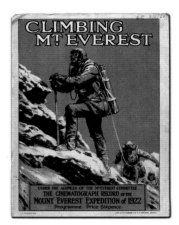

ABOVE: Cover of the program to Captain John Noel's film of the 1922 Everest Expedition and Lizzie Hawkins-Whitshed's 1895 *Hints on Snow Photography*.

LEFT: A page from the 1936 Everest album showing contact prints of many of the Sherpas who took part in the expedition, including a young Tenzing Norgay, who can be seen in the first picture third row down. The portraits were all created by Jim Gavin, 1936.

From the 1950s colour photography was beginning to be used widely by the general public, and Alfred Gregory, official photographer of the 1953 expedition, applied it brilliantly. You can find a couple of his photographs in this book. Sherpas manfully bear their loads; skies pulsate in electric blue. His friends rest in camp, waiting for a new day of adventures to begin. You can catch a glimpse of wild excitement in their eyes.

Yet it was Sir Edmund who created the most famous Everest shot. But there is no picture of Hillary on the summit that morning in May. Tenzing didn't

> Photographs allow us to see the mountain's face, and to journey closer toward its sacred summit.

know how to use a camera and, as Hillary joked, 'it was not the moment to teach him!' Hillary's shots of the mountains below them, not the summit portrait itself, were the important images. It would have been easy to forge shots of any member of the team, zipped deeply into his jacket, goggles on, posing manfully on some compact pinnacle of snow with the indigo-blue void stretching out behind him. Some people have done this since, here and on other mountains, falling short of their goals yet hoping to deceive once they descend. But to simulate a complete view from the roof of the world would have been impossible. Hillary's photographs allow us to gaze across the Himalayas – 'snaking glaciers, outcrops of bare rock, pure white snow, and billowing clouds' – appreciating that the summit had finally been reached, but not overcome. 'It is not the mountain we conquer', Hillary later wrote, 'but ourselves'.

Portraits provide a glimpse into the heart of mountaineers and their achievements. The Western gaze still raises the highest mountains to the summits of expectation and they are places where it is easy to invest our hopes and fears. I'm lucky to have climbed in the shadow of Everest, to have struggled up high passes in drifting snow; admiring the summit ridge catching the first rays of the sun, trekking to base camp and chatting with those whose desires are firmly set on that ridge and beyond. But since most will never have the chance to travel in the Himalayas, photographs help us feel a connection to its history, its drama, and the people who live there. Photographs allow us to see the mountain's face, and to journey closer toward its sacred summit.

RIGHT: Members of the Vaux family, annual visitors from Philadelphia, make their way up the seracs of the Illecillewaet Glacier to pose for photographs, Selkirk Mountains, 1905. First photographed by the family in 1887, their images here formed the basis of the first long-term studies of glaciers in Canada and now help modern-day researchers better estimate the extent of glacial loss. The snout of this vast ice mass of ice has retreated some 2,000m since this picture was created.

BECAUSE WE ARE MOUNTAINEERS

In 1923 Mallory was lecturing widely in an effort to drum up funds for a new expedition. When pressed by sceptics to justify the endeavour, he spoke eloquently of the pull of the hills:

> I suppose we go to Mount Everest, granted the opportunity, because – in a word – we can't help it. Or, to state the matter rather differently, *because we are mountaineers*. To refuse the adventure is to run the risk of drying up like a pea in its shell ... Have we vanquished an enemy? None but ourselves. Have we gained success? That word means nothing here. Have we won a kingdom? No and yes. To struggle and to understand – never this last without the other ... we go, for the stone from the top for geologists, the knowledge of the limits of endurance for the doctors, but above all for the spirit of adventure to keep alive the soul of man.

This book, *Mountain Heroes*, hopes to capture something of this spirit of human adventure. Reinhold Messner, a hero to many, who became the first man to scale Everest without oxygen in 1978, described a 'state of spiritual abstraction' when he reached the summit. 'I no longer belong to myself and to my eyesight', he wrote. 'I am nothing more than a single narrow gasping lung, floating over the mists and the summits'. Hillary's response to reaching the top of the world was more succinct. 'Well, we knocked the bastard off', he told his companions on returning to safety.

Once this book is finished I will go to the mountains again. Perhaps, simply, I shall just sit awhile in the open air, by the crag or on the soft turf at a river's side. I may join friends to scramble amongst the Alps, feeling the rock under my hands, and climbing high just to stop and listen to the nothing that is everything. I'll drink in the breeze on the cliffs that tumble from the edges of the moor here in Cornwall, their feet wrapped in the Atlantic swell. I will not climb well, but well enough to remember the joy that it brings. We all face our own mountains. The pleasure is in overcoming what challenges us, and realizing more of life as we go. There are countless people in these pages who provide this sort of example – bravely making the first ascents, slowly but surely cutting steps up steep ice, hanging on the end of a rope as the storm approaches, and all to bring something of the experience home for us – yet most importantly, they do it for themselves. They are all heroes in different and surprising ways. This is their story.

St Ives, 2011

Mumm 1907. 6/8
Garhwal etc.

Nanga Parbat.
N. Collie 1895 6/9

NORWAY.
Collie & Spencer 5/4

Everest 8/1
1924 end.

Canada 5/8
Robson area
Collie & Hun

Misc.
Everest aerial 8/5
Sella - Caucasus

THE MOUNTAIN FACE

One day's exposure to mountains is better than cartloads of books.

JOHN MUIR, 1896

I've always hated the danger part of climbing, and it's great to come down again because it's safe ... but there is something about building up a comradeship – that I still believe is the greatest of all feats – and sharing in the dangers with your company of peers. It's the intense effort, the giving of everything you've got. It's really a very pleasant sensation.

SIR EDMUND HILLARY, 1977

There are two kinds of climbers, those who climb because their heart sings when they're in the mountains, and all the rest.

ALEX LOWE, 1997

GALLERY

THE MOUNTAIN FACE
HUW LEWIS-JONES AND COLIN WELLS

This is a gallery of one hundred remarkable people; an album of lives shaped and inspired by the mountains. It is neither complete nor definitive. Coming face to face with a selection of individuals in this way, we hope to celebrate the range of human activity and adventure amongst the everlasting hills and deep in our wildest places.

Though the history of humankind's relationship with the great mountain ranges can be read in many ways, photography provides us with a glimpse of more recent ambition and achievement. From those who make their homes in the shadows of these hills, to those who strive to their summits, we recognize the joy and the opportunity that these regions offer us. We have gathered together some of the finest images from the world's leading alpine collections and borrowed personal treasures from a range of private archives, whilst also creating striking new portraits of interesting and inspiring characters whose hopes and dreams are connected to the mountains.

In this brief snapshot, we encounter those who have spent their lives at altitude; explorers and mapmakers, pioneering travellers, alpinists and photographers, artists and outdoor film-stars, ice-climbers and extreme skiers, anthropologists and geologists, and many others who make their home among the hills. We join the visionaries and innovators who would change the nature of mountaineering forever. We hear from the hell-raisers and the eccentrics, some of the bright young things, as well as so many of the craggy veterans of the traditional climbing scene. We can learn from their experiences, listen to and respect their achievements and, perhaps encouraged by their example, we can head out on our own adventure.

Within these pages meet a group of characters that have risen to the top – in a combination of hard work and boldness that is often breathtaking. Our portraits speak of people who have been inspired by the wilderness, and that feeling of rock beneath their hands, to dare the impossible, to push themselves to the limits of their skill and courage, and to survive to tell the tale. There are some here who were not so lucky. The mountains have been cruel. They lie alone, perhaps entombed in drifting snow, or high on some remote and exposed spot, their bones bleached by the sun and scoured by the wind. But they remain too in those beautiful places to which they came both for peace and for challenge, with good friends and shared hopes – all drawn to the hills, to experience that special something that is the meaning of life.

St Ives and Hope, 2011

PREVIOUS PAGE: The Alpine Club in London houses an eclectic photographic collection – drawers of magic lantern slides, boxes of glass plates, stacks of prints and private albums, to endless cases of modern film negatives – a genuinely untapped trove for the researcher willing to carefully work through this avalanche of material.

CUMBRIA, 2011
SIR CHRIS BONINGTON 1934-

For many years the public face of British climbing, Chris Bonington undertook a score of impressive early ascents in Britain on both rock and ice, but it was in the Alps that he first established his reputation. He became one of Britain's most successful post-war alpinists, and then went on to shape the way Greater Ranges climbing developed.

Born in London, Bonington went into the Army in the 1950s. He began climbing in the Alps and during the early 60s built up an impressive portfolio of routes including the first British ascents of the South West Pillar of the Dru in 1958 and *Cima Grande Direct* in 1959. In 1961 he teamed up with Don Whillans, Ian Clough and the Polish climber Dlugosz and made the celebrated first ascent of the Central Pillar of Frêney on Mont Blanc. As if this wasn't enough, later that same year Bonington achieved the long-sought first British ascent of the *Eigerwand*.

A successful expedition to Patagonia, where he overcame the difficult granite spire of the Central Tower of Paine was to be Bonington's last climbing expedition for seven years as he developed a career as an adventure photojournalist. He had originally resigned his commission in the Army to join an expedition to Nuptse, and he less reluctantly turned down a job with Unilever to go on another. 'I had to choose between selling margarine and adventure. I chose adventure'.

Bonington soon realized he preferred being in front of the cameras rather than behind them and returned to climbing. In 1970 he masterminded the ascent of the South Face of Annapurna. It marked the start of a new era of Himalayan climbing; never had such a huge and steep face been tackled at such altitudes. Bonington would subsequently lead two high-profile attempts on Everest's South-West Face in 1972 and 1975. The 1972 attempt failed but the 1975 expedition was a resounding success, albeit marred by the death of charismatic climbing cameraman Mick Burke.

The expedition hastened the passing of an era of juggernaut-sized expeditions and, as with most elite mountaineers of the period, Bonington chose to pursue 'alpine-style' ascents of big peaks from then on. Among the highlights are his 1977 first ascent of the fearsome Ogre in the Karakorum with Doug Scott, which involved a nightmare retreat after Scott broke both legs and Bonington several ribs. In 1981 Bonington led a team to the top of the remote Chinese peak of Kongur (7,720m) and in 1985 he reached the summit of Everest himself.

Numerous climbing expeditions followed: to Greenland, Antarctica, the Caucasus, the Karakoram and Himalaya, and writing countless books. The mountains have been a life-long passion for Sir Chris and, although now eligible for a bus pass, there seems little chance of him hanging up his boots just yet. He continues to rock climb to a respectable standard, pioneering new routes recently in Morocco, and still climbs Grade VI snow and ice in Scotland – impressive for a chap approaching his eightieth birthday. He chuckles at the thought. 'Yes, not bad'.

YOSEMITE, 1969
YVON CHOUINARD 1938-

Yvon Chouinard isn't just any old climbing superstar. In terms of global significance he's definitely Top 10 and, in the view of many observers, he may well be Number One. 'The fact of the matter is, he's a genius, period', says his erstwhile climbing buddy and business partner Tom Frost, himself somewhat of an American climbing legend.

Frost is alluding to the fact that although climbing history is punctuated by plenty of individuals who have made a difference – by dint of outstanding climbs, a new approach to the game or a technological innovation – it's almost unheard of for someone to tick the boxes in all these areas. And then to export that influence so that it touches every single person whoever puts on a harness wherever they may be on the planet. That is why Yvon Chouinard is arguably the single most important climber of the twentieth century.

To even begin listing those areas in which he has made major advances begins to sound like a roll call of recent climbing evolution itself. His invention of the mini-piton, the RURP, supercharged the development of Yosemite and, hence, big-wall climbing all over the world. His Rockies climbs with Fred Beckey began serious lightweight alpinism in North America. He was a major reason the British-inspired 'clean' free climbing ethic swept across 1970s America. His pioneering advocacy of environmental sustainability in the manufacturing sector is beginning to influence major corporations too. Basically, without Chouinard world climbing today would probably look very different indeed.

Born into an impoverished French Canadian expatriate community, the Chouinard family relocated to California when he was seven in what Chouinard calls a 'Grapes of Wrath' experience. 'I think my early life there basically taught me the necessity of self-reliance'. Chouinard would be part of the hard climbing boom of 1960s Yosemite (he took part in the first ascent of the *North America Wall* among many other significant climbs) and applied his technically adept mind to not only designing better pitons, but also manufacturing them himself using a mobile forge in the back of a pick-up truck before moving to proper facilities in Ventura and building a highly successful business. In this stunning portrait by celebrated climbing photographer Glen Denny, Chouinard is sorting out his gear at Camp 4 in Yosemite, ahead of another day's hard, and no doubt innovative, climbing.

Always possessed of a heightened sense of environmental awareness though, he became appalled by the damage his iron pitons were doing to the rocks he loved as the climbing population grew. In 1971 he stopped making them altogether even though they brought in seventy percent of his income. In their place, heavily influenced by the traditional natural protection ethics of Britain, he started a 'Climb Clean' campaign which championed nut protection and began manufacturing aluminium wedges; the famous 'Chouinard Stoppers'. Such equipment, including his other invention of curved ice picks allowing direct traction on steep ground, revolutionized climbing around the world and changed mountaineering forever.

Meanwhile, he continued to climb hard, making numerous trips to the Andes, Russia and the Greater Ranges. But by the beginning of the 1980s, Chouinard was becoming increasingly disenchanted with the climbing scene. 'I never realized there would be so many climbers', he says. He felt that sheer weight of numbers was loving the mountains to death and didn't like the idea of being a direct part of promoting it. So he sold Chouinard Equipment to concentrate on the clothing manufacturing company he had founded in 1972, Patagonia. 'I couldn't help myself', he says. 'I'm an innovator, I could have started ten companies'. Despite this, Chouinard doesn't mind admitting he despises the 'Suits' and he still considers himself a dirtbag climber at heart: 'I never wanted to be a businessman', he protests, with a smile.

BOULDER, 2011
LYNN HILL 1961-

In 1993 Lynn Hill became the first person – male or female – to free climb El Capitan's world-famous 1,000m route the *Nose* in Yosemite. A year later the five-foot, seven-stone American was back, and did it again, this time under twenty-three hours. 'I wanted to do something that had meaning to me', she says. 'I love being outside, I love natural rock, I love the whole experience. I chose the *Nose* because it had never been done before, and it was one of the most beautiful things in the world that I had seen. When you see the valley, tears come to your eyes'.

It was the crowning glory of a remarkable rock climbing career, exceptional by any standards, but especially so by a women who proved you could take men on at what many of them had smugly assumed was 'their' game – and beat them. Hill began climbing as a diminutive fourteen year old, following a solid grounding in gymnastics, but hated the way 'girls had to smile and do cutesy little routines on the floor. I had this reputation as this tomboy that rebelled against traditions anyway. I didn't like it, but I thought, if I'm different then I'll just be me and I'll do what I feel like doing. That gave me a certain freedom'. With this rebellious streak, Hill became a regular of the legendary Camp 4 'climbing bum' scene of Yosemite, living off little income and spending the maximum time climbing.

However, the advent of competition climbing allowed her to turn her passion into a lucrative career. In addition to making many new routes and hard repeats she spent much of the 1980s doing indoor and outdoor competition climbing, winning over thirty international titles. With nothing left to prove, she spent the 1990s challenging herself on bigger, riskier free-climbs, and making bold first ascents on many hard rock climbs and mountain faces. Famed US climber John Long gives his verdict: 'I have been all over the world and have had the fortune of doing things with many special people, some famous, some anonymous. But the biggest little hero I've ever known is Lynn Hill'. He pauses. 'The rest of us are just holding her rope'.

LONDON, 1910
EDWARD WHYMPER 1840-1911

Edward Whymper perhaps did more than any other individual to bring mountaineering to wide public prominence, thanks to his skill as a writer and illustrator, and a burning ambition to achieve renown on the highest peaks of the Alps. The fact he was at the centre of the most notorious mountaineering accident of the Victorian period also helped enormously. His tragedy-packed ascent of the Matterhorn was a tale of high drama, which precipitated the world's first global mountaineering media story.

Whymper began his career as a lowly young wood engraver in London. But he harboured a dream: impressed by the glorious adventures of the Royal Navy's polar explorers, he too desired to become a national hero in the mould of a Ross or Franklin and saw alpine climbing as a means to this end. Unlike many of his contemporaries, he served no apprenticeship in climbing, instead flinging himself at unclimbed summits right from the word go and was soon chasing trophy peaks, especially the charismatic Matterhorn. In 1865, following several abortive attempts, and feeling he had been betrayed by his former partner, Jean Carrel, who was now mounting his own assault, Whymper cast about desperately for a means to beat him to the summit. This resulted in a hastily assembled party featuring three climbers of vastly different experience and four guides all speaking different languages. It comprised the eighteen-year-old rising star of the Alpine Club, Lord Francis Douglas, and his guides the Taugwalders, together with the great guide Michel Croz plus his client Charles Hudson. Fatefully, Hudson insisted on bringing along his young friend: the inexperienced novice climber Douglas Hadow.

The unwieldy party set forth from Zermatt and despite the oddball mix they made triumphant progress to the summit, beating Carrel's Italians. But while descending Hadow slipped, pulling off all but Whymper and the Taugwalders who were tied to the rest of the chain by a weak sash line – which broke under the strain. The accident resulted in a press furore with some dark mutterings about Whymper's role in the affair.

Following this trauma Whymper switched attention to pioneering climbing in Greenland and the Andes. But he remained trapped in a terrible paradox; sensitive to reminders of the 1865 accident, he was nevertheless compelled to constantly tour and lecture about it. In 1894 alone he gave forty-eight lectures to over 50,000 people. Like a soap opera celebrity doomed to becoming typecast, he had to recognise the terrible truth that his fame rested on a single memorable role that everyone was keen for him to reprise.

To give Whymper himself the last word: 'There have been joys too great to be described in words, and there have been griefs upon which I have not dared to dwell, and with these in mind I say, climb if you will, but remember that courage and strength are naught without prudence, and that a momentary negligence may destroy the happiness of a lifetime. Do nothing in haste, look well to each step, and from the beginning think what may be the end'.

SHARTSE, 1974
KURT DIEMBERGER 1932-

It is no overstatement to say that Kurt Diemberger is a living legend in the world of mountaineering. Following a tough apprenticeship in the Alps, proving his mettle on hard climbs including the Eiger *North Face*, the Austrian became one of the leading high altitude alpinists during the 'golden age' of post-war Himalayan mountaineering. He was part of the team that made the first ascent of Broad Peak in 1957 – which was also the first 8,000m peak to be climbed 'alpine-style' without high altitude porters and supplementary oxygen – and also the first ascent of Daulaghiri in 1960. He remains the only person alive to have made the first ascent of two 8,000m mountains.

This striking portrait has become iconic in its way, shorthand for a person whose life in the hills has been one of huge success, extreme risk, tough weather, and perilous descents. Kurt was pleased to offer this photograph to this project. 'The icebeard portrait – as it has become known – is one of my favourites. It was taken on the 7,500m summit of Shartse at its first ascent in 1974 by my good friend Hermann Warth. It was pre-monsoon, and we'd just climbed through a cruel storm. Hermann froze the tips of a couple of his fingers in a matter of a few minutes up there, working his camera to get some shots. We wanted to pioneer this 'great ridge of Everest', as far as we might be able, but had to stop on this summit. We were only a small expedition, and with that terrible weather we could not have gone on much further. Standing on top of Shartse, I was looking toward banners of windswept snow in the air on Peak 38, then to Lhotse Shar, and the magnificent summit of Everest and feeling undescribably content, to be there with a good friend, and close to the fulfillment of a great dream. First steps to the future!'

In later years, Kurt would go on to make a series of superlative ascents, climbing the 8,000m peaks Everest, Makalu, Gasherbrum II, and K2. Tragedy, however, has also stalked his career. Following triumph on Broad Peak, Kurt was the last person to see the famed climber Hermann Buhl, before the German fell to his death through a cornice during their attempt on the neighbouring peak of Chogolisa. After his ascent of K2 in 1986 Diemberger was one of only two survivors after a storm engulfed the mountain, resulting in the death of five climbers. He suffered severe frostbite during the battle to descend and had to undergo amputations.

Despite these harrowing experiences, Diemberger has also built a reputation as writer, film-maker and photographer, with his autobiographical books *Summits and Secrets, Spirits of the Air* and *The Endless Knot* now regarded as classics of mountaineering literature. Aged eighty, he is still climbing and visiting the Himalaya. 'I am happy because there is no end of discovering there', he says. 'I don't do things for glory and I don't believe in speed records either. I think going slow and steady is the secret to success'.

Chitral, 1904.

Photo by Lt. Hon. Arthur Murray, 1/5th Gurkhas (later, Lord Elibank)

Major Hon. Charles Bruce, 1/5th Gurkhas. One of the best of men.

CHITRAL, 1904
CHARLES BRUCE 1866-1939

A career soldier, who introduced short trousers to the Indian Army, jaunty Brigadier-General Charles Granville Bruce was a larger than life character, whose massive appetite for fun – and for food – never got in the way of his prodigious mountaineering activity. 'Now he was a big, big man', remembered his later contemporary Kenneth Mason. 'His laugh was a tonic throughout the Himalayas, and he was an enormous eater. He didn't believe in mountain sickness. He always said it could be put down to too much tinned salmon the night before'.

Bruce hadn't always been such a jovial bear of a man, however. A member of the Fifth Gurkha Rifles Regiment, he had begun his association with the mountains by way of shooting the people who lived amongst them. As a specialist in small unit combat, Bruce spent much of the last decade of the nineteenth century fighting assorted hill tribes in the North-West Frontier Province of the Raj, alongside his Gurkha troops. During one engagement in Waziristan he single-handedly attacked a pillbox whilst under continuous fire and slaughtered the five defending Wazir riflemen with a *kukri* knife.

In 1892 he joined Martin Conway as logistics manager on his pioneering mountaineering trip to the Hispar and Biafo Glaciers. Bruce's ebullient character made a deep impression on Conway, who described him as the 'goods-train plus luggage' of his expedition and claimed he was 'worshipped by his Gurkhas'. Following the Conway expedition, Bruce explored the length and breadth of the Himalaya whenever he could get time off, usually accompanied by handpicked men. To keep fit in between trips, he used to run around the foothills of the Khyber Pass carrying his orderly on his back. He also kept in relative trim by taking on professional Punjabi wrestlers and once allegedly managed to throw three of his Gurkhas out of a wrestling ring simultaneously.

Bruce's mountaineering activities were also impressive, spending ten seasons in the Alps and in 1895 joining Fred Mummery's pioneering alpine-style attempt on Nanga Parbat. In 1907 Bruce was on Trisul with Tom Longstaff where they discussed an expedition to Everest, the first people to seriously contemplate such a venture. Following the Great War – in which he was badly wounded at Gallipoli – Bruce took command of the 1922 and 1924 Everest expeditions. His leadership style was unusually laid back. As a fluent Nepali speaker he was able to banter away to the Sherpas like a local and made friends in the villages through which the expedition caravan passed by presenting each headman with a bowler hat.

During the 1924 expedition, he partied like a teenager, going on a tiger shoot, and celebrated his fifty-eighth birthday by downing a bottle of rum. Combined with a dose of malaria, even he had to accept he was a little under the weather as the expedition wore on, and reluctantly relinquished leadership to Edward Norton. Following Everest Bruce began to slow down a bit but took time out to pen one of the most entertaining books of pre-war Himalayan exploration, the autobiographical *Himalayan Wanderer*, before he died of a stroke in 1939.

KIENTAL, 2009
STEPHAN SIEGRIST 1972 -

Based in the Bernese Oberland, leading all-round Swiss climber Stephan Siegrist is arguably best known for his spectacular first ascents in Patagonia, the Himalaya and Central Asia. In his 'local patch', the Alps, he has tackled several of the most difficult climbs on the notorious Eiger North Face. Remarkably he has climbed the *Nordwand* a grand total of twenty-seven times to date.

Siegrist was actually born far from the mountains in Meikirch and first encountered the Alps as an eleven year old on a ski tour. He was a teenager before he discovered climbing but became extremely enthusiastic, becoming a full-time climber from the age of nineteen and a mountain guide in 1998. In 1999, he attracted international attention following the first winter ascent of Cerro Torre's West Face with Thomas Ulrich, David Fasel and Greg Crouch. Since then his expeditions have drawn acclaim, such as the North-West Ridge of Thalay Sagar (6,904m) in 2004 and his demanding mixed route *Lightning Strike*, on the 6,352m Arwa Tower in India's Garhwal Himalaya with exciting German photographic alpinist Thomas Senf and Denis Burdet.

In 2010, Siegrist with fellow Swiss climber Dani Arnold and Senf made the first winter ascent of Torre Egger in Patagonia. Siegrist is also now hugely respected for his climbs in unexplored parts of Antarctica, such as three first ascents on Holtanna and Ulvetanna in 2009 with dynamos Alexander and Thomas Huber and Max Riechl. In recent years Siegrist has also embraced the new mountain sports of BASE-jumping and slacklining. He has literally taken this to extremes by jumping from the top of the Eiger's *Magic Mushroom* route after having made the first free ascent of the phenomenal 21-pitch 7c+ climb.

This unique portrait shows Stephan in a private moment. He is 'safe' at a belay after a hard ice climbing pitch of the forbidding *Eisteufel* WI6, in Kiental. He describes the scene. 'I just came back from Queen Maud Land in Antarctica and this was my first climb that winter. I was cleaning the ice of debris, as I was working my way upwards, and a large chunk hit me square in the face. I still had to climb another twelve metres or so, to the safety of the next belay. Suddenly you feel something unusually warm on the cold skin of your face. Then you taste blood in your mouth and see deep red gushing all over the white ice. It always bleeds much more from the face. Luckily, it's never usually as bad as it looks. You feel shocked at first, then a little bit embarrassed. This is just a scratch actually, compared to some of the scrapes we normally get when climbing really hard. Business as usual, I suppose?'

GLEN COE, 1960
ROBIN SMITH 1938-1962

Scotsman Robin Smith was one of the most outstanding climbers in post-war Britain. This is all the more remarkable given his tragically short climbing career – just six years of blistering achievement before it was snuffed out on a foreign snow-field.

As a youngster Smith began climbing on the tempting but illegal Salisbury Crags, the magnificent volcanic outcrop that dominates the Edinburgh skyline. Fending off Holyrood Park security guards while learning how to climb steep rock, he became renowned for a bold – almost reckless – disregard for difficulty and conditions. Contemporary descriptions of Smith depict a slightly mad individual, dressed in unkempt climbing clothes with a fraying rope coiled round his shoulders and a lopsided grin permanently plastered across his face which frequently emitted giggles. His nickname 'Wheechie' was a reference to the high-pitched cry he would routinely deliver towards fellow climbers he saw struggling on routes.

While a philosophy student at Edinburgh University in the late 50s Smith began creating some of the hardest climbs in the country such as *Shibboleth* (E2) and *Yo-Yo* (E1) in Glencoe and *The Needle* (E1) in the Cairngorms. During a celebrated week in February 1960 when he and Jimmy Marshall made six cutting-edge winter climbs on Ben Nevis, Smith contrived to drop his single ice-axe on no fewer than three occasions, remaining casual despite the most desperate of ascents. Such was his intellectual ability that he was able to frequently skip lectures and seminars to go climbing, but still managed to graduate with flying colours.

In addition to his climbs Smith was revered for his writing. In the words of Jeff Connor: 'He had discovered the gift of capturing the essence of the chaotic, anarchic and yet essentially disciplined business of climbing'. As a consequence, his best-known essay 'The Bat and the Wicked', describing an epic ascent of the eponymous Ben Nevis route with Dougal Haston, is widely recognized as a classic, and is one of the most frequently anthologized climbing essays, as well as achieving the accolade of being made into a film. In 1960, just two days after arriving in Chamonix, Smith and Gunn Clarke made the first British ascent of the *Walker Spur*, then regarded as second only to the Eiger North Face for difficulty and seriousness. The following day an all-star cast of predominantly English climbers – Chris Bonington, Don Whillans, Les Brown, John Streetly, plus token Scot Hamish MacInnes – toiled up to repeat the route under the misapprehension they were about to lay claim to the prize. 'The discovery of jammed rope slings (peculiar to British climbers) and Smartie packets en route aroused the suspicions of MacInnes, confirmed by the appearance of the dishevelled but exultant Smith as the second party came off the mountain'.

By the early 1960s the future of Robin Smith, and Scottish climbing, looked exciting. But in 1962, it was suddenly all over. The bright young hope, roped to Wilfrid Noyce – a figure from a previous generation of British climbing legends – fell to his death on Peak Garmo in the Pamirs, cutting short, in the words of Jim Perrin, 'a career of richer promise than perhaps any other figure in British post-war mountaineering possessed'. When asked about him a few months ago, his dear friend Jimmy Marshall summed Robin up in these perfect words: 'He was a really brilliant climber, with the ability and intellect to take climbing out into orbit, yet keep his feet on the ground'.

LOCH GARTEN, 2011
JIMMY MARSHALL 1929-

In one legendary week on Ben Nevis in February 1960 Edinburgh architect Jimmy Marshall and philosophy student Robin Smith advanced the sport of winter climbing a full ten years. On consecutive days they climbed six first winter ascents of very hard climbs including *Orion Face Direct*, a climb of alpine proportions, and also made the second ascent of the legendary *Point Five Gully* in just seven hours – a route that the first climbers had laid siege to over six days, using three hundred metres of fixed rope and more than sixty rock and ice pegs. The fact that Marshall and Smith achieved this using the extremely strenuous technique of step-cutting appears, from the remove of the twenty-first century, to be almost unbelievable.

Marshall's skill was such that he could lead routes almost faster than some of his talented seconds could follow. The doyen of Scottish mountaineering in the 1970s, Dougal Haston, famously remembered that his experience of partnering Marshall on the first ascent of the Ben's *Minus Two Gully* was 'a stunner and a mind-awakener'. He admitted that, '...it was taking us as long to second as Jimmy to lead. His experience and ability were still beyond ours. He seemed able to cut steps like a machine'.

But Marshall was just as skilled an operator on rock and his futuristic climbs were an inspiration to others to push the standards of the day. He became a prime mover behind the post-war resurgence of the Scottish Mountaineering Club, leading by example. Only a few years older than his youthful 'apprentices', he became known as 'The Old Man', a term of respect as much as an ironic reference to his maturity. Young climbers of the 1960s like Jim Stenhouse remember he was a great tutor. 'You couldn't have had a better teacher than Jim Marshall', he says. 'He was just incredible, and he was like a sort of Godfather – I suppose he still is'.

Marshall is now retired and has moved from the city to the Highland village of Dulnain Bridge from where he can keep his keen mountaineering eye on the Cairngorms. A romantic at heart, he says, 'I'm not a hermit or a recluse, but I just love empty spaces. But, you know, I don't really love mountains themselves, but rather the tough challenge of it all – they are inspirational, particularly in winter, when it's *sturm und drang*, as the great German climbers of the pre-war era would say'.

LONDON, 1895
SIR MARTIN CONWAY 1856-1937

Mountaineering art critic and cartographer, Martin Conway began his varied career in alpinism in 1872. Despite struggling at first on hard, technical ground he was driven to persevere by a desire 'to see what is on the other side of any range of hills'. It was this impetus that drove him to mount one of the earliest expeditions to the Greater Ranges – a famous caravan of climbers, artists and scientists who trooped up the mighty Hispar and Biafo Glacier systems of the Karakoram in 1892.

Conway's expedition mapped the glaciers, the biggest outside the polar regions, and moved on to the great Baltoro Glacier, which led on to a further glacier stretching to the foot of the world's second highest peak, K2. Their climbing achievements, although modest, reached heights of over 6,700m. The expedition was influential, setting a trend for large-scale expeditions in the area, and was the first to probe the approaches to K2, mapping some 5,180 square miles of the Karakoram in the process. As a consequence, Conway received a knighthood, and in 1896 he used his growing skills to complete the first crossing of Spitsbergen. By 1898 he was following in the footsteps of Whymper to the Andes.

Aconcagua, the highest mountain in the region, was the great prize, but they warmed up first on smaller 6,000m peaks of the Bolivian Cordillera Real, unaware that the indigenous Indians were seriously considering killing them for profaning the summits of their sacred peaks with their presence. The eventual assault on Aconcagua failed just below the top, and after exploring Tierra del Fuego, Conway lost interest in South America, and climbing in general. The bureaucracy had killed the romance for him: 'Mountains had called me as things of beauty and wonder, things terrible and sublime, and instead of glorying in their splendour here I was spending months in outlining the vagrant plan of them on a piece of paper. That realisation ended my mountain career'.

In later life he served as a Member of Parliament and in 1931 became a Peer of the Realm, as the first Baron, Lord Conway of Allington. At the Paris exhibition of 1900 he was awarded a gold medal for his mountain surveys, and was later honoured with the prestigious Founders Medal of the Royal Geographical Society. President of the Alpine Club from 1902, he also became the President of the Alpine Ski Club at its inaugural meeting in 1908. He also continued his stellar academic career, finishing as Slade Professor of Fine Arts at Cambridge University; it's sister chair in Oxford at one time occupied by the venerable John Ruskin. Conway was also a passionate collector of photography, and was happy to sit for the celebrated society photographer Alexander Bassano at his Old Bond Street studio, where this portrait was created. Very active to the last, Conway still found time to write several books about art history and co-edit the first series of alpine guidebooks with William Coolidge – helping to spread the practice of 'guideless' climbing, something rather ironically, that both men, traditional in their outlook, professed to deplore.

KARAKORAM, 1978
PETER BOARDMAN 1950-1982

After climbing Everest in 1975 Pete Boardman found he had become a mountaineering celebrity. Uneasy with this status, he still felt he had to prove something to his peers. Accordingly, the next year he teamed up with Joe Tasker to launch himself at what was then probably the hardest Himalayan climb yet made – the technically ferocious West Wall of Changabang.

Boardman had begun climbing when he was in his early teens, joining his local Stockport climbing club. His first visit to the Alps enthralled him and his life's course was set. A degree in English Literature at Nottingham University – where as President of the student mountaineering club, and led a trip to the Hindu Kush – was followed by a spell as an instructor and then a climbing bureaucrat with the British Mountaineering Council. Following Everest, Boardman became the Director of the glamorous International School of Mountaineering at Leysin in Switzerland. In addition to a punishing series of lecture tours Boardman had also embarked on a career as a perceptive writer, publishing an account of his ascent of Changabang, *The Shining Mountain*, to critical acclaim in 1978.

The same year Boardman attempted a new route on the West Ridge of K2, but plans were aborted after a windslab avalanche killed team member Nick Estcourt. This personal portrait shows a cheerful, if a little weary, Boardman getting dry again having crossed yet another river on the walk in to their basecamp, before the tragedy unfolded. In 1979, partnered with Tasker, Doug Scott and Georges Bettembourg, he pulled off a highly impressive alpine-style ascent of Kangchenjunga. It was among the most influential ascents of the 1970s, epitomising an approach that would

thenceforth become the only acceptable way to climb for any ambitious alpinist. There was scarcely time to recover before he was off to do the long, exposed and intricate West Ridge of Gauri Sanker. Somehow, Boardman still found time to write about these trips in his second book, *Sacred Summits*, destined to appear posthumously. The following year a small alpine-style team of Boardman, Tasker, Scott and Dick Renshaw nearly died on K2 when avalanches almost swept their camp from the mountain.

The partnership with Tasker prospered, despite an obvious rivalry. 'There was continual banter between them, which seemed to open up the chinks in each other's armour and Pete's presence seemed to induce in Joe a show of hardness and outrageous behaviour,' observed Renshaw. 'They sometimes seemed like an old married couple'. Boardman's final expedition was to Everest's North-East Ridge in 1982. He disappeared with Tasker at around 8,200m. Boardman's body was discovered in 1992 by three Kazakh mountaineers. 'It was as if he had lain down in the snow, gone to sleep and never woken,' thought Chris Bonington after seeing photographs. 'We shall probably never know just what happened, but we lost two very special friends and a unique climbing partnership whose breadth of talent went far beyond mountaineering'. They left a legacy both of inspiring, innovative ascents, but also of influential books – their exceptional abilities as writers, not least as thinkers, raising the 'expedition genre' out of an increasingly formulaic mire. The prestigious Boardman-Tasker Prize for Mountain Literature was instituted as a fitting tribute to both men's climbing and literary prowess.

RONGBUK GLACIER, 1924
HOWARD SOMERVELL 1890-1975

Although a native of the English Lake District, Somervell waited until heading south to Cambridge University before taking up climbing. Here, however, he proved to be an ace alpinist and a skilled artist too, a passion he continued all his life. During one six-week trip to the Alps with Bentley Beetham he notched up thirty-five routes, bringing both men to the attention of the Mount Everest Committee, then recruiting for the 1922 expedition. On the mountain Somervell performed as well as predicted, reaching nearly 8,300m without bottled oxygen. 'His recuperative capacity was unique', said one admiring colleague. At the height of his physical and mental powers – he had earned a Double First in Natural History from Cambridge University, and served as a front-line surgeon during the horrors of the War – Somervell displayed, not unsurprisingly, a touch of arrogance. 'Somervell is the most urbanely conceited youth I have ever struck – and quite the toughest,' thought Tom Longstaff in grudging admiration of the young Everester. The 1922 expedition leader Charlie Bruce thought likewise: 'An absolute glutton for hard work, and a wonderful goer and climber. He takes a size 22 hat. That is his only drawback'.

During the expedition Somervell formed a close friendship with George Mallory, and the two famously read Shakespeare to one another in their tent at night. Together they established camp on the North Col at about 7,000m, then the highest man had ever camped. They later set a world altitude record, but turned around when they realized they had no hope of reaching the summit before dark: 'better to live to fight another day', Somervell said at the time. He was selected to return with the ill-fated 1924 expedition for his climbing credentials and also because he was 'on the doorstep', having decided to work in India as a medical missionary. Somervell played a major role on the trip, first rescuing four porters marooned by storms and then making a bid for the summit without bottled oxygen with expedition leader Edward Norton. At 8,500m Somervell was forced to turn back because of breathing difficulties. Unbeknownst to him, he had developed frostbite in his larynx.

Norton ploughed on solo, reaching an incredible 8,570m before turning back, plagued by double vision and hallucinations. It was an altitude record that would not be broken, with certainty, until 1952. He carefully picked his way down to rejoin the ailing Somervell and returned to the North Col, but not before Somervell had almost choked to death. A section of his throat lining came loose in a coughing fit and blocked his windpipe. 'I could not, of course, make a sign to Norton, or stop him, for the rope was off now; so I sat in the snow to die while he walked on. I thought, "Oh well, this is the end. Cheerio everybody"'. In quite literally a last-gasp attempt to breathe, the medically minded Somervell attempted a dramatic form of artificial self-respiration. 'Finally, I pounded my chest with both hands, gave one last almighty push – and the obstruction came up'.

Exhausted, the two men recuperated while Mallory and Irvine prepared to make their do-or-die summit attempt; which ended in tragedy. Somervell found the strength to shoot a series of photographs and panoramas, then the highest point in the world's mountains at which photographs had been taken. It was Somervell who lent Mallory his Kodak 'Vest Pocket' camera to snap the hoped-for moment of triumph on the top of the world. After Everest, the compassionate Somervell turned his back on a lucrative surgeon's job that could have been his in London to instead devote himself to medical care in Asia, becoming head of one of the largest mission hospitals in the world at Neyvoor in Travancore, India. He served for nearly forty years as a medical missionary before returning to the Lake District for a well-earned retirement.

HAMPSHIRE, 2008
GEORGE BAND 1929-

At the age of twenty-three, George Christopher Band, a former President of the Cambridge Mountaineering Club, was the 'baby' of the 1953 British Commonwealth Everest Expedition, selected on account of his excellent Alpine record. Band proved his mettle on the trip and went one further when, two years later, together with superlative climber Joe Brown he made the first ascent of the world's third highest peak, the 8,586m Kangchenjunga. It remains the highest mountain first ascended by Britons.

Despite being a 'talented amateur' – George pursued a long and successful career in the oil and gas exploration industries – the ensuing decades would see him active in the Karakoram, Andes and the Caucasus in addition to the Alps and back home in Britain. Since the mid-1980s he has been Chairman of the Mount Everest Foundation, President of the Alpine Club, on the Council of the Royal Geographical Society and President of the British Mountaineering Council. Currently Chairman of the Himalayan Trust UK, he continues to support the late Sir Edmund Hillary's work on behalf of the Sherpa of Nepal

George describes the day his portrait was created. 'The young photographer and keen climber Ed Luke was beginning his work on creating a series of portraits of well-known British climbers. He asked if he could include me, so I invited him to my home in Hartley Wintney, Hampshire, for a photo shoot. After a session in my study, we wandered through the kitchen to go into the garden to seek further inspiration. The green door of the kitchen intrigued him as a natural frame and backdrop, so this became his preferred portrait. He showed me his interesting portfolio, so we encouraged him to mount them as a small exhibition. I was delighted when the Alpine Club agreed to host a modest world premiere of sorts, the display was called *Rock Stars*. Compared to today's exciting top athletes, you know, I felt privileged to be included!'

'Success on Everest back in 1953 changed the lives of most members of the team', George tells me, some time after his shoot. 'There were three great spin-offs which continue to this day: the Mount Everest Foundation, supporting young climbers on innovative explorations; the Duke of Edinburgh's Award of which John Hunt was the first Director; and Ed Hillary's Himalayan Trust, building schools and hospitals in the Everest area that will be a perpetual memorial to his life and achievements. I would love to have gone higher on Everest, and fortunately had the chance to grab a summit myself with Joe on Kangchenjunga two years later, on Charles Evans' very happy expedition'. As befits his pose in this stylish yet simple portrait, Band remains a gentleman, considerate and humble, no doubt about that. His courtesy for others was there that historic day in 1955 too. The British expedition honoured the beliefs of the Sikkimese, who hold the mountaintop sacred, by stopping a few feet short of the actual summit. Most successful summit parties since then have followed this tradition.

LONDON, 1967
ERIC SHIPTON 1907-1977

Thanks to their exploratory mountaineering activity, Eric Shipton and Bill Tilman are often credited with 'inventing' the notion of the *lightweight* approach, best summed up by Tilman's cherished assertion that: 'Any worthwhile expedition can be planned on the back of an envelope'. It is ironic therefore, that outside of mountaineering circles, Shipton became famous chiefly for his role in leading old-fashioned siege-style assaults on Everest. But Shipton's heart always lay in low-key, low-impact mountaineering and he was never happier than when pushing new ground over unexplored passes and valley systems.

Born into a middle-class family on a tea plantation in Sri Lanka, Eric Earle Shipton became hooked on climbing after visiting the Alps. Anxious to escape the formal constraints of conventional society, the restless Shipton headed out to a coffee plantation in Kenya, where a chance meeting with Bill Tilman would change the course of both their lives. Despite their odd-couple pairing – Shipton the dashing ladies' man who made the colonials' wives swoon when they peered into his azure eyes, Tilman the premature fogey and laconic curmudgeon – they hit it off, making one of the most celebrated partnerships in mountaineering history.

Shipton had climbed Kamet in 1931, an experience that opened his eyes to the huge untapped potential of exploratory mountaineering in the Himalaya and whetted his appetite for more. Although he would undertake more 'traditional' excursions to Everest in 1933, '35, and '36 the experiences left him with grave reservations about the value of large-scale expeditions. 'I sometimes thought that bedsores were a more serious hazard than frostbite or strained hearts', he wrote in his journal. So, during the rest of the 1930s he teamed up with Tilman to roam across the Himalaya like mountaineering nomads, undertaking a seven-month exploratory climbing expedition to make the first traverse of the Rishi Ganga Gorge, the first exploration of the Nanda Devi 'Sanctuary', and a four-month trip across the Karakoram.

Following the Second World War Shipton became embroiled in the national obsession with Everest once again, being sent by the Joint Himalayan Committee in 1951 to reconnoitre a route up the mountain from Nepal. But, spooked by the near success of the Swiss on Everest in 1952, they ousted the popular, but laid-back Shipton from leadership of the 1953 expedition, and replaced him with a 'thruster'; the no-nonsense logistics expert Colonel John Hunt. Though this very public demotion frustrated him hugely at the time, it was to turn out to be a blessing, allowing him to return to an arena that he knew and loved best; the small, free-ranging exploratory trip. Shipton's final great exploratory mountaineering would take place in the late 1950s and 1960s in Patagonia's Tierra del Fuego, on its remote ice caps and storm-lashed sub-Antarctic ranges which few had penetrated, making the first ascents of several peaks, including Mount Darwin and Mount Bove.

The last decade of Shipton's life was partly spent as a celebrity lecturer with trekking groups or on cruise ships to exotic locations. The charismatic half-plate portrait by the Bassano studio is from this period, as Shipton had become the well-respected elder statesman of British, in fact, global mountaineering. For a man who cut a fine figure in the smartest of Savile Row suits, London society was not his natural habitat, and he was too brilliant a man to have any real interest in the glittering cocktail parties of the fashionable set. Wilderness was his terrain, and there are few men in history who have had such mastery, and a sensitivity, of travelling through it and upwards to its summits. His was no conquest of the mountains, but a profound respect and pleasure to spend time in these places. And it was the simplicity of this approach that sets him apart from other, more publicly famous climbers. He died in 1977 following prostate cancer, the same year as his great old partner Tilman was lost at sea somewhere off the Falklands. 'If I had another life I'd like to be a Yaghan Indian', he once told a Chilean friend. 'Just a pot and matches and go fishing'.

SOUTH COL, 1953
GEORGE LOWE 1924-

When George Lowe met Edmund Hillary while working in New Zealand's Southern Alps just after the war and struck up a friendship, little did he know it would be the beginning of a journey to the highest altitudes and latitudes on the planet.

In 1951 Lowe joined the first New Zealand expedition to the Himalaya, exploring the Indian Garhwal and was part of the team that climbed Mukut Parbat. This led to his being invited to join Eric Shipton's Everest Reconnaissance expedition of 1952 during which he was tasked with investigating high altitude physiology and the effects that differing flow rates from bottled oxygen apparatus might have on climbing performance.

The following year he was an integral part of the successful 1953 Everest expedition during which his friend Hillary summitted along with Tenzing. Lowe, together with Alf Gregory and Ang Nima Sherpa supported the summit pair, placing a final advance camp just 300m below the 8,850m summit. This personal portrait, by Hillary, shows a typically cheerful Lowe at Camp VIII on the South Col. More expeditions followed: to Makalu in 1954, again with Hillary, although the mountain was not climbed. Then, after meeting Sir Vivian Fuchs, he and Hillary were invited to join the Commonwealth Trans-Antarctic Expedition. The ever versatile Lowe was given the job of filming the first crossing of the continent. His superlative still imagery and footage from this pioneering expedition are a lasting tribute to his skills, and his courage, as an explorer and man of a bewildering array of talents. 'He was', Hillary described, 'just such a good bloke. Gentle, brilliant, and humble. Simply first-class'. High praise indeed, from this most respected of mountain men. After the Everest frenzy had abated a little, Hillary returned to New Zealand and got married and it was Lowe who was there at his side as his best man.

Following Everest, Lowe felt he ought to get a proper job and became a teacher in England. Exploration was not forgotten, however, and he was involved in many trips with school pupils to Greenland, Greece and Ethiopia, as well as 'grown-up' trips to Everest again and to the Pamirs with John Hunt. Following a spell as director of a school in Chile he returned to England to become a schools' inspector. He helped to found the Sir Edmund Hillary Himalayan Trust in 1989, succeeding Sir Chris Bonington as Patron in 2008, and helping to continue its wonderful work among the people of Nepal.

It was Lowe who first congratulated Hillary and Tenzing, as they made their way successfully down from the summit of Everest, that brilliant May day back in 1953. Lowe had been observing their progress from high on the Col, and climbed up to the couloir above the Col to meet them as they descended. He brought with him a thermos of warm tomato soup and a hug, to shelter them for a moment from the wind. Hillary unclipped his mask, grinned a tired greeting and then sat down on the ice for a rest. Finally looking up to his old friend, he said in his matter-of-fact way: 'Well George, we knocked the bastard off!'

CONISTON, 1894
JOHN RUSKIN 1819-1900

It might seem strange that a man who said, 'all the best views of hills are at the bottom of them', and 'the real ground for reprehension of alpine climbing is that it excites more vanity than any other athletic sport', would have such a profound impact on the development of mountaineering. But is it likely that climbing would never have evolved in quite the same way without the Victorian artist and reforming intellectual John Ruskin.

With his perceptive prose Ruskin cut through the soft-focus haze generated by the Romantic poets and painters, yet also abhorred the concept of mountaineering for fun. 'True lovers of natural beauty', he declaimed with almost Cromwellian fervour, 'would as soon think of climbing the pillars of the choir at Beavais for a gymnastic exercise, as of making a playground of Alpine snow'. Ironically, his writings about the Alps had quite the opposite effect, encouraging a much greater awareness of the superb mountains lying across the Channel, and stimulating a desire in others to climb up them.

Ruskin was born into a well-off London family who followed the fashionable habit of leisurely summer tours across Europe. His first visit to the Alps captivated him; an emotional experience he would later encapsulate in his assertion that mountains are 'the beginning and end of all natural scenery'. He advocated the idea that mountains could play a spiritual role in human life, that one didn't necessarily have to be a natural historian to be interested or appreciate them. For Ruskin, travel amongst mountains could help mankind to learn more about itself.

Such ideas helped to definitively bring to an end the era when such landscapes were regarded as threatening, ugly and dangerous. Yet Ruskin never felt able to climb much himself. His suspicion of the motives of those wishing to climb the peaks he held in such sacred regard was probably strengthened by his accidental encounter in Chamonix with the 'Barnum of Mont Blanc', Albert Smith, when the showman arrived from his successful ascent. The sight and sound of salutes fired from cannon in celebration and general razzmatazz was probably what led Ruskin to later denounce 'sporting' climbing, saying mountains were being used, 'as soaped poles in a bear-garden', which too many people 'climb and slide down again with shrieks of delight'.

This elegant portrait was created by Fred Hollyer in September 1894 at Ruskin's home Brantwood, a lodge commanding views over Coniston Water in the heart of the Lake District. Then Ruskin was in fading health and in fear of losing his mind – 'the monsoons and cyclones of my poor old plagued brains'. Though he professed to disliking having his portrait taken, Ruskin is known to have sat for well over 100 paintings and, wittingly or not, for over eighty photographs. He was 'always at his best full face', one journalist described, 'as his profile sometimes assumes a predatory appearance with his prominent beak-like nose. As a young man he was quite handsome; as an old man his looks betokened the prophet and sage that he was'.

ESTES PARK, 2011
THOMAS HORNBEIN 1930-

Tom Hornbein began his climbing career at the age of thirteen when he ascended Signal Mountain in Colorado, after a childhood of climbing trees and houses in his hometown of St Louis. All else that followed, he tells me, 'really unfolded from that point onwards, and mountains were at the heart of everything – climbing, mountain rescue, medicine, family and friends, and as the spiritual place to season a life of adventures of many flavours'.

Tom began making first ascents in the Estes Park and Long's Peak area while studying geology at Boulder in the 1950s and this pioneering theme would continue throughout his life. His curiosity about how the human body reacts to high altitude led him to swap sciences to study medicine at Washington University in St Louis and he soon turned his climbing attentions to the Himalaya.

In 1960 he joined an expedition to Masherbrum, which led to an invitation to join an American expedition to Everest in 1963. Partnered by Willi Unsoeld he made both the first ascent of the mountain's formidable West Ridge, and the first traverse of the peak by descending the South-East Ridge (bivouacking on the latter at 8,530m). It was a climb that mountaineer and award-winning author Jon Krakauer has declared to be 'one of the great feats in the annals of mountaineering'.

As a result, Tom is one of the few people to have a feature on Everest named after him: the Hornbein Couloir, which formed part of their traverse route. Tom allowed climbing to take second place to his medical career following his literal high point on Everest and went on to become professor and chairman of the Department of Anesthesiology at the University of Seattle. He now makes his home in Colorado, where photographer Claudia López tracked him down to create this portrait.

Tom is an 'exceptional' man, veteran mountaineer Doug Scott describes, and the West Ridge ascent is 'in a class all its own, when one considers the history of Everest'. When Unsoeld and Hornbein left their top camp, with more than 600m of extreme terrain above them, they were genuinely stepping out into the unknown. 'The price of climbing in Himalayan style is that only a part of the expedition has a chance to summit. The rest are forced to invest their own desires for the realization of something more worthy and lasting. This was the case with the West Ridge, where team spirit was seen at its best. The positive energy generated by Dick Emerson, Al Auten, Barry Corbett and the Sherpas during the final buildup went to the top with Horbein and Unsoeld. Really there was a bit of all of us up there; the rather sizeable bit that wants to know what we do not know about the world we live in, but mostly seeks to know about ourselves'.

The story of Everest belongs to many men but in Hornbein the mountain accepted a man equal to its challenge. 'It's a place I find so hard to describe, it's so difficult to sum it all up. The drama, the hardship, the toiling up windswept heights, as well as the day-to-day reality of it all – the grubby unbathed living, of hours of sweaty boredom and moments of fun or introspective aloneness. I can't speak of today's mountain and those who travel the world to go and slog up it. But, I can say, at that moment back in 1963, it was a magnificent setting where men were human beings, nothing more … and nothing less'.

TRIVOR, 1960

WILFRID NOYCE 1917-1962

Described as 'the last of the scholar-mountaineers', in many ways Noyce represented the end of an era in British mountaineering that had often been characterised by earnest, privately educated Oxbridge men. An amateur poet and intellectual, he was known for exploring the spiritual side of climbing in his writing, whilst also being phenomenally gifted in perilous situations on remote mountains the world over. That is, until the day a mountain took his life.

As a teenager, young Cuthbert Wilfrid Francis Noyce became well known for his exploits on Welsh rock, putting up climbs such as *Soap Gut* on the Milestone and seconding John Menlove Edwards on the first free ascent of *Munich Climb* also on Tryfan. In late adolescence, Noyce had a short-lived affair with Edwards, which would have devastating psychological effects on the tortured soul of the troubled and sensitive Liverpool climbing genius. Noyce later collaborated with Edwards in compiling the guidebooks to Tryfan and Lliwedd and the pair spent a good deal of time climbing together.

It was during his time that Noyce suffered his first major accident when in 1937 he fell from near the top of *Mickledore Grooves* on Scafell in the Lake District. Noyce was unconscious for three days and needed plastic surgery on his face – the results of which were to give him a strangely youthful appearance for the rest of his life. There were further accidents in 1939 when he badly broke a leg on Ben Nevis and in 1946 when he fractured the other falling off a climb on Great Gable. 'I was blown bodily off an easy rib of the climb, and my leg just crumpled under me', he later wrote. Unfairly, perhaps, but unsurprisingly, his contemporaries secretly regarded him as accident-prone. Nevertheless, Noyce quickly recovered from most of his injuries and came back climbing harder and in more innovative ways.

Already noted for his rapid climbing feats in the Alps, Noyce became one of the leading post-war British alpinists, achieving early repeats of climbs such as the *Welzenbach Route* on the north face of the Dent d'Herens, and extended his range to the Himalaya where he was on the first ascents of the ferocious Machapuchare, Fluted Peak and the 7,577m Trivor in the Karakoram, the 'Unknown Mountain'. This is where this striking summit portrait was taken, just as the clouds rolled in great silvery billows. No photographs existed of the mountain face that the expedition had intended to climb, and even officials in Pakistan were unable to locate it on their maps. This abstract, unexplored landmass stimulated Noyce to write a brilliant account of the adventure when he returned to England, touching on the magic of the mountain and the hold that these high places have in both the heart and the mind's eye. Once on the climb itself, the expedition was broken up by sickness, and until the last day it seemed as though the summit would escape them. 'But summit-taking alone does not send out expeditions to the Himalaya', Noyce later reflected, 'it is the knowledge of Nature and of *self* gained in the ascent, along with an interest in the peoples who live in the shadow of great peaks. The mountain remains unknown as before, but those who climbed it know themselves a little better, for the climbing'.

Noyce was also selected as a member of the 1953 British and Commonwealth Everest expedition, where he played a major role in breaking the route to the South Col. He finally met his maker on a British-Soviet expedition to the Pamirs in 1962, after a successful ascent of the 6,595m Mount Garmo. On the descent, when roped to his climbing partner Robin Smith, one of them slipped on a layer of soft snow over ice, pulling the other, and they both fell some 1,200m to their deaths.

LOCH GARTEN, 2011
ANDY NISBET 1953-

Seen here dusted in snow on the shores of Loch Garten in the Cairngorms, Andy Nisbet is in his natural element. For if Britain has ever produced anyone who could be described as a 'Mountain Man', it is surely the Aberdonian Nisbet. As proverbially tough as the granite of his native city, but renowned for his gentle temperament, he has been committed to a life of mountaineering action since a child. From the age of nineteen, when he became the then-youngest person to have completed all the Munros, scarcely a day has passed when he has not been climbing, or planning his next campaign, most often in his beloved Scottish Highlands.

Nisbet is especially revered for his winter climbs. Along with other Scots in the late 1970s such as Colin MacLean, Murray Hamilton and Kenny Spence, Nisbet led the way in pioneering the imaginative use of modern ice-tools on mixed ground which led to such huge leaps in technical standards. However, of them all it is Nisbet who has consistently maintained his enthusiasm and drive over many hard winter seasons. In an unfussy manner and helped by an unsurpassed knowledge of Scotland's mountains, he has contributed over 800 new routes in the past three decades. And of the 600-or-so climbs in Scotland currently graded V or over, Nisbet's name features on the first ascent details of a quarter of them.

Furthermore, it is a record that has been gained in one of the toughest climbing areas on the planet. The Highland's remote cliffs, mountain faces, gullies and summits are prone to storms and winds of Patagonian ferocity and nearly always entail an arduous approach over bog and moor. In this savage arena Nisbet has survived huge falls, been raked by rockfall and been carried down the mountain in an avalanche.

Nisbet has not only recovered from such setbacks but, in a mark of the true enthusiast, remains as keen as ever. He seems as content to pioneer a new Grade II as much as a IX, and he appears to be showing no let-up in productivity despite reaching his mid-fifties and acquiring a new hip (required after suffering a series of nasty motoring accidents in addition to his climbing injuries). Throughout it all, he has retained a characteristic serenity, a stillness not dissimilar to this morning beside the great Loch in this portrait, shortly before the winter storm clouds gathered once more. 'Don't let the pace of modern life dominate', is his advice to younger men. 'Make time for your climbing. Life is simpler in the mountains. I go there so I can focus on what I'm enjoying in order to achieve the very best from it. Simple, really'.

NANGA PARBAT, 1953
HERMANN BUHL 1924-1957

Hermann Buhl remains one of the most iconic of European mountaineers. He made significant climbs in a highly fluid style before he died at the height of his powers. Among mountaineers the Austrian's legacy lies in his influence in bringing 'Alpine-Style' dash and élan to climbing the big mountains of the Greater Ranges.

His solo ascent of Nanga Parbat in 1953 in particular was a *tour de force*. Buhl was so far ahead of the rest of the German-Austrian team in terms of speed and ability that on the summit bid day he simply left his partner behind and made for the top despite technically difficult ground and the knowledge that this dangerous mountain had already claimed thirty-one lives, including a significant proportion of the inter-war German climbing elite. Buhl spent a night at over 8,000m with no shelter, before returning after forty-one hours alone, hallucinating with frostbitten toes. This famous portrait, arguably one of the most iconic in mountaineering history, was taken as Buhl made his descent. Buhl's book about his adventure, *Nanga Parbat Pilgrimage*, became a classic of mountaineering literature that would inspire thousands of climbers.

Buhl was born in Innsbruck and began climbing as a teenager in the Austrian Alps, rapidly becoming an expert and joining a mountain rescue team. During the Second World War he served with the Alpine troops, seeing action in Italy before being captured. Following the war he trained as a guide and was clearly technically ahead of most of his peers at this time. He made many spectacular climbs in the Alps, often solo, and was particularly skilful at negotiating loose rock.

One of his most severe tests of character came in 1951 during an ascent of the Eiger North Face. Buhl and Sepp Jochler became trapped by bad weather high on the notorious face. The rock soon became coated in verglas and the climb turned into a battle to survive. Three other parties with a total of seven climbers were also on the face, including the famous experts Gaston Rebuffat and Guido Magnone. Buhl took the lead and fought his way up the Exit Cracks despite near-impossible conditions. Rebuffat remembered that: 'On the fourth day Hermann gave his all for us on one rope length for four hours. And then at the top suddenly flipped over and was hanging head down. So naturally I went up to him and had to turn him right way up, and seeing he was no longer in a fit state to lead, I had no option but to take over. Buhl had not only achieved absolute mastery, he had climbed above all the others'.

The experience would serve him well on Nanga Parbat in 1953. 'Mountaineering is a relentless pursuit', he described in 1956. 'One climbs further and further yet never reaches the destination. Perhaps that is what gives it its own particular charm. One is constantly searching for something never to be found'. The following year on Broad Peak he and his companions proved that, without any help from high altitude porters, a small team could climb an 8,000m mountain. But it was Buhl's last summit. Some days later, attempting Chogolisa, he fell through a cornice to his death.

NANGA PARBAT, 1978
REINHOLD MESSNER 1944 -

By climbing all the 8,000m peaks in the world Reinhold Messner became one of the most influential Himalayan climbers of the twentieth century, if not indeed one of the most impressive ever. There is little need for debate about this. It is a fact. His demonstration that it was possible to climb the highest mountains without the use of supplemental oxygen raised the bar for others wishing to emulate his feats, while his ethical views about clean styles of climbing continue to hold great currency amongst the élite performers of the sport.

Born in Italy's South Tyrol, the German-speaking Messner's reputation originally lay with his accomplishments in the Alps during the 1960s, where he made over 500 ascents and many significant new routes. But in 1970 he joined an expedition to attempt the vast and fearsome Rupal Face of the Karakoram's Nanga Parbat, the highest rock face in the world. Messner succeeded in reaching the summit with his brother Günther, but tragedy struck on the descent when Günther was killed in an avalanche. Shaken by the loss of his brother and suffering frostbite injuries (six toes were amputated), it was two years before he returned to high-altitude climbing, beginning again in stunning fashion on the totally unknown South Face of Manaslu. From then on he began to pick off all the fourteen 8,000m peaks, startling the world with his and Peter Habeler's ascent of Everest without using supplementary oxygen in 1978 and reaching his final 'eight-thousander', Lhotse, in 1986. In between, Messner made expeditions to other mountains, most notably Denali, Aconcagua and Kilimanjaro and also revisited some of the 8,000m peaks to make innovative styles of ascents. Following his high altitude odyssey, Messner switched his focus to polar exploration and more general wilderness travel. Following a spell as a Green Party politician he is now concentrating his energies on building an ambitious series of mountain-themed museums in his native Tyrol.

Two climbs stand out in a long career of superlatives. His oxygen-less solo climb of Everest's North-East Ridge in 1980 was the first time that the world's highest peak had been climbed in such a manner, while his ascent of a new route up Nanga Parbat's Diamir Face, without oxygen and porter support, broke considerable new ground. Having tried three times to create a new route, he finally achieved his dream, using up every last ounce of courage and energy to claw himself to the summit on 9 August 1978. This was the first solo ascent of any 8,000m mountain. Using his ice-axe as a tripod, Messner was able to photograph himself on the summit that day. There he left a parchment copy of the first page of the Gutenberg Bible: 'In the beginning God created...' He had been there once already, with his younger brother. They had hugged each other. It had been their first eight-thousander. It was also to be their last together. After an hour or so alone at the top, Reinhold shouldered his pack, and began his descent through the drifting snow. Asked to choose a favourite portrait for this book, over a lifetime in the mountains, Messner offered this image. It is not hard to understand what this photograph means to him.

GANESH, 1955

CLAUDE KOGAN 1919-1959

In 1959 the diminutive French swimwear designer and accomplished alpinist Claude Kogan set out for the 8,200m summit of Cho Oyu, the world's sixth-highest peak. She was joined by her friend, a Belgian, Claudine van der Stratten. They were never to return. Their top camp was struck by a devastating avalanche killing the two women and their two Sherpas. It brought a tragic end to the most ambitious mountaineering venture then undertaken by an all-woman team, and to the life of one of France's most striking and accomplished female alpinists.

The pioneering womens' trip to Cho Oyu – which was notable for not only its all-female contingent but by being international – was Kogan's brainchild. It had been born from what Kogan described as 'a boiling, impotent rage' after failing to climb the mountain with famed Swiss climber Raymond Lambert. Stymied, within reach of the summit, Kogan felt they had not tried hard enough and was left with a desire to prove that women were every bit as determined and tough as male mountaineers.

Kogan, at just over five feet tall, certainly did not fit the stereotypical image of the post-war testosterone-fuelled macho-mountaineer. Born in Paris to an impoverished mother, she left school at fifteen and became a seamstress. She was introduced to climbing by her future husband George Kogan in Nice. When France was occupied by the Nazis, they sought refuge in the Mercantour massif. Following the war they resumed a clothing business in the south of France where they had a small clothing factory. Kogan designed the swimwear and among their early customers was Christian Dior.

In 1951 the Kogans joined a Franco-Belgian Expedition to the Cordillera Blanca of Peru. Claude and Nicole Leiniger reached the summit of Alpamayo (5,947m) and Qjitaraju (6,100m). Later that year Claude was widowed after George died, but her passion for climbing remained undimmed. In 1952 she returned to the Andes and made the summit of Salcantay (6,081m) with Bernard Pierre and the following year she was part of his Himalayan expedition to Nun in the Kashmir. After most of the climbers had been caught in an avalanche, she and Pierre Vittoz successfully made the first ascent of the mountain. Her second Himalayan expedition was the attempt on Cho Oyu in 1954 when she and Raymond Lambert were only some 500m from the top when turned back by bad conditions. Nevertheless, her altitude record for women of 7,600m lasted many years. The following year she achieved her second Himalayan summit climbing Ganesh I. Keen to return to Cho Oyu, Kogan secured financial backing from *Paris-Match*, and set about recruiting twelve women climbers from Britain, France, Belgium, Switzerland and Nepal before meeting her untimely end, swept off the mountain by a wave of tumbling snow and ice.

e Nés bien
amicalement
Claude

GANESH. HIMALAYA.

FRÊNEY, 1961
DON WHILLANS 1933-1985

One of the great characters of British climbing, Don Whillans epitomized the changes that swept through British society in the post-war period. In the 1950s, with his partner Joe Brown they rapidly established themselves as the best climbers in the country, with Whillans' sometimes raucous behaviour, blunt character and mordant wit signifying an anarchic working-class takeover of a hitherto predominantly middle-class activity.

Brought up in Salford, Manchester, Whillans trained as a plumber and began hillwalking on the nearby Pennines. Within two weeks of being introduced to steeper terrain he was leading 'Very Severe' climbs. In 1951 he met Brown, and together they rewrote the rulebook of British climbing, powering up steep, serious lines in the Peak District, Wales and Scotland, and establishing a standard of climbing which had been regarded as impossible by the pre-war generation of climbers. Whillans also blazed a trail for a British revival in the Alps, climbing with a range of partners and making many impressive ascents. Whillans' most significant contribution to European climbing was, arguably, his role in the first ascent of the difficult Central Pillar of Frêney on Mont Blanc, an action-packed affair during which a 'race' developed between a Continental team led by René Desmaison and the British/Polish team comprising Whillans, Chris Bonington, Ian Clough and Jan Djuglosz. This famous portrait shows Don high on the Frêney Face, in typical pose: flat cap on head and well-earned cigarette in his mouth.

After Frêney, Whillans concentrated on expedition climbing – and socialising, as his increasing girth began to testify. Once asked why he drank so much beer he replied, 'I have a morbid fear of dehydration'. In the early 1960s he was successful in Patagonia on *Poincenot* and the Central Tower of Paine but arguably his greatest mountaineering moment arrived on the summit of Annapurna in 1970 when, with Dougal Haston, he battled up extremely arduous rock on the mountain's South Face against all the odds.

Whillans also brought to bear a strength of character to match his physical prowess; in his encounters with officialdom, and other climbers, he rarely came off worse. He had a reputation as a mean brawler, with many stories circulating including one in which he punched a conductor from a moving bus. One local newspaper headline reporting Whillans' unwilling arrest for drink-driving memorably read: 'Five-foot Climber Floors Six Coppers'. A legend was born; hence his nickname 'The Villain'. Earning himself a cult following, he also designed mountaineering equipment, including the 'Whillans Harness', once described as an innovation to safely transport beer-guts to great height. But, sadly, it was his copious drinking that would eventually hasten his downfall. 'I don't worry about when I'm sixty-five', he once said. 'Many people don't get that far anyway, and there's no guarantee that I will'. Whillans was just fifty-two when he had a fatal heart attack while gearing up for a climb in Wales.

BAFFIN ISLAND, 1998
GREG CHILD 1957-

Australian Greg Child began his climbing career with hard new routes on Mount Arapiles before moving to the USA in 1980. There he became a leading pioneer of the era in Yosemite, making new routes on El Capitan before switching his attention, and considerable skills on rock, to extreme mountaineering. He has since made over thirteen mountaineering expeditions to the Himalaya and among his accomplishments are climbs to the summit of Everest and K2, a new route up Shivling, the first ascent of the North-West Ridge of Gasherbrum IV and a new route up the Trango Tower. Child has also made first ascents of peaks in Baffin Island and Alaska.

In this striking photograph by Gordon Wiltsie, Greg ascends his fixed rope high on Great Sail Peak, above a blanket of subzero fog in the Stewart Valley. From Arctic lows of minus 30, as the sun cleared later in the expedition on the north-facing wall, summer temperatures soared. The two men were on assignment for *National Geographic*, pioneering a climb, and creating a story, among these remote and mostly impregnable stone ramparts.

Also well known for his award-winning climbing writing, photography and film documentaries, Child has recently concentrated on more general mountain exploration. In 1999 he penetrated little-visited jungles in India to seek out unclimbed peaks on the Indo-Tibet border, his expedition team becoming the first Westerners to encounter the Bungaroo people of the upper Kurung Valley in the process. Other typical recent adventures include a 150km lightweight backpacking traverse of Comb Ridge, a stretch of the Arizona-Utah desert that encompasses the heartlands of the ancient, and vanished, Anasazi Indian culture. 'For all the complexities that exist in climbing, it's actually a very primal thing for those who do it,' says Child. 'It's true that climbing meets some kind of basic need in me'.

EVEREST, 1980

KRZYSZTOF WIELICKI 1950-

Krzysztof Wielicki epitomizes the spirit of a generation of incredibly tough Polish mountaineers who dominated Himalayan climbing through much of the mid-1970s to the late 1980s. And Wielicki was one of the toughest – choosing to specialize in arguably the most arduous forms of high altitude climbing: winter and solo ascents. Wielicki's passion for climbing transcended the problems caused by having to operate under an economically constrained communist regime. As a youngster he had to improvise. 'We had no access to decent equipment', he recalls. 'I remember walking around in the wintertime in the Karkonosze Mountains with an alpenstock cut out in the woods from a root'.

He also shrugged off climbing accidents and injuries that would have stopped the careers of lesser climbers dead. In his first year of climbing he fell, breaking his back. 'At the clinic, they stuffed me into a plaster corset up to my neck. The only problem was, it was the end of April, 1970, the beginning of end-of-term examinations. My brother was getting married and my mother simply couldn't know that I was climbing at all. I was afraid of how she might react. For my brother's wedding, I cut the plaster with a knife edge. I escaped from the hospital through the balcony and out across the roof'.

In another mishap in the Dolomites in 1973 a rock smashed Wielicki's helmet and injured his head – but he kept on climbing anyway despite temporarily losing consciousness and 'dripping with sweat and blood'. Though a doctor advised him to stop, he continued the climbing trip for another fortnight with stitches in his scalp. Another learning experience occurred on an expedition to Afghanistan in 1977. Wielicki and his two companions dropped a rucksack containing all the food while in the middle of an alpine-style ascent – resulting in an eight-day starvation scramble to return to base camp. After such experiences, scaling Himalayan giants in winter seemed comparatively benign and in 1980 he became the first person to climb Everest in winter. This characteristic portrait was created by Bogdan Jankowski just after he came back from the summit. Returning home to a hero's welcome, Wielicki was rewarded by a grateful Polish government with the gift of a colour television.

During the 1980s, like many of his fellow Polish mountaineers, Wielicki funded his expeditions by working in rope access, painting factory chimneys, power station cooling towers and the like. 'I painted almost the whole of Silesia', he joked. In the summer of 1984 he made a world record on Broad Peak by becoming the first person to climb an 8,000m mountain in under twenty-four hours. Wielicki went on to become the fifth man to climb all fourteen 8,000m peaks, with another two of them (Kangchenjunga and Lhotse) as the first winter ascents and four (Lhotse, Dhaulagiri, Gasherbrum II and Nanga Parbat) solo. It was, however, not achieved without cost: a rock avalanche shortened his spine on Bahirati II, while he has been avalanched three times and fallen into crevasses. Despite the injuries, and the deaths of many friends, he still loves the mountains. 'You can change your hobbies, not your passion', he says. 'With time, it fills all spheres of your life'.

LONDON, 1902
SIR LESLIE STEPHEN 1832-1904

The privilege of a wealthy background allowed Old Etonian Leslie Stephen to become one of the first obsessively competitive mountaineers in the world. Unlike many of his peers, who preferred traditional pursuits such as fox hunting, Stephen was keen on a sport that would take him to foreign fields. 'Bagging' virgin Alpine peaks became his thing, and he was exceptionally talented at it.

Between 1858 and 1877 he was the 'Golden Age of Mountaineering' personified, making dozens of first ascents or new routes up the now classic peaks of the western Alps such as the Zinarothorn, Alphubel and Monte Disgrazia. More remarkably, unlike others who were attempting to formulate the protocols of early mountaineering activity, he eschewed the subterfuge of scientific exploration and openly admitted he did it for sporting challenge – thereby making respectable the notion that there was no necessity to invoke special pleading to justify climbing mountains. This did not impress everyone. 'He made a fetish of his athleticism', thought a Cambridge University contemporary.

But Stephen didn't feel the need to intellectualize his climbing – he did enough of that off the mountain. Among many other things he was a one-time Anglican clergyman, journalist, a serene literary biographer, a philosophical historian, theorist, and pioneer of evolutionary ethics. The literary trend spilled over into his domestic life – his first wife was William Thackeray's daughter, while among his children by his second wife was the great novelist Virginia Woolf. It is therefore perhaps unsurprising that Stephen wrote arguably the first (and still one of the best and most entertaining) mountaineering books, *The Playground of Europe*, which, together with Whymper's *Scrambles Amongst the Alps*, can be reckoned to have initiated the genre of mountaineering literature.

Stephen though had no illusions about the importance of mountaineering within the grand scheme of things. 'When history comes to pronounce upon men of the time', he said, 'it won't put mountaineering on a level with patriotism or even with excellence in fine arts'. In later life, he still loved travelling in the mountains, although he dearly missed being able to climb them. Writing to a friend: 'I wander about at the foot of the gigantic Alps, and look up longingly to the summits ... I lately watched through a telescope the small black dots which were really men creeping up the high flanks of Monte Rosa, and I lingered about the spot with a mixture of pleasure and pain in the envious contemplation of my more fortunate companions'.

This charismatic half-plate glass negative was created by George Beresford, the popular family photographer in his studio on London's Brompton Road. Stephen had been taken for a sitting by his beloved daughter Virginia, as he was just about to go into hospital. It was surgery from which he struggled to recover. This would be his final photograph. Virginia later described her father in a private letter to a friend: 'He was beautiful in the distinguished way a racehorse, even with an ugly face, is beautiful ... and he had such a fling with his hands and feet'.

EL CAPITAN, 2005
STEPH DAVIS 1973-

One of the leading female rock climbers in the world, Steph Davis is renowned for her 2003 one-day ascent of Yosemite's El Capitan – only the second woman ever to achieve this feat. Furthermore, in 2005 she completed the first female free ascent of the *Salathé Wall* and made a one-day speed ascent of the fearsome Torre Egger in Patagonia. This stunning portrait, by renowned adventure photographer Jimmy Chin, captures Steph in her element, high on El Capitan, pushing her skills and her courage to the limit.

Also famed for her hard solo climbs – Davis is likely to be the only woman to have soloed a climb graded as hard as 5.11+ – in 2007 she soloed *The Diamond*, a 1,000-ft route on Colorado's Long's Peak, four times for a film, before BASE-jumping from the summit. With a famously chilled personality, Davis has eschewed a conventional career in order to pursue these adrenaline mountain sports, extreme climbing, jumping and wing-suit flying. 'Frankly, I really dislike shopping', she says. 'It's necessary to purchase things like food and gear, of course, but my goal is usually to spend as little time possible doing this task'.

Needless to say, she lasted just five days at law school before quitting and moving to Colorado, and living out of her car (initially her grandmother's hand-me-down Oldsmobile Cutlass Ciera, later upgrading to a Ford Ranger pickup), guiding, and waitressing to feed her climbing habit. Eventually, she made Moab her home by 'acquiring a storage unit and a library card'. 'You know, when you live in a trailer, it really keeps you honest,' she says. 'You shouldn't have any kind of mess that doesn't look good. Immediately, it's trashy!'

As a consequence, although she may have missed out on the dollars, she has gained a richness in mountain experience few others can claim, having travelled the world to pursue her climbing dreams. Davis has been on expeditions to create new routes in alpine, big wall, and solo styles, in Pakistan, Kyrgyzstan, Baffin Island, Italy, and South America, becoming the first American woman to summit Fitzroy in Patagonia and to summit all seven major peaks of the Fitzroy Range.

'I love being in the mountains because I feel happiest in natural, pure places where my direction comes from the elements', she tells me, when we talk a little about her experiences, and that truly ground-breaking ascent of El Cap back in 2005. 'I'd always seen the *Salathé* free as an ultimate dream climb. There is very little moderate climbing at all on the route, and the headwall pitches are sustained, strenuous and technical, and super exposed. It's an amazing route but, as you know, there is just so much to celebrate by getting out there in amongst the mountains, whatever you're climbing. Spending time in wild places will always remind you that in the great scheme of nature, the universe, and geologic time, you are just the tiniest smidge of all the other energies at play. And I think this is really good for people to remember'.

LONDON, 1992
BARON JOHN HUNT 1910-1998

Born in Simla in 1910, Henry Cecil John Hunt was the eldest son of an Indian Army Officer. Following in his late father's military footsteps, he became a high-flier at Sandhurst where he gained the nickname 'Thruster John'. Hunt was introduced to skiing and mountaineering in the Alps, and took his new-found passion back to Asia while serving with the Indian Army, first attempting Saltoro Kangri in 1935. He was turned down for the 1936 Everest Expedition on the grounds of a medical examination, which suggested he had a weak heart. He was even advised to take care going up stairs. Undeterred, he set off into the hills, reconnoitring the eastern slopes of Kangchenjunga, climbing the South-West summit of Nepal Peak and making the third ascent of the Zemu La.

In 1940 Hunt was called from the heat of the sub-continent and swapped his Shalwar Kameez for a Kilt to become chief Instructor at the Commando Mountain and Snow Warfare School in Braemar. In 1943 he was on the Italian front, winning a DSO during desperate action. With the war over, a call came from London to take command of a new British and Commonwealth expedition to Everest.

The British had permission to try the mountain in 1953, but should they fail, French and Swiss teams were lining up to make their own attempts. A feeling close to high anxiety appeared to have gripped the decision-makers in London. In their eyes there was more than climbing a mountain at stake; national prestige depended on it. In a series of political manoeuvrings, they ousted the popular, but laid-back civilian Eric Shipton from leadership, and replaced him with the 'thruster', and by then a colonel, John Hunt. 'We've got this one chance, and if we don't get it right we've had it. And dammit, it's our mountain', the Himalayan Committee's secretary told Hunt. An old-fashioned amateur approach was decisively squashed by a new corporate managerialism. Though many of the climbers felt a strong loyalty to Shipton, and were unhappy by his replacement, Hunt's attractive personality and frank admission that the change had been badly done, soon won the men over.

To quote Jim Perrin, 'the 1953 venture was less expedition than expeditionary force'. The British were determined not to fail and, for once, everything seemed to go in their favour. The weather was reasonable, Hunt's revered organizational ability lived up to expectations, the team was a strong and happy one and, arguably most importantly, they had got the science right. On 29 May Edmund Hillary and Tenzing Norgay gained the summit. The news filtered back to Britain just in time to coincide with the coronation of the new Queen Elizabeth on 2 June. The country, still rationed and under austerity measures after the war, was beside itself with pride.

Hunt found himself in great demand for various worthy public offices after his success on Everest; he served on myriad national committees and was responsible for founding the Duke of Edinburgh Award. He was awarded the National Geographic Society Hubbard Medal and the Founder's Gold Medal from the Royal Geographical, among countless other gongs and honorary degrees. He was made a life peer by the Queen for his work with young people, gazetted as Baron Hunt of Llanvair Waterdine. Hunt later represented the Liberal Democrats in the House of Lords, where this elegant portrait was created by Nick Sinclair. When Hunt passed away in 1998, friends from around the world paid tribute. Sir Edmund Hillary, though fiercely loyal to Shipton in those early days, was the first to recognize all that he owed to Hunt. 'John had been such a brave and good man, and crucial to our success on Everest. I had come to admire and respect him enormously'.

YOSEMITE, 1963
GALEN ROWELL 1940-2002

Ask some Americans to name a landscape photographer and the chances are that they will respond with Ansel Adams. Ask for another and it is likely that many will cite his fellow Californian Galen Rowell. The fact that the two men are often mentioned in the same breath is a measure of the popularity that Rowell's powerful wilderness images attained over the last quarter of the twentieth century. A man of considerable substance and spirit, and a fine climber too, Rowell became a cult figure to climbers and photographers alike, before becoming a household name. Now still a hero to a new generation, his vision has shaped the way many thousands, perhaps millions, of people have come to view the mountains and nature's treasured places.

Like his predecessor, Rowell sought to use his pictures to help further the cause of conservation. While Adams lovingly captured the haunting beauty of California's Sierra Nevada and Yosemite, Rowell's canvas encompassed the wild places of the entire globe. His exquisite colour photographs achieved a worldwide currency, thanks to regular exposure in publications such as *National Geographic* magazine, as well as countless books, including some eighteen titles written by Rowell himself. Yet this super portrait, by Ed Cooper, shows a very young Rowell climbing high in Yosemite, long before he had taken up a camera in earnest.

Rowell participated in the so-called 'golden age' of Yosemite climbing, helping to put up many first ascents on the sheer granite cliffs. At the same time, he started to record this new era of adventure sports using photography with the eye of an artist. Lightweight 35mm cameras began appearing in the 1960s and, combined with innovative saturated-colour Kodachrome filmstock, allowed energetic, mobile photographers like Rowell to get into positions undreamed of by previous landscape or sports photographers to produce images of stunning impact. Typical of the trademark style Rowell developed at this time are images of climbers clinging to dizzyingly vertiginous Yosemite cliffs, and figures on mountain ridges beautifully backlit by early morning light.

In 1972 Rowell took the bold step of becoming a full-time professional 'outdoors photographer', a concept virtually unheard of then. From the mid-1970s onwards, Rowell went on to become one of the most sought-after wilderness landscape photographers in publishing. Many of his pictures have become the best known and most frequently reproduced 'outdoors' images in the world. Typical examples include an Alaskan grizzly bear captured by Rowell's lens peeking above the cover of foliage – and displaying a very obvious and menacing eye contact with the viewer. Another celebrated Rowell image features the climber Ron Kauk hanging, bare-torsoed, from a precipitous Yosemite cliff, framed perfectly by a rainbow glowing from the spray of an adjacent waterfall.

And arguably his most famous image, that of a rainbow striking the rooftops of the Potala Palace in Lhasa, Tibet, owed everything to Rowell's legendary anticipation and fitness. Spotting a rainbow developing during an oncoming storm, he guessed the shooting position from where an ideal composition might be made and ran flat out across the Tibetan plateau with his camera for several hundred yards at 12,000ft altitude. The picture was so 'perfect', that it initially failed to find many buyers as it was assumed it must have been a fake.

His was a life of mountain beauty, and in the end, mountain tragedy. Rowell and his wife died returning from a photographic assignment in Alaska when the light aircraft they were travelling in crashed. Rowells' photographic legacy lives on, however. 'Leave only footprints and take home only happy memories and good photos – that was something I always believed in when I was lucky to travel to wild places. Memory is a sieve that keeps the nuggets and releases the rubble,' he once wrote. 'I wanted my photography to do the same'.

RORAIMA, 1973

JOE BROWN 1930-

Joe Brown is arguably *the* British climber of the twentieth century; his skill and vision opened the doors to the modern concept of the sport of rock-climbing, while his mountaineering achievements were genuinely world-class. Brown's legacy comprises over six hundred UK rock routes, of which many continue to be the most exciting, challenging and sought-after in the country. Brown began serious climbing in 1947 while an apprentice builder in Manchester and, typically, some of his earliest efforts were bold and almost at the cutting edge of the day – all the more remarkable in retrospect given that he was climbing in nailed boots.

In spite of the profligacy of his pioneering, Brown only fell off nine times in his first nine years of climbing. Then he didn't fall off for the next twenty-six years. Crags such as Snowdon's Clogwyn d'ur Arddu would almost become synonymous with the Mancunian, as would parts of the Peak District where extreme routes now graded, such as *Right Eliminate* (E3 5c) and *Great Slab* (E3 5b), showed how far advanced he was. The post-war rock revolution initiated by Brown was completed after he encountered a climber of equal ability but different qualities to make the ultimate 1950s climbing dream team: fellow Manchester man, tough guy Don Whillans.

Together they formed the core of the informal 'Rock and Ice Club' whose happy-go-lucky members were destined to become the dominant influence on hard British climbing through much of the 1950s. Brown and Whillans rolled their campaign of hard climbing into the Alps, making record times on extreme routes such as the West Face of the Petit Dru and becoming the first British alpinists to compete on equal terms with top continentals, despite operating on a shoestring budget. Brown remembers the day after that historic climb: 'Louis Lachenal, one of France's foremost guides, came to pay his respects. He was dressed immaculately and was escorted by a gorgeous girl. He found the party lounging on the ground in filth and squalor, like a band of brigands. Goodness knows what he thought of us'.

Brown's success on domestic rock and in the Alps secured him an invite to join Charles Evans' expedition to the third highest mountain in the world, the 8,586m Kangchenjunga. Climbing with George Band, he made the first ascent of the mountain via a hard jamming crack – later avoided by subsequent climbers – which then marked the hardest technical climbing achieved at high altitude. As well as setting up a highly successful climbing equipment business, from the 1970s Brown continued to go on many expeditions, visiting Everest and Denali (climbing the Cassin Ridge), Latok II, Cho Oyu (descending by parapente) and continuing to pioneer rock climbs in Britain and abroad, especially Morocco. This evocative portrait shows Brown relaxing in a hammock, deep in the dense Venezuelan jungle, en route to climb the sheer overhanging wall of the unclimbed Great Prow of Mount Roraima, the remote mountain that inspired Conan Doyle's *The Lost World*. The climb itself was challenging in the extreme, were it not made more so by the bushmaster snakes, scorpions and bird-eating spiders.

RAKEKNIVEN, 1997

GORDON WILTSIE 1952-

With a career spanning four decades, and more than a hundred overseas expeditions, Californian Gordon Wiltsie is one of the world's leading professional adventure photographers, specializing in capturing stills from the wildest corners of the earth.

Some of his more famous projects have included documentation of mountaineering, skiing and dog-sledding expeditions to the edges of the known world. His expedition to Antarctica's Queen Maud Land in 1997, with Conrad Anker, Jon Krakauer and Alex Lowe, made the first-ever big-wall climb on the continent, Rakekniven, 'the Razor'. In this dramatic portrait, by the fine mountaineer Rick Ridgeway, Gordon jumars up a rope to get into position for the summit push. It was Gordon, in fact, who was the first to reach the top – to be ready with his camera for the climbers who had opened up this challenging face. Another memorable highlight has been the first ascent of Great Sail Peak on Canada's Baffin Island in 1998 – then the biggest, hardest and northernmost cliff yet attempted.

Wiltsie was inspired to pursue his profession after a chance meeting with the doyen of adventure photographers. 'When I was seventeen I met a guy called Galen Rowell. He wasn't even a famous photographer at that time, but he'd had stuff printed in various magazines, and I thought: "Wow, if this guy can do it then so can I." To make that kind of assumption was a bit ridiculous, but I went on to assist him and he became my mentor. I learned a lot from him'.

Over the years Wiltsie has also had plenty of non-photographic adventures. One epic ski trip with two friends involved travelling across the Himalaya from Ladakh to Kashmir. They nearly ran out of food and fuel after a two-day storm and then were avalanched over a cliff. Despite crushing two vertebrae, breaking several ribs and injuring his knee he managed to ski 40km to safety.

Among many other ascents, Wiltsie has attempted a very difficult, unclimbed route on Baruntse (7,129m), near Mount Everest in Nepal, only being turned back after all its technical challenges, by winds in excess of 180kmph. Fluent in Nepali, Hindi and Tibetan, he has also helped train Sherpa mountaineers in safe climbing techniques and is increasingly drawn towards documenting the cultural life of mountain peoples. 'People sometimes call me a landscape photographer, but I'm not. I enjoy the human spirit, and our human story. More than anything, I suppose, I'm a people photographer', he says. 'Gordon, simply, is not only a great extreme photographer, probably the best in the game, but he's also a fine climber and he uses these skills to dramatic effect', describes Conrad Anker, the revered American alpinist. 'He combines captivating stories and inspiring photography to convey the joy and intensity of the expedition life in a way that all can understand. The breadth and diversity of his epic work answers our primal calling for adventure'.

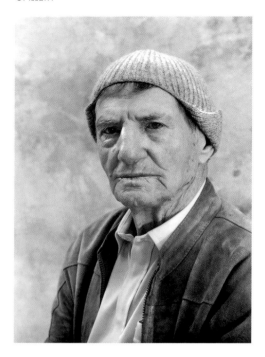

MILAN, 1999
ANDERL HECKMAIR 1906-2005

As a member of the so-called 'Munich School', the group of highly talented and innovative climbers hailing from the Bavarian city in the 1920s and 30s, Anderl Heckmair was one of the leading German climbers of the inter-war period. He began his climbing career in the Wilder Kaiser and, thanks to the ensuing economic depressions, found plenty of time to practise the sport due to unemployment. He qualified as a mountain guide in 1933.

Among his many great climbs is the first ascent of the Charmoz North Face and he also endured several hard attempts on the Walker Spur. Heckmair is most well known, however, for leading the team of four who made the first ascent of the North Face of the Eiger in 1938, earning his place in the history books in the most dramatic and profound way. It was a climb of such skill, endeavour and then, as now, technical difficulty, that it changed the nature of mountaineering forever.

Heckmair led the most difficult pitches on the ascent, aided by the novel use of newly-developed twelve-point crampons. 'Anderl led like a hero all the way up the climb – a real hero, quietly doing the job and serving his friends', wrote Heinrich Harrer in his classic account, *The White Spider*. His climb of the face, which had repelled all previous attempts and taken the lives of six climbers, was a true *tour de force*, with Heckmair taking several falls and battling against all the odds despite food poisoning.

The Eiger climb brought him fame and an audience with Adolf Hitler, but Heckmair remained resolutely unimpressed by the Nazis, refusing to join the Party. It may have been this reluctance that meant he was shown no favours on the outbreak of war, posted to the Eastern Front where his Eiger climbing partner Vörg fell on the first day of the Russian campaign. Following the war Heckmair worked as a mountain guide in his native Bavaria, and helped form a professional association. He continued to climb in places as diverse as the Andes, Ruwenzori and the Himalaya and often hiked alone in the hills well into his nineties. This elegant portrait was created by celebrated Canadian photographer Craig Richards, who travelled specially to Italy to meet this most interesting of mountain men.

'In the mountains, freedom rules', Heckmair reflected, shortly before his death. 'To climb in the cleanest way possible – that was my desire. How others climb is their business, and nobody has the right to interfere. For me mountains are a personal challenge. I don't want to consider mountaineering as a *sport*. There is no doubt about the importance of achievement, but what is of primary significance is still the climbing experience. Everything evolves constantly, and rightfully so. It does not cause problems in sport to always go faster, farther, higher; but alpinism has a different soul, it has traditions, ethics and romance. Modern climbers will soon realize it's not all about technical perfection, but rather the manner, the style in which mountaineering is done. I may be getting old, but I don't need to go out looking for even greater difficulties. I like to feel the nature of mountains, to sleep in simple mountain huts, and talk to the people who live in the hills ... I want to be with the mountains as a human being and an admirer, to experience rather than to conquer or to win'.

TRANGO, 2009
THE HUBER BROTHERS
ALEXANDER 1968 - THOMAS 1966 -

With a farmer-turned-mountain-guide father who had a reputation for climbing alpine routes very fast, it was perhaps inevitable that Bavarian brothers Alexander and Thomas Huber were destined for a life of extreme mountain climbing. Counted among the world's greatest all-round climbers, together they made a special impact on the smooth granite faces of California's Yosemite Valley after achieving several significant 'firsts', including hard routes on El Capitan such as *El Niño, Zodiac* and *Free Rider*, the first free ascent of an El Capitan route within one day.

In a climb that grabbed headlines around the world, in 2007 they also set a new speed record on the thirty-one pitches of El Capitan's *Nose*, clocking in a time of two hours, forty-five minutes and forty-five seconds. Since then they have also teamed up to make big-wall ascents in Antarctica and Pakistan, where they achieved the first free ascent of the classic thirty-five pitch route *Eternal Flame* on that immense granite needle, Trango Tower. When invited to contribute a special portrait from their private collection for this project, it was to this redpoint climb that they looked. 'There's no doubt we were extremely lucky though', Alexander says. 'The weather was great, which meant the cracks were free of ice. I take my hat off to the achievement and free climbing instinct of the first ascenders, who have passed on the best and most beautiful free climb on the globe. We are thrilled that we could play a little part in developing this route!'

But the brothers also take sibling rivalry to the ultimate lengths with their individual reputations, making hard solo climbs on big cliffs, such as Thomas' winter solo of the Eiger North Face, or Alexander's solo of the vertiginous *Direttissima* (500m, 5.12a) of the Cima Grande in the Italian Dolomites. There are perhaps too many more notable climbs to mention, but to give just a few: Alexander's first ascents of exceptionally difficult sport routes such as *Open Air* (5.15a/9a+) in Austria, while Thomas has made hard Himalayan climbs, such as the first ascent of the direct North Pillar of Shivling (6,543m) with Iwan Wolf in 2000, which won the *Piolet d'Or*. Further dispelling any idea that they might be any kind of climbing twins, the brothers display other divergences in character: Alexander is a keen physicist, while Thomas is the enthusiastic lead vocalist with the alt-rock band 'Plastic Surgery Disaster'. But one thing is certain: they are one of the strongest partnerships in world alpinism and, no surprise really, as there is no one better to share the challenge and brilliance of the mountains than your best friend, your brother.

OTTAWA, 1960
SIR EDMUND HILLARY 1919-2008

It was perhaps inevitable that the first person to clamber atop the planet's biggest mountain would turn out to be a larger-than-life character himself. Edmund Hillary, a bold, brash beekeeper from New Zealand had already enjoyed a more eventful career than most before the climactic events surrounding his moment of triumph on Everest with Tenzing Norgay in 1953.

A redneck upbringing in New Zealand led to adventures in that country's alps, where Hillary learned the craft of ice-climbing. It was while on a shoestring Kiwi expedition to the Indian Garhwal in 1951 that he cheekily 'hitched' aboard the British Everest reconnaissance expedition, led by the laid-back Eric Shipton. Impressed by Hillary's sound mountain-craft and fortitude at altitude, he was invited onto the following year's training expedition to Cho Oyu and then the 1953 Everest attempt. His infamous Antipodean directness was exemplified by his description of the triumphant moment of conquest on the peak: 'Having just paid our respects to the highest mountain in the world, I then had no choice but to urinate on it'. He followed up this robust christening with a frank appraisal of his achievement which he gave to his dear friend George Lowe at the South Col, and repeated to expedition leader John Hunt back at base camp: 'We've knocked the bastard off'. His language, he joked, was slightly moderated when he received his knighthood from the Queen.

Although several mountaineering ventures followed his Everest triumph, Hillary ironically suffered from ever more severe bouts of altitude sickness, ensuring that his energies were increasingly channelled into adventures on horizontal planes rather than steeply inclined ones. In 1956-58 he drove a converted farm tractor all the way to the South Pole, as part of Bunny Fuchs' phenomenal Commonwealth Trans-Antarctica Expedition. Hillary was, in his own words, 'Hellbent on the Pole', and neglected his orders to make an audacious dash there, risking both fuel and supplies for the later party, although it is fair to say that his work in pioneering a route up the Skelton Glacier and establishing depots on the polar plateau were crucial to the expedition's overall success. Hillary and the 'Old Firm' – Mulgrew, Bates, Ellis and Wright – were the first men to reach the Pole overland since Captain Scott, back in 1912.

Hillary later immersed himself in river-rafting expeditions, before turning to the equally choppy waters of political life, made more difficult for him, no doubt, because of his kindness, honesty and fundamental decency, something seldom found among those of great fame. Hillary was also heavily involved in addressing welfare issues of the Sherpa in Nepal, to whom he devoted a lifetime of help with aid programmes via his foundation, the Himalayan Trust, building mountain airfields, bridges and schools, clinics and hospitals, and renewing remote Buddhist monasteries; all told, the work he regarded as his finest achievement. On summing up this most incredible of lives, it's best to give Hillary the last word: 'I have had much good fortune, a fair amount of success and a share of sorrow, too. Ever since I reached the summit of Mount Everest the media have classified me as a hero, but I have always recognized myself as being a person of modest abilities. My achievements have resulted from a goodly share of imagination and plenty of energy'.

LONDON, 2011
KENTON COOL 1973 -

Living up to his surname, Kenton Cool is remarkably relaxed in the face of adversity. He suffered a huge fall from a hard route on Welsh slate in 1996 which shattered both his heel bones. Doctors gave him the bad news he would never walk without the aid of a stick and would certainly never climb again.

Following three operations, a month in hospital and three and a half months in a wheelchair, Cool recovered from a year of physiotherapy to rapidly develop into one of Britain's leading alpinists. He helped pioneer 'single-push' alpine tactics with his forty-seven-hour continuous ascent of a new route, *Extra Terrestrial Brothers*, on Denali, while his first ascents span Europe (L'Olan Central Couloir, to name just one), the Himalaya (the North Face of 6,369m Kusum Kanguru and the South-West Ridge of 7,555m Annapurna III), as well as remote locations in Greenland. Together with Ian Parnell and John Varco he was nominated for the prestigious *Piolet d'Or* award for his ascent of Annapurna III.

Cool has also achieved repeats of major climbs such as the *Denali Diamond*, in addition to success on the hardest winter routes in Scotland. With an appetite for adventure, anywhere and anyhow he can find it, its no surprise to discover he has repeated extreme climbs on such esoteric climbing media as crumbling southern English chalk cliffs as well as more conventional venues such as the sport cliffs of Thailand (where he has achieved F7b+ routes) and Yosemite big walls, for example, *The Shield*. Now a professional mountain guide he has completed eighteen successful expeditions in the Greater Ranges and summitted Everest eight times – the most by any Briton. In addition, he holds records for skiing, becoming the first Briton to complete a ski descent of an 8,000m peak, when he descended Cho Oyu in Nepal in 2006, following this up in 2010 with a ski descent of Manaslu.

Veteran polar expedition photographer Martin Hartley finally dragged him into a studio shoot for this portrait. Cool was in London for meetings with a new sponsor; Hartley had a small window of opportunity, having just returned from an expedition up the Niger River and overland to Timbuktu. I had an email confirming it was finally going to happen, sent by mobile phone from the Alps, followed by a sat-phone call from the middle of the Sahara. Back in town, Hartley had just one day before heading out again, this time to photograph adventurers on the floating pack ice of the Arctic Ocean. Some time later, a brightly coloured postcard arrives for me from overseas. It's from Hartley, sent the previous month from Timbuktu: 'You'll be reading this mate, chained to your laptop with that deadline looming, whilst I'm mucking about on expedition. Remember, remember. Keep writing mate!' Some people, Hartley and Cool clearly, get the best jobs...

'Yes, it's a good life being out in the wild', Cool agrees. 'Mountains have defined my time since I was a young bloke, and I'm lucky now, I pretty much live and breathe them. A normal year will see me spending two hundred plus days in the hills. I'd be pleased never to have to sit in front of a computer ever again! For a long time climbing was just for pleasure, and though I'm now able to earn my living as a guide my love for the mountains still isn't diminished. Everest has been pivotal in my life since 2004. I've been every year since, spending more time there than any other place in the world. It's a region of astounding beauty, full of history and myth. I don't know any other mountain like it – I really think I'm in love with the place and the people, the strong proud Sherpa, who live there'.

YOSEMITE, 2002
DEAN POTTER 1972-

American Dean Potter might be regarded as the ultimate 'extreme sports Renaissance man'. First making his name as a climber, he has since smashed physical and psychological barriers as an alpinist, BASE-jumper and slackliner.

Potter made waves in 2006 when he made a speed climb of what was then regarded as the hardest aid climb in the world, *Reticent Wall* on El Capitan, which he, and companions Ammon McNeely and Ivo Ninov, ascended in under thirty-five hours, shaving five days off the previous fastest time. Hard alpine climbs in Patagonia were tackled the same year and he began soloing hard rock climbs such as the famed *Separate Reality* in Yosemite. BASE-jumping has become his major passion. In 2009 he jumped from near the summit of the Eiger to complete the longest BASE-jump ever, covering some 3,000m in vertical height and nearly four miles in a two-minute fifty-second flight. Slacklining – essentially extreme tightrope walking using a stretchy climbing rope, between craggy outcrops at huge heights – has become another Potter speciality. This so-called 'Highlining' reached amazing levels when Potter traversed a bouncing 100ft slackline completely untethered, over the yawning abyss at Yosemite's Taft Point. He then soloed it four times more. Perhaps unsurprisingly Potter's sell-out lecture shows have titles such as 'Embracing Insanity'.

Combining all these audacious skills Potter has now arguably taken solo climbing to its most extreme form to date. Allying his skill in BASE-jumping with climbing, he has helped create the new sports of BASE-lining and free BASE: slacklining and climbing, respectively, while wearing only a parachute as protection from a fall. In 2008 he free-soloed the overhanging climb *Deep Blue Sea* on the Eiger route wearing a BASE parachute as his only safety back up. 'Soloing for me is about being completely in the moment, not worrying about the past or future, but just being right here, right now. That's why I do it', he says. Some, of course, view his antics with consternation and concern, but more often than not the response is one of jaw-dropping amazement. 'Dean Potter outgrew the title of climber and became something other, something that defies definition', says *National Geographic* Magazine. 'He is awe-inspiring, maybe crazy, and most definitely badass'.

FAIRWEATHER RANGE, 2010
JEREMY JONES 1975-

A legend in big-mountain snowboarding, with more than twenty action-sports films to his credit, Jeremy Jones has travelled the world from the Caucasus to the Andes to pioneer the best lines down huge mountain faces. He is eight-times winner of *Snowboard* magazine's 'Big Mountain Rider of the Year' award. In this portrait, by renowned shooter Greg Von Doersten, Jones relaxes during a day off at his remote base camp in the heart of Alaska's Fairweather Mountains while shooting his most recent snowboarding film, *Deeper*. A project many years in the making, it saw Jones creating epic first descents of mountains out of reach of ski lifts, snowmobiles and even helicopters – setting up camp, studying the mountain face up close, and climbing hard and high with his board on his back. 'Returning to basics in this way', he says, 'well, the possibilities for a richer experience are now almost endless'.

Although Jones's name had become almost synonymous with helicopter-borne snowboarding in remote backcountry, completing some of the most challenging lines of the last decade, he has increasingly turned his back on most mechanical aids, concerned by the climate-change deterioration he has witnessed in the mountains and a desire to minimize the carbon footprint of his sport. In 2007 Jones founded Protect Our Winters (POW), a non-profit organization dedicated to combating climate change by raising awareness, acting as a campaigning umbrella group for the winter sports community. More often that not, these days Jones chooses to hike and climb as his sole means of accessing these formidable mountain faces. 'You can never be unhappy if it's snowing!' he says.

LONDON, 1926
DOROTHY PILLEY RICHARDS 1893-1986

One of the leading lights of the early all-female Pinnacle Club, Dorothy Pilley was one of the few women climbers operating during the 1920s. She ranged throughout the Alps and crags of Britain, actively seeking the company of other women to climb with in preference to men. Such pioneering feminist credentials – or 'feminine' as she preferred to characterize her philosophy – were showcased in her graceful semi-autobiographical 1935 book *Climbing Days*, which charted her adventures in Wales, the Lake District, Scotland and overseas. She was part of a new generation that increasingly saw rock climbing not only as training for the snow-clad peaks of the Alps, or majestic mountains in more remote corners of the world, but also as a demanding and worthwhile business in itself.

The mountains were for Pilley, as they are for many, a region of solace and retreat: a place for the thrill of a challenge but more so for the beauty and stillness to be found there. She hated returning home to the city. 'How the contrast shook one! To go back to gloves and high-heeled shoes, pavements and taxicabs. Walking with an umbrella in Piccadilly one felt as though one could easily become a case of divided personality. This time yesterday! One lay munching a dry sandwich on a rocky ledge, plucking a patch of lichen and listening to the distant roar of the white Ogwen Falls. It wavered, faded, and grew again louder as the breeze caught it ... the strangeness of the dual life made, in those days, a cleft, a division in my mind that I struggled in vain to build some bridge across. Kind, firm friends would say, "All good things come to an end", or, "You can't expect all life to be a holiday". But to me, and to climbers before and after me, this was no question of holidays. It went down into the very form and fabric of myself'.

Pilley found further happiness marrying Ivor Richards, the eminent literary critic, classical archaeologist and sometime climber. It was in company with him, on their honeymoon in fact, and supported by the mountain guides Joseph and Antoine Georges, that she truly cemented her reputation as a credible and talented alpinist, when they made the first ascent of the tricky North Ridge of the Dent Blanche in 1928. She had already impressed many in the clubbish climbing community of London with success on the notorious Grépon in her first season in the Alps and the following year, with her friends Annie Wells and Lilian Bray, completing an ascent of the Mittaghorn with no men on the rope to help them. But it was 1928 – the season she referred to as her 'Great Year' – that would make her name. Pilley later wrote that at one particularly steep section of the Dent Blanche climb, where she and her new husband were jammed together into a tiny space on the otherwise vertical cliff, clinging to a single handhold scarcely sufficient for one, their guide looked them up and down and said with a smile, 'Ah, les amoureaux!'

Pilley was also unusual in that she was one of the few people – male or female – who managed to undertake a considerable amount of climbing during the Second World War. A respected journalist and author, she travelled widely in China and became something of an authority on its art and religion. However, Pilley's climbing energy was sadly curtailed after 1958 when a drunk driver crashed into the back of her car, severely injuring her hips. 'Afterwards', she wrote with characteristic elegance, 'well, the scale of the Alps, and of much else, is strangely changed'. Nevertheless, often in the company of her husband, she still explored mountain ranges all over the world, especially in North America. And even at the age of ninety-three, Pilley would be seen spending Hogmanay at a climbing hut in Skye, quaffing whisky and loudly enthusing about the simple, eternal joy of the mountains.

CHAMONIX, 1993
ALISON HARGREAVES 1962-1995

At five feet four inches tall, Alison Hargreaves appeared at first sight to make an unlikely elite mountaineer. However, beneath her motherly exterior lay exceptional strength, energy and an immense ambition. Hargreaves hailed from rural Derbyshire where she came under the influence of PE teacher Hillary Collins – later the wife of top British climber Peter Boardman – who inspired an interest in outdoor pursuits. Such was Hargreaves' natural talent that by the time she left school she was leading E3, making her one the best British women rock climbers of the late 1970s. As a consequence she caught the eye of local caving and climbing shop owner, and small-scale equipment manufacturer, Jim Ballard and began working in his shop.

Soon to become Hargeaves' husband, Ballard became her *de facto* manager and sports coach combined. Unusually for a female climber in the mid-1980s, Hargreaves also excelled in the alpine arena, making the first British woman's ascents of several *Grandes Courses,* including the North Face of the Matterhorn. In 1986 she travelled with the Americans Tom Frost, Jeff Lowe and Mark Twight to the Solu Khumbu, making a number of first ascents including a difficult line on the North-West Face of 6,856m Kantega.

Although becoming increasingly well known amongst the British climbing community it wasn't until she made headlines with an ascent of the North Face of the Eiger in 1988, at six months pregnant, that Hargreaves became much talked about by the wider public. The birth of two children put her climbing career on hold for a few years but by the early 1990s, with a family to support and worries about financial security, she made a conscious decision to tackle a series of prestigious and media-worthy ascents. There followed a whirlwind of publicity after she soloed six alpine north faces in the summer of 1993 and a 'competition' between her and the glamorous French climber Catherine Destivelle was manufactured by sections of the press. Upping the ante, Hargreaves began a campaign to climb 8,000m peaks and made an impressive solo ascent of Everest's North East Ridge without bottled oxygen in 1995. It was in attempting K2 later in the same year, while descending, that she was killed after being blown off the mountain in a freak storm.

NORTH DEVON, 2010
DAVE BIRKETT 1968 -

Dave Birkett is one of the great traditional climbers of our time, if not the greatest. It's a title he doesn't covet though. The modest backwoodsman of British climbing, he performs modern miracles of extreme climbing in tough and unfashionable mountain settings. 'I wouldn't have it any other way, no farting about in lycra in the sunshine for me', he says. Rightly proud of his Cumbrian heritage, with his pick-up truck and unabashed love for Country Music, gnarly Birkett was brought up by his hill-farming grandfather and was destined for a life as a shepherd until he discovered, as a teenager, his true talent. His roots are reminiscent of the 'native climbers', like the famous Victorian farmer John Robinson of Wasdale or the early European Alpine guides; people who worked and walked the land of their home mountains, got to know them intimately and then climbed in them, sometimes for fun, sometimes for work. And, just as unusually, Birkett remains essentially an amateur, generating the bulk of his income as a stonemason and with other farm contracting work.

There is definitely nothing old-fashioned about Birkett's climbs. His reputation is built on pioneering the hardest imaginable routes on some of the most remote mountain crags. For the last two decades Birkett has dominated Lake District climbing. *If Six was Nine* on Iron Crag was a climb that ushered in the E9 grade to the region. Many more '9's have followed, on Pavey Ark and especially Scafell, the highest mountain in England and his favourite. 'I just love it up here', he says when asked why he makes the regular calf-sapping pilgrimage up to Lakeland's loftiest crag. 'I'm happiest when I'm hanging around on a rope in the mist – which is where I started I suppose, waiting in the clouds for Granddad while rounding up our sheep'. At present only two of Birkett's eight E9s have been repeated.

In 2003 he climbed James McHaffie's E8 6c, *Fear of Failure*, on Dove Crag 'onsight' - without any prior knowledge of the holds or pre-inspection by abseil. It remains arguably the only true E8 onsight achieved to date. Nor is his talent restricted to the summer months: in winter 2010 he established *Never Ever Say Never*, a desperately thin but aesthetic ice climb at Grade VIII on Scafell. Most recently, as shown in this stunning action portrait by Alastair Lee, Birkett has been sending some ridiculously tough routes on sea cliffs too. Having mastered James Pearson's 'E12' test-piece *The Walk of Life* on the monster slab Dyer's Lookout on the North Devon coast – also re-climbed and downgraded by Dave MacLeod, a still very respectable E9 – Birkett has now put up his own line there. In this shot, he is reaching the hard moves on the upper reaches of his brilliant E9 6c, *Once Upon a Time in the Southwest*.

Although Birkett still climbs most in his home mountains of the Lakes, he continues to put up hard new routes in Scotland and repeats cutting-edge lines throughout the rest of the UK and overseas. Despite his prodigious climbing talent, he remains a cragsman at heart, fuelling up on local ale after an honest day repairing dry-stone walls, or forming a one-man sheep mountain rescue service for his neighbours when members of their flock become stuck. He relishes the Lakeland fells for their beauty as much as their climbing. 'This is the best place in the world', he says.

THAME, 2003
APA SHERPA 1962 -

Although only five feet four inches and a mere 120 pounds, Apa Sherpa has the nickname 'Super Tiger'. And for good reason: he holds the record for reaching the summit of Mount Everest more times than any other person, a mind-boggling twenty times.

Born in the early 1960s – he admits he doesn't know exactly when – Apa hails from Thame, the same Nepali village as Tenzing Norgay. After his father's death, when he was just a boy of twelve, Apa had to help support his mother, two sisters and three young brothers and left school to earn money working as a porter. Apa – known too by his more formal full family name, Lhakpa Tenzing Sherpa – then worked for many years as a trekking porter and kitchen hand, until his strength and fitness singled him out as a hugely capable high-altitude porter. He first set foot on the glacier in 1985 and by 1990 had literally risen through the ranks to reach the summit of Everest.

Apa's subsequent role as Sirdar, or head porter, for many high-altitude expeditions enabled him to reach the summit every year between 1990 and 2010, except 1996 and 2001. In 1992 he climbed to the summit twice and with the money earned from his expeditions he built a lodge, appropriately named 'the Everest Summiter', and settled in his native Thame. He married in 1988 and when this touching portrait was created by photographer John van Hasselt in 2003, Apa was contemplating his future as a porter and guide. With five mouths to feed, his children and wife Yanji would have preferred he didn't climb the mountain anymore and risk injury or worse, since his next trip would be his thirteenth, an unlucky number here as elsewhere.

Nonetheless, he felt the call of the mountain – and, not to forget, the money that could rightly be extracted from the wealthy tourists flocking to walk up it – and so donned his crampons once more. Apa moved with his family to Utah in the USA in 2006 in order to take advantage of better educational opportunities for his two sons and daughter. When not on expedition he works for Diamond Mold, a precision machining company in Salt Lake City. In 2009, he founded the Apa Sherpa Foundation dedicated to the improvement of education and economic development in Nepal. At the time of writing, Apa was headed back to Everest for a twenty-first summit attempt. 'They wanted me to go and be a base camp manager,' he said. 'I told them if I go to base camp for two months, then I am going to climb to the top. Sitting there is no fun at all'.

NEW YORK, 1925
ANNIE SMITH PECK 1850-1935

Like so many Victorian career mountaineers, Annie Smith Peck's name was made following a climb of the Matterhorn in 1895. Thirty years after its first ascent the mountain still held the mystique sufficient to attract public attention – especially when it was a rare ascent by a woman, and a glamorous American one to boot. But Peck had been climbing enthusiastically for a decade, adding such pioneering activity to her already considerable academic achievements in the fields of archaeology and classics.

Born into a wealthy Rhode Island family, Peck nevertheless needed to support her travel and climbing habit by becoming a public performer. In this delightful and elegant rare portrait, she is photographed by a press reporter arriving in New York at the beginning of a new lecture tour. It was said of Peck that she possessed 'a pleasant voice' and this, together with her 'feminine appearance', 'captivated her audiences, which had expected a muscular, masculine-looking woman'.

In her fifties, Peck set upon the notion of climbing a peak higher than any other woman. In 1908, she scaled Huascarán in Peru, supported by two Swiss mountain guides. Estimating the height to be 7,300m, the peak was declared the highest mountain in South America, and Peck received international recognition as holding the female altitude record. However, she had a formidable rival to her mountaineering claims in the form of the doughty Fanny Bullock Workman. The parallels between the women were striking: both were from wealthy American families, both had enjoyed expensive educations in Europe, both pioneered female emancipation and suffrage – and both enjoyed mountaineering and were hungry for the fame accorded by holding the altitude record.

Workman claimed her ascent of the 7,100m Pinnacle Peak, a subsidiary in the Nun Kun massif of the Karakoram, was higher and vigorously – and expensively – defended her claim against Annie Peck's by engaging a team of French surveyors to measure the height of Huascarán by means of triangulation. The revised height was calculated to be 6,648m (now known in fact to be some 6,768m). Nevertheless, this still left Peck with the American record in the western hemisphere. Peck continued to climb, travel, write and lecture into old age, making further first ascents in Peru, including unfurling a 'Votes for Women' banner atop the summit of the 6,425m Corpuna in 1911 aged sixty-one, whilst also pioneering long-distance air travel across the continent. She climbed her last mountain, Mount Madison in New Hampshire, indulging her passion for the hills as a treat for her eighty-second birthday.

KWANGDE, 2009
INES PAPERT 1974-

'I have spent most of my life in the overtaking lane,' admits Bavarian climber Ines Papert. Born in the flatlands of Saxony, Papert trained as a physiotherapist before moving to Bechtesgaden just north of the Austrian Alps, where she began her meteoric career on steep ice. 'I started doing lots of ice climbing on waterfalls. I liked the feeling a lot, totally free to choose my own line and how much protection I would use'. No sooner had Papert begun to lose herself in the climbing life, she became pregnant. Instead of seeing the birth of her child in 2000 as an impediment to further sporting progress, Papert merely changed goals so that she could accommodate childcare into training regimes and adventures. This entailed entering into the fray of the competition circuit. Just a year on from giving birth, Papert achieved first place in the women's category of the ice-climbing World Cup followed with victories in 2002 and 2003 and four World Championships.

But the event that really shook up the competitive ice scene – massively significant for women's sport on a broader level too – was her overall victory at the 2005 Ouray Ice Festival in Colorado when she not only beat all the women but the men as well. In an era when huge media fuss is generated over professional sportswomen competing with men in less physically arduous sports such as golf, the fact that an eight-stone woman with the delicate build of a dancer achieved a stunning win in an activity with a premium on sheer brute strength was nothing short of ground-breaking.

Everyone agrees, however, there is nothing brutal about Papert's style of climbing. Elegant is the word most frequently used to describe her ascents. Despite her fame on ice, Papert also has an outstanding record on pure rock, regularly onsighting 5.12d and redpointing 8b and having accomplished some of the hardest routes in the Alps. Surviving a bad fall after a hold broke in the Dolomites in 2005 – 'there were two operations and they put a lot of metal in my leg, thirteen screws and a plate', she says – Papert's climbing has gone from strength to strength. After winning the women's final at Ouray and the women's ice World Cup title again in 2006 she gave up competitions to concentrate on 'real climbing, on real mountains'.

This portrait was created by Cory Richards as Papert prepared in base camp for her first major foray into extreme Himalayan winter climbing. In the weeks that followed, Richards and Papert reached the summit of the 6,093m Kwangde Shar in Nepal's Thame valley. The two weaved a brilliant new line, dubbed *Cobra Norte* (WI5, M8), up the cold North Face, narrowly avoiding a cascade of rockfall, before breaking left to join the French route on the East Ridge and continuing up to the summit through a maze of mixed terrain. Good to her word, Papert has also begun visiting Scotland to immerse herself in its completely traditional winter climbing ethics. Immediately mastering the medium, she has made the hardest Scottish climbs by a woman to date, on sighting established Grade XIIIs on her first trip and creating a new IX. 'There is nothing comparable in other countries', she enthuses. 'We need to get the real adventures back'.

EL CAPITAN, 1964
GLEN DENNY 1939-

Born in Modesto, California, Glen Denny first experienced the state's wild mountain landscapes during fly-fishing trips into the Sierra Nevada with his father. Curious to explore further, he moved to Yosemite in 1958 to learn to climb and was inspired by witnessing Warren Harding's epic battle to make the first ascent of El Capitan. 'At El Cap Meadow, I ran into a traffic jam of people watching. Through binoculars I could see tiny people inching up a magnificent wall. I instantly realized I had come to the right place'.

Denny himself was soon making first ascents and climbing the most challenging routes in Yosemite Valley, including the third ascent of *The Nose* and mixing with many of the big-wall pioneers of the early 1960s, such as Harding, Royal Robbins, Yvon Chouinard and Chuck Pratt. He would later go on to make first ascents in the Cordillera Huayhuash in Peru and the Hindu Kush in Afghanistan. So often hidden behind the camera, in this on-the-face 'mountain portrait' Denny becomes the subject himself, photographed by his climbing companion Tom Frost. They are relaxing on the Mazatlan Ledge on the pioneering second exploration ascent of El Capitan's *North American Wall*. It is the sweet spring of 1964.

Originally self-taught, Denny began photographing the nascent Yosemite climbing scene before studying photography and film-making at San Francisco State University. His subsequent climbing films have garnered awards at many film festivals, while his photography has been extensively published. His celebrated 2007 book, *Yosemite in the Sixties* is a visual chronicle of that 'Golden Age' of hard Yosemite big-wall climbing. Denny has majestically captured the vast vertical landscapes, and those pioneering climbers within it, allowing too an insider's view of the life of the notorious 'climbing bum' scene of Camp 4 in its heyday.

'One of the strange things about climbing is the number of climbers who want to write about it', Denny says. 'I too felt the urge. I didn't want the experience to disappear, but how to describe it? If I stayed with the facts, the page was clear, but cold. If I said how it really felt, the page ran hot with embarrassing confessions. I couldn't get it right. So, I combed the library shelves and read the mountaineering classics. In some of those books I came across photographs that made me say to myself, "Yes, that's it!" Towering, icy peaks, smooth walls with ant-like climbers on them, haggard faces after frosty bivouacs: those indelible images told the story as effectively as words could. I realized I could show what it was like, and not have to explain it. So a camera strap was added to the clutter of slings around my shoulders. Under my right arm nestled a small folding camera, as handy as my hammer; when the image of the experience appeared, it had to be captured *right now*, before it disappeared. Unlike writers, I couldn't wait. My climbing partners got used to annoying new phrases like "Hold it," "I'm changing film", and the dreaded, "Could you do that again?"'

'I didn't say those things to Royal Robbins while he was leading the third pitch of the *North America Wall*', Denny describes. 'He had placed a long line of marginal pitons, and the situation was tense. But the light on the rock was beautiful. He had been on his last pin for quite a while. It seemed solid, so I raised the camera. Suddenly he got bigger in the viewfinder, and the belay line started zinging out as if I'd hooked a marlin. I dropped the camera and grabbed the rope with both hands. It hurt like hell, but there was nothing to do except grab harder. After what seemed like a long time, things stopped moving. I looked up. Royal was a lot closer now. He looked down and said, "Nice catch". The gradual arrest had pulled out only a few pins; I didn't tell him why it had been so dynamic. The rope burns made my palms look like raw salmon fillets'.

EL CAPITAN, 1970
PETER HABELER 1942-

Peter Habeler and Reinhold Messner stunned the mountaineering world in 1978 when they made the first ascent of Everest without supplemental oxygen – a feat previously thought to be humanly impossible. Habeler set a further record by descending from the summit to the South Col in only one hour. Nevertheless, he remained circumspect about this achievement. 'I have not conquered Everest', he said. 'It has merely tolerated me'.

Habeler was born in Austria and started climbing as a six year old. Among his early accomplishments were first ascents in the Rocky Mountains and being among the first Europeans to climb on the big walls of Yosemite. This striking portrait was captured by Doug Scott, as Habeler belays him below the headwall, on the epic face of El Capitan's *Salathé Wall*. Later in 1970 Habeler teamed up with Messner, with both men taking a serious sports training approach to alpinism that was unusual at the time. Messner was delighted to have found a climbing partner who was as fit and enthused as himself. 'He's like a sky rocket', he said of Habeler, 'really impressive once the fuse is lit'.

Together they began making fast ascents of difficult peaks in the Alps – including a then record-breaking time of ten hours for the North Face of the Eiger in 1974 – and then the Himalaya. In particular, their ascent of Hidden Peak in 1975 in just three days was highly influential, ushering in an era of alpine-style ascents of 8,000m peaks. Habeler went on to climb several others, including Cho Oyu, Nanga Parbat and Kangchenjunga. In the 1990s he founded the Peter Habeler Ski and Mountaineering School in his Austrian hometown of Mayrhofen. Despite all his success and international prestige Habeler still maintains that climbing is so much more than a career. 'Mountaineering is about friendship', he says, 'it's about raising people up'.

CUMBRIA, 1934
GEOFFREY WINTHROP YOUNG 1876-1958

Young was one of the leading Edwardian-era British alpinists. Often climbing with the top local guides of the day, such as Joseph Knubel, he completed many impressive routes between 1905 and 1914 including the South Face of the Taschhorn, the East Face of the Zinal Rothorn and the Mer de Glace Face of the Grépon. This was achieved despite the disapproval of his father Sir George Young who, although himself a former alpinist, had forbidden all mention of climbing when Geoffrey was a child following the death of his brother while mountaineering.

Geoffrey therefore took up the sport illicitly while at Cambridge University during reading weeks at Wasdale Head in the Lake District and on university buildings and church spires, producing a guidebook *The Roof-Climber's Guide to Trinity*. The climb which made Young's reputation more than any other was his futuristic first ascent of the South Face of the Taschhorn in 1906, climbed with the Lochmatter brothers and eccentric Irish climber V.J.E. Ryan. The climb was an epic, involving an all-day battle on technical ground in a terrible snowstorm with falls, gymnastic moves and rope tricks, and the outcome in doubt until the very last – not at all normal fare in Edwardian alpinism. The climb was not repeated for another thirty-six years until a strong Swiss party armed with all sorts of gadgets managed it. 'Even with all the resources of modern techniques,' said the leader Georges de Rham, 'such as pitons, clasp rings and rubber shoes, I thought it was exceptionally severe'.

Young would go on to climb many other important routes before the First World War intervened. He initially covered the early battles as a war correspondent before helping set up an ambulance unit formed predominantly of non-combatant Quakers. They served first at Ypres then transferred to the Austro-Italian front. It was here in 1917 that his left leg was smashed by shrapnel. It was amputated soon after.

Following the war, Young married Eleanor, the daughter of revered climber and Norwegian pioneer Cecil Slingsby. After a brief honeymoon Young resumed climbing, now with a wooden leg, ascending the Matterhorn in 1928. He also threw himself into writing books and poetry and into climbing politics, serving on the Joint Himalayan Committee. As a former schoolteacher he had an interest in education and helped the persecuted German progressive educationalist Kurt Hahn escape the Nazis and set up a British school. The result was Gordonstoun School, and Young became the first Chairman of Governors. Young would expand his interests in this direction by promoting the founding of the Outward Bound movement, as well as helping to establish the first modern outdoor education centre at White Hall in Derbyshire.

Young's most lasting achievement, however, probably lies in his being the driving force behind the creation of the British Mountaineering Council in 1943, the umbrella group for climbers in the UK. He died peacefully in 1958, leaving as his legacy his ideas on outdoor education, the successful BMC, and one of the most quoted lines of mountaineering poetry: 'Only a hill, but all of life to me, up there between the sunset and the sea'.

EIGER, 1966
DOUGAL HASTON 1940-1977

With a reputation as a laconic Edinburgh 'hard-man', Duncan Curdy McSporran 'Dougal' Haston rose from humble baker's son to become director of the International School of Mountaineering in Leysin and an alpinist of genuine world renown. His legacy remains compelling and he still commands a cult following among the climbing fraternity; an enigmatic character with very human flaws – a kind of 'rock'n'roll hedonist' renowned for his boozing and brawling – he nonetheless conceived and then mastered some of the finest climbs of his generation, becoming something of an 'A-list' celebrity in the process. The 'blue-eyed boy and sharp dresser with a penchant for polka-dotted neckerchiefs', Haston arrived at this point via a series of spectacular climbing achievements including an ascent of the cutting-edge rock route *The Bat* on Ben Nevis with Robin Smith. His breakthrough to true stardom was a winter ascent of a direct route up the Eiger's North Face.

Haston was part of the Europe-wide televised ascent of 1966 in which the celebrated American alpinist John Harlin died. Harlin had made the first American ascent of the North Face's original route in 1962 and hatched the plan to climb the mountain once more: this time by the *direttissima*, 'the most direct', route. Having made excellent progress up the 'great wall', the party were battered by storms and they dug in for shelter, waiting for a clear window of weather before a dash to the top. However, on continuing the climb Harlin's rope broke and he plummeted to his death. Haston, who was climbing with Harlin, recovered from the tragedy to reach the summit with a German party following the same line. Haston had frequently asked for thicker ropes in the preparation stages of the assault, and it was he who ensured that the direct line was renamed the 'Harlin Route' in honour of a departed friend.

Yet, he always remained something of a loner, seeking solace in the wilderness and taking himself off into the mountains when the media frenzy threatened to overwhelm him. 'For me', he once said, 'it is hard to have a friend who is not a climber. He needs to have shared the many close-to-death experiences, and not have panicked; backs one up through trouble, and is not jealous of success. On this basis, I have few friends'. Scottish legend Jimmy Marshall, who was indeed a friend and early mentor to Haston and other young climbers, showing great fondness, would still describe him as 'a superb mountain man, but one evil bastard'.

After the Eiger, Haston was a regular on the elite expedition circuit of the day. He climbed Annapurna with Don Whillans via its South Face in 1970 and the South-West Face of Everest (dubbed, 'The Hard Way') in 1975 thereby becoming one of the first two British climbers – along with Doug Scott – to climb this most famous of mountains. It was a spectacular turnaround of fortunes for a man who, only a few years before being catapulted to the top echelon of world climbing, had languished in Glasgow's notorious Barlinnie prison as a result of killing someone while drink-driving in Glen Coe. Observers have speculated since whether the guilt Haston felt as a result drove him to extreme life-risking behaviour on these most challenging of climbs. He was prepared to die doing what he loved, he frequently told those who became close to him. Haston later turned novelist and in the manuscript of *Calculated Risk*, which was published posthumously, his hero out-skis an avalanche on the notorious slopes above Leysin. In a grim coincidence, aged just thirty-six, Haston was caught in an avalanche whilst skiing alone there and he suffocated to death.

K2, 1954
LINO LACEDELLI 1925-2009

'One of the finest climbers of the 1950s' – in the words of Reinhold Messner – Lino Lacedelli first made his name as a member of the *Cortina Squirrels*, an elite Italian climbing club with the fearsome reputation as being the best climbers in Europe in the immediate post-war period. Lacedelli's mettle was proven in 1951 after he made the second ascent of the *Bonatti-Ghigo* on the East Face of the Grand Capucin – then one of the most difficult routes in the western Alps – in well under a day and no bivouac. It was a style which the next fifteen teams to climb the route could not repeat.

The following year his fame grew when he climbed the South-West Face of Cima Scotoni in the Dolomites; regarded at the time as one of the hardest rock climbs in the world. Lacedelli then became focussed on tackling the most difficult Alpine climbs in winter. He was chosen to join the prestigious 1954 Italian expedition to K2 and successfully joined Achille Compagnoni to become the first men to stand on the 8,611m summit, the second highest peak on the planet, salving the wounded pride of a nation humiliated by the failures of fascism and its wartime defeat. It is still fairly regarded as the golden page in the history of Italian achievements in the mountains. This remarkable portrait, from a private family collection, shows Lacedelli exhausted but victorious, having reached the summit on 31 July 1954. Compagnoni lost a glove taking this photograph, and Lino quickly gave him one of his own. He would have to have his thumb amputated back in Italy, its life frozen out of it on the perilous descent.

The expedition, however, had been an acrimonious affair. Its leader Ardito Desio was almost universally reviled by his climbing team, while the climbers themselves became factionalized. One of the main bones of contention would end up revolving around Walter Bonatti's contribution to the final summit push. His supporters depicted him as selflessly ferrying crucial oxygen supplies up to the lead pair, Compagnoni and Lacedelli, at their high camp, only to find they had moved their tent higher than agreed and along a dangerous traverse, thereby ensuring Bonatti and his Hunza porter companion, Amir Mahdi, had to endure a dangerous night out in the open at 8,000m. This resulted in terrible injuries for Mahdi in the paralysing cold. Lacking high-altitude boots, he lost all his toes and most of his fingers to frostbite.

The official view portrayed the whole thing as a mix-up rather than a conspiracy. But behind the scenes there began a whispering campaign against the young thruster Bonatti – the rising star of Italian alpinism – suggesting that he had tampered with their oxygen apparatus, and that he had been attempting to beat the lead climbers to the summit, thereby putting all their lives in danger. In the years afterwards, the squabbling over the truth as to how the expedition had been conducted almost eclipsed the event itself. The matter rumbled on for an incredible half century.

Throughout this period one man maintained a notable silence: Lino Lacedelli. But when he was eighty-one, shortly before his death, he finally decided to offer his side of the story, largely vindicated Bonatti's take on events. Photographs, like this one, also proved the summit team had, and used, oxygen that day. Lacedelli defended his decision to keep quiet while Desio was still alive on the grounds that if he had spoken out before he 'would have been destroyed'. Given the treatment meted out to Bonatti and others by Desio's use of media spin, this is a credible claim. Despite global fame, and the loss of a thumb to frostbite on K2, Lacedelli had returned home and continued working as a plumber, before setting up a small shop selling new climbing kit. He quickly returned to rock climbing in the mountains on his doorstep, the Dolomites, and established many more hard new routes. One final brilliant, and often ignored achievement, is that Lacedelli participated in some 163 mountain rescues during his lifetime.

SNOWDONIA, 2011
ERIC JONES 1936-

For over twenty years, right through to the 1980s, Eric Jones was one of the most prolific and daring solo climbers in the world. And it wasn't just contemporary cutting-edge rock climbs that he was calmly edging up ropeless, but major alpine routes such as the *Bonatti Pillar* on the Petit Dru. His solitary ascent in 1969 – the first solo climb since Walter Bonatti had surged up it in 1954 – epitomizes the amazing mental discipline with which the Welshman was able to keep it together in extraordinarily stressful situations. On an initial attempt he was knocked off by stonefall while trying a difficult free move on the crux section. Miraculously, he was saved by a small hook tied to his harness, which caught on a nubbin of a rock as he fell. Jones managed to retreat despite a gushing head wound. After two day's quality recovery time in the 'Bar National', he returned to the fray and completed the route, followed by a solo of the *Gervasutti Pillar.*

Such coolness in tough conditions became a Jones trademark, and some of it was caught on film thanks to an innovative documentary by Leo Dickinson that used helicopters to follow Jones' solo progress up the Eiger North Face in 1982. Despite advances of time and technology, it still remains one of the most gripping climbing films made, an air of tension palpable despite the steady, calm progress of the man sporting a dragon on his helmet.

Despite this Jones' innate modesty has ensured that he has retained a low profile, making his living from running a popular climbers' café at Tremadog in North Wales. As a result many have underestimated his ability. A classic example of this occurred during Messner and Habeler's historic ascent of Everest without oxygen in 1978. Jones was part of the filming support team and assigned the job of tracking and filming the two stars as long as he could keep up. In spite of the burden of heavy camera equipment he kept pace behind the stars comfortably and ended up sharing their top camp before the summit push. The two lead climbers hadn't counted on company and a lack of extra bivouac equipment meant Jones had to hunker down on his own in a spare tent without any insulation, resulting in no sleep and very cold limbs by the morning. He was forced to go down, but one wonders if history might have turned out differently if he could have had a little warmth that night.

In recent years Jones seems to have lost none of his appetite for extreme adventure. In 1990 he flew a hot air balloon over Everest, crash landing in Tibet, while in 1997 he became the oldest person to BASE-jump the spectacular Angel Falls in Venezuela. When asked how he would like to be remembered, his reply was typical: 'as a modest man, that's all'.

LONDON, 1890

JOHN TYNDALL 1820-1893

John Tyndall was one of the outstanding scientists of the Victorian period. A research collaborator with Faraday, he succeeded him as President of the Royal Institution. Among his friends were the likes of Louis Pasteur, Charles Lister, Thomas Huxley, Leslie Stephen, Thomas Carlyle and Tennyson. Among many outstanding achievements were his theories explaining why the sky is blue, pioneering the measuring of atmospheric pollution and his suggestions that changes in water vapour and carbon dioxide could be related to climate change – ideas which would lead to modern theories of global warming.

This was a remarkable achievement for the son of a lowly Irish Police Constable in County Carlow, who had begun his academic career in the common school education system and been denied a university education until well into his thirties. It was Tyndall's academic curiosity that first drew him to the Alps, where he was involved in the debate over the functioning of glaciers with his great rival James Forbes. After publishing his last word on the subject in 1860 – in *Glaciers of the Alps*, one of the sixteen books and some 145 scientific papers he generated during his indefatigable career – he turned his competitive energies towards climbing and immediately became embroiled in the race to climb the two highest remaining unclimbed peaks in the Alps with Edward Whymper. Tyndall struck the first blow in the fight for glory between the two when he made the first ascent of the Weisshorn. He then made successively higher attempts on the Italian side of the glamorous Matterhorn but Whymper eventually revenged his defeat with his eventful ascent of the peak in 1865.

Later in life, Tyndall entered politics, campaigning against Gladstone and the Home Rule Bill. He remained a touchy individual who was quick to take offence at perceived slights, famously resigning from the Alpine Club when he was Vice-President after humorous comments by Leslie Stephen denigrating scientific pursuits in the mountains struck a raw nerve. His rows with Forbes over their differing views about glaciers were legendary. Tyndall remained a bachelor until he was fifty-six, when in 1876 he married Louisa Hamilton. Their marriage was an extremely happy one, until in 1893, while experimenting with drugs to try to combat his insomnia, his wife Louisa accidentally administered an overdose of chloral, killing him stone dead.

SOLSBURY HILL, 2011
STEPHEN VENABLES 1954-

The late 1970s and 80s marked a transitional period in Greater Ranges mountaineering when the era of the large, often nationalistic 'siege-style' expeditions of the post-war period was all but finished, but the commercial guiding and trekking industry was yet to seriously invade the Himalayan stage. There followed a brief 'Golden Summer' of amateur British alpine-style mountaineering in the understated mould of Tilman and Shipton. Prominent among the leading players of this new wave was the witty and avuncular Stephen Venables.

Venables began his journey to the highest summits on earth on the lowly boulders of Fontainebleau while a schoolboy on holiday in France. Following Oxford University and a spell in theatre management and teaching he decided to commit to full-time climbing. From 1977 onwards, when he made three new routes in the Hindu Kush, he threw himself into a series of high-profile and charismatic expeditions throughout the 1980s. Memorable highlights included the first ascent of the Kishtwar-Shivling with Dick Renshaw in 1983, and 'almost' summiting the 7,385m Rimo in the Indian Karakoram via a highly-technical ridge. After completing six gruelling days of difficult climbing, and with all the major obstacles out of the way, Venables dropped his rucksack – forcing him, and his remarkably sanguine partner Victor Saunders, to descend without gaining the summit. Himalayan ventures were interspersed with trips to South Georgia and Venables became known for his expedition books, the first of which won the coveted Boardman-Tasker Prize.

Venables' fame widened in 1988 when he became the first Briton to climb Everest without bottled oxygen, following a hard new route up the Kangshung Face. It was not achieved without cost, however, with frostbite claiming several toes. In 1992 he was back having epic adventures, when an abseil anchor pulled following the first ascent of Panch Chuli V in India. Trapped at 6,700m with both legs broken, the ensuing high-altitude rescue, with an Indian Army helicopter straining at the very limit of its altitude ceiling, its rotor blades just inches from the steep snow slopes, has entered mountaineering legend.

LONDON, 1892
FRED MUMMERY 1855-1895

Albert Frederick Mummery, a myopic, stooped tannery owner from Dover with a cheeky wit and a forceful climbing ability, is often credited with writing the manifesto of modern alpinism. 'The essence of the sport lies, not in ascending a peak, but in struggling with and overcoming difficulties', he wrote. In other words: it was the way to the summit, rather than the summit itself that was important – a radical assertion in the Victorian period.

Mummery had begun his alpine climbing career traditionally enough, employing guides and tackling the famous peaks, but he soon blossomed into a new breed of self-reliant climber by dispensing with their services and setting his sights on new and challenging routes. Mummery's magnetic personality attracted a talented entourage of climbers, amongst them Norman Collie, Geoffrey Hastings and Cecil Slingsby. In 1891 he almost pulled off the futuristic ascent of the North Face of the Aiguille du Plan, a huge cascade of steep ice which was not climbed for a further thirty-three years. This epitomized Mummery's bold style, which may have had something to do with a physical deformity to his spine. It meant he could not carry heavy loads – he simply *had* to go fast and light. He was also intensely short-sighted, which possibly accounted for his legendary hopelessness at route finding.

This seems to have caused him to blunder into ground-breaking technical situations from which he then had to climb his way out.

From 1892 Mummery embarked on a long campaign of difficult rock routes, often accompanied by talented climber Lily Bristow, a good friend of his wife, leading to his famous ironic comment that, 'all mountains appear doomed to pass through three stages: An inaccessible peak – The most difficult ascent in the Alps – An easy day for a lady'. Mummery went on to lead the first guideless ascent of the steep Italian side of Mont Blanc, and pioneered climbing in the Caucasus and Greater Ranges, engaging the 8,126m beast Nanga Parbat in 1895, the first expedition in recorded history to have attempted one of the Himalaya's eight-thousanders. It was here that he disappeared, probably the victim of an avalanche whilst trying to pioneer a route on its Rakhiot Face. It was a mountain that would go on to earn a fearsome reputation – with some thirty-one men losing their lives on its slopes, before a dramatic first ascent by the legendary Austrian alpinist Hermann Buhl. Returning from the summit in 1953, it was Mummery, chief among others, that Buhl praised in his moment of triumph, describing him as 'one of the greatest mountaineers of all time'.

BONDASCA VALLEY, 1987

RICCARDO CASSIN 1909-2009

Another of the all-time greats, Riccardo Cassin was born into modest Italian family in Friuli and began scrambling as a youth on the limestone crags near Lecco. He joined a leading group of climbers known as the 'Lecco Spiders', attracting the attention of the famed Italian pioneer climber Emilio Comici, from whom he learned advanced techniques in the use of pitons. In the mid-1930s Cassin began to establish hard new climbs on the cliffs of the Dolomites, such as the first ascent of the Piccolissima of the Tre Cime di Lavaredo.

By the close of the decade he solved one of the last two 'great problems' of alpine climbing: namely the North-East Face of the Piz Badile in 1937 and the legendary *Walker Spur* of the Grand Jorasses in 1938. His ascent of the *Walker Spur* for example – a fierce, soaring ridge line that had defeated the attentions of so many talented climbers – was even more remarkable given that Cassin and his party had never even been to Chamonix before and were completely unfamiliar with the mountain terrain there.

Following the war, in which Cassin had fought as a partisan resistance leader against the Nazis, he turned his prodigious talents to the Greater Ranges. In 1957 he led the Italian expedition to Gasherbrum IV that made its first ascent and in 1961 he led his entire party to the summit of Denali by its South Ridge, now named the Cassin Ridge in his honour. Cassin also started a highly innovative and successful mountaineering equipment manufacturing business. After leading ambitious expeditions on the West Face of Jirishanca in the Peruvian Andes and the South Face of Lhotse in Nepal, Cassin retired from elite alpinism in the mid 1970s.

Nevertheless, he remained extremely active and in 1987 at the age of seventy-eight he celebrated the fiftieth anniversary of his first ascent of the North-East Face of Piz Badile by repeating the climb. In this rare, family photograph specially chosen for this project, Cassin is seen relaxing at the Sasc Fura hut shortly after his impressive second ascent of this most imposing of granite faces. The *Cassin Route* is still considered one of the superlative climbs in the history of the range and is hugely popular today, a testing ground for all aspirant alpinists. In 1937, as one of the six 'Great North Faces' of the Alps, it was a climb of epic proportions. The Como team of Mario Molteni and Giuseppe Valsecchi were already on the face when Cassin and his team started out, and on his quickly reaching them they decided to join forces. In the event, Molteni died of exhaustion and exposure on the summit, whilst Valsecchi fell to his death descending the south ridge just before reaching the safety of the hut.

KATHMANDU, 2011
ELIZABETH HAWLEY 1923 -

Although she cheerfully acknowledges to never having climbed a mountain in her life, the diminutive eighty-eight year old American Elizabeth Hawley is a force to be reckoned with in the Himalaya, possessing the power to reduce rough mountaineers to quivering bags of nerves.

For Hawley has become the *de facto* gate-keeper to the portals of Himalayan climbing fame; if any mountaineer wants recognition that they have reached the summit of the most prestigious peaks in the world, they first need to persuade the legendary sharp-tongued American. 'I don't mean to frighten people, but maybe I've acquired this aura of being the arbitrator,' she says. 'It could also scare them into telling me the truth, I suppose, and that might be useful'.

Hawley has lived in a modest flat in Kathmandu since 1960, after moving from America. As a journalist working for *Fortune* magazine in New York, she fell in love with Nepal during a round-the-world trip and decided to stay. There, she became a correspondent for Reuters and has been recording mountaineering feats since 1963. On first-name terms with many of the world's most famous climbers – such as Reinhold Messner and the late Sir Edmund Hillary – she has nevertheless crossed swords with others she suspects of being 'economical with the truth'. Some refuse to be interviewed by her; one even accusing her, grossly and unfairly, as being 'a senile old woman'. Most, however, welcome her role.

Hawley does not seek the limelight and, notoriously camera-shy, she was finally persuaded to have a new portrait appear in the pages of this book by young photographer Cory Richards, who travelled to Nepal to meet her. 'One of her biggest contributions is keeping the mountaineers honest', says mountain guide Dawa Steven Sherpa. 'The climbers like to be in the database', insists Hawley. 'They like to have their name in print amongst other mountaineers'. Whatever the truth of this, unless an expedition's records are subjected to Hawley's scrutiny and deemed to pass muster, they are likely to remain tainted by doubt. In the competitive world of high-altitude mountaineering, as well as the highly-lucrative business of guided ascents, it is still thankfully the case that a gentlewoman with well-kept records can keep the most burly of mountain men in check.

PARIS, 1950
MAURICE HERZOG 1919-

In 1950 Maurice Herzog and Louis Lachenal became the first people to climb an 8,000m peak when they reached the summit of Annapurna – at 8,091m, the tenth highest in the world. As befitted such a historic ascent, their climb proved to be an epic. The French team's approach was also remarkable for its era, in that the mountain was climbed without the use of supplementary oxygen and that their pioneering route was explored, developed and climbed all within the same season. It was a mountain sensation only surpassed that century when Everest was 'knocked off' so spectacularly by Hillary and Tenzing in 1953.

Such élan on Annapurna was not achieved, however, without a severe price. The lightweight boots that the lead climbers has elected to use to speed movement on the summit attempt proved insufficiently warm and both men were to lose toes to frostbite. To compound the matter, Herzog lost his gloves close to the summit and, forced to endure a high-altitude bivouac during the descent, the resulting freezing ensured that Herzog would eventually lose most of his fingers too. The expedition doctor was forced to perform emergency amputations in the field without anaesthetic. Such grisly details ensured that Herzog's classic book of the expedition, *Annapurna*, became a bestseller upon his return to France, and to date it has sold over eleven million copies in countless languages combined, more than any other mountaineering book. In this elegant portrait the conquering hero poses for a press photographer in a Parisian apartment. Though dressed in a beautiful suit, his mountain injuries could not pass unnoticed.

Following Annapurna, Herzog turned his energies to politics, serving as a French government youth and sports minister in 1958-63 and the Secretary of State in 1963-66. In a long and distinguished public service career he has also been the Mayor of Chamonix and Deputy to the National Assembly from Haute-Savoie. But, it is the story of Annapurna, with its tragedy and triumph – not to mention some ongoing controversy over the precise details of the summit day – that ensures Herzog his place as the 'mountain hero' of so many people around the world. His book, with it's stirring last line calling us to answer the challenges of life, continues to inspire each new generation of mountaineers: 'There are other Annapurnas in the lives of men'.

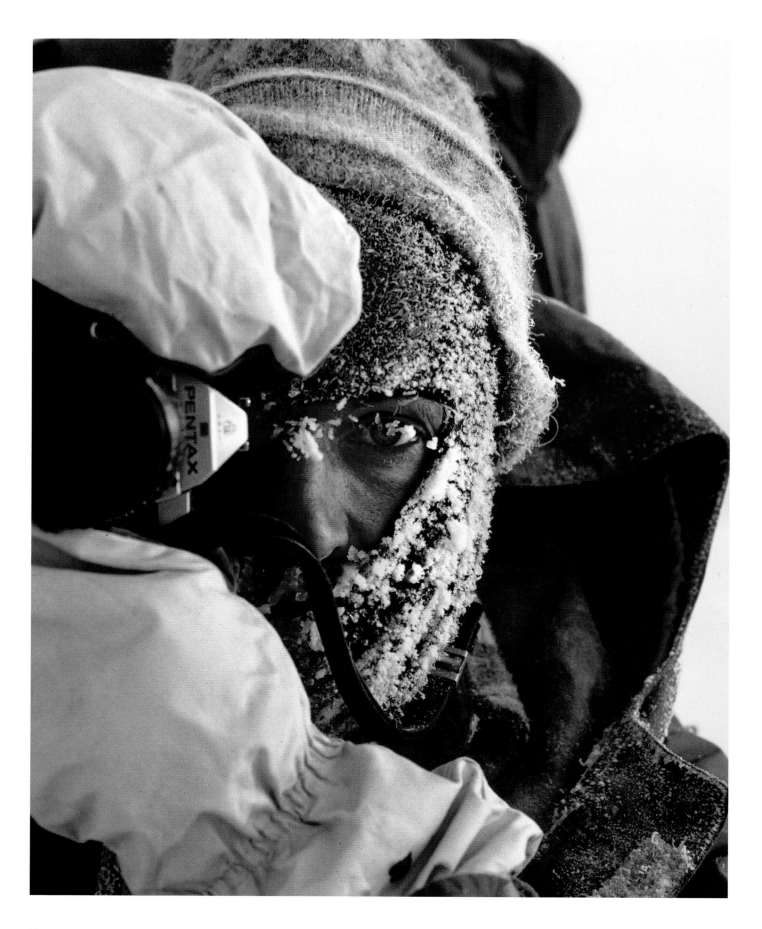

ELLESMERE ISLAND, 1984
PAT MORROW 1952-

Pat Morrow achieved national fame in 1982 when he became the second Canadian to stand atop the summit of Everest. But wider international acclaim followed four years later when he became the first person to climb the highest peaks on each of the seven continents, based on the list devised by Reinhold Messner. This represented a considerable mountaineering feat back in the mid-1980s, which was rightly recognized by the Canadian government awarding him the Order of Canada. 'I can attest to the fact that I didn't set out to earn this kind of recognition in the first place', says the famously modest Morrow. 'The main reward was reaching my goal and all the things I learned along the way'. The quest took Morrow over fourteen years to complete.

These days, although by no means easy, the marathon of climbing the 'Seven Summits' has become devalued in the eyes of many serious mountaineers, due to its increasing commercialization and its pursuit by trophy-hunters and wealthy tourists rather than competent climbers, as Morrow himself reflects. 'I was able to solve the formidable political and physical logistics of getting to remote mountains, like Antarctica's Mount Vinson, or Indonesia's Carstensz Pyramid, and those logistics have remained in place for all subsequent climbers. While you might think this is a nice legacy to leave behind for the climbing community, it's a double-edged sword. Now anyone with disposable income can hire a guide to shepherd them up these peaks. In the case of Carstensz, guide operators have fixed ropes in the most difficult parts of the climb, reducing the accomplishment of reaching the summit of the technically most difficult of the Seven to a mere jumaring exercise. And, sadly, on Everest there have been fixed ropes from high camps to the summit since the early 90s'.

As a result, Morrow's pioneering 'pristine' round can arguably never be bettered, as befits the well-respected mountaineer who, in partnership with his wife Baiba, has pursued a superlative career as a photographer and film-maker. In choosing his portrait for this book, Morrow fondly remembers a remote shoot in the Arctic wilds of Canada's Ellesmere Island. 'Not long to pose for a portrait that day though, it was approaching a soul-sapping minus 50 degrees! In the beginning, I suppose, I went to the mountains and deep into the wilderness for the challenge of climbing and documenting these beautiful places', he says. 'These days, I go there to be nurtured'.

ATACAMA, 1956
MATHIAS REBITSCH 1911-1990

During the 1930s and 40s, Tyrolean Mathias 'Hias' Rebitsch was one the world's leading climbers. His first ascents in the Karwendel, Kaiser mountains and Stubai Alps are now recognized as among the most difficult of the era, commanding respect from today's most innovative climbers. Rebitsch was remarkable, not least in that he eschewed the trend followed by most of his peers towards the use of pitons for aid in difficult sections of a climb, advocating instead the use of 'purer' free-climbing techniques. As a result, some of his technically advanced climbs were actually of a difficulty level not 'officially' recognized until 1977, as the new UIAA 'Grade VII'. Given the relatively unsophisticated equipment and protection available at the time, some have suggested that Rebitsch may have been the best free-climber of the twentieth century.

Rebitsch was scarcely less adept on ice: more widely acclaimed internationally was his outstanding attempt on the Eiger's North Face in 1937 with Ludwig Vörg. Rebitsch essentially found the key to unlocking the mystery of the infamous *Nordwand* and, despite hellish weather, such was his skill that both returned alive after a hundred hours on the face. In 1938 he reached the 'Silver Saddle' at 7,450m, as part of the Austro-German attempt on Nanga Parbat, narrowly escaping death when he fell on brittle ice but managing to reflex ice-axe brake in the nick of time.

Following the war, in which he served in the Arctic and as an instructor at the Army's mountain school, he returned to hard climbing in the Tyrol and in 1947 made a 700m ascent of the Laliderer North Wall that remained the most difficult rock climb in the Northern Limestone Alps for many years. When the iconic Austrian climber Hermann Buhl came to repeat it he declared it was the hardest climbing he had ever encountered. He also suggested that Rebitsch's route on the Goldkappel South Wall was the 'once in a lifetime' climb.

In some ways these climbing feats would remain Rebitsch's high mark. In 1951 he suffered a serious motorcycle accident that effectively ended his extreme climbing career. Nonetheless, as a trained chemist who had wide interests in philosophy, there was much to occupy his brilliant and inquisitive mind. He also became increasingly interested in archaeology and would contrive to twin his love of mountains with this pursuit to roam on several campaigns deep into the Andes, such as his 1956 Austro-Swedish Atacama expedition. During the trip, Rebitsch unearthed some unique Inca figures of hammered silver near the summit of the Argentine caldera Cerro Galàn. In 1958 he carried out extensive high-altitude excavations on the 6,730m Chilean volcano Llullaillaco and made other expeditions continuing this important archaeological work. A free-spirited hedonist, a mountaineering purist and a peerless explorer: all these things have ensured that Hias Rebitsch continues to inspire those climbers that follow him.

EVEREST, 1963
JIM WHITTAKER 1929-

Jim Whittaker became internationally famous in 1963 after reaching the summit of Everest – the first American to do so. When asked to contribute a personal photograph for this project, it was no surprise that Whittaker offered this classic summit shot. It is the first day of May. Though he ran out of oxygen in the final climb, with the help of Sherpa Nawang Gombu he finally managed to reach this sacred spot to plant the US flag proudly in the snow there. 'You never conquer a mountain, they can't be conquered; you conquer yourself', he has said many times since. Nonetheless, this photograph has become iconic in its own way, shorthand for a lifetime's achievement and high endeavour.

The Everest climb had a profound impact on the course of Whittaker's life, leading to an invitation to the White House and a friendship with the Kennedy family. When John F. Kennedy was assassinated, Bobby Kennedy, the President's younger brother and then US Attorney-General, asked Whittaker to guide him up the Yukon mountain newly named in JFK's memory, and then the highest peak in North American that had yet to be climbed. When Bobby Kennedy later decided to make a bid for the Presidency as Democratic candidate, Whittaker took him aside, warning him: 'Do you understand that what you are doing is a lot more dangerous than climbing mountains?' As fate would have it, just four months later, Whittaker was a pallbearer at his friend's funeral, Bobby having suffered the same tragic end as his brother.

Whittaker would go on to lead the successful 1978 American K2 expedition and in 1990 led the large 'Earth Day International Peace Climb', which put twenty climbers from the USA, Russia and China on the summit of Everest, starting from the Chinese occupied Tibetan side of the mountain. He has also been busy in the business world, as the first full-time employee of the pioneering Recreational Equipment Incorporated co-operative business in the 1960s. Today he is chairman of the board of Magellan Navigation, the leading GPS manufacturer. After a lifetime of outstanding achievement in climbing and business, Whittaker remains far from complacent. 'A lot of people my age act like they've seen it all and have nothing much else to learn', he says, 'but I'm still a learner'.

TIAN SHAN, 1913
CHARLES HOWARD-BURY 1883-1963

As leader of the very first Everest expedition in 1921, Howard-Bury secured a niche in mountaineering history, although he was never a notable mountaineer in the technical sense. A graduate of Eton and Sandhurst, he joined the British Army in 1904, serving in India. Fond of travel in mountain terrain, he was rebuked by the Viceroy of India for taking an illegal jaunt into Tibet in 1905. Ironically, as one of the few Britons to have penetrated the country, this would give him the credentials to lead the Everest venture.

The intrepid bachelor Howard-Bury poses in this rare photograph, deep in the Tian Shan mountains on one of his explorations, mostly spent hunting, writing and womanizing, whilst hacking about on his travels. During the First World War Howard-Bury would win a DSO and was mentioned in despatches seven times, before being captured. By the close of the war he had seen action at the Somme, Passchendaele and Ypres, and he was one of only fifty survivors from his battalion in the King's Own Rifles.

Following the war the Joint Himalayan Committee was short of cash after a minor cashier absconded with a large proportion of their funds. Howard-Bury went on fact-finding mission to Tibet at his own expense in 1919 and 1920, which resulted in his being made overall leader of the first Everest expedition. During the expedition itself it was hardly surprising that the liberal-minded George Mallory didn't really get on with his arch-conservative leader. 'I don't find myself greatly liking him,' Mallory wrote to his wife. 'He is too much the landlord with not only Tory prejudices but a very highly developed sense of hate and contempt for other sorts of people than his own'.

Despite all his efforts, and considerable personal expense, the Everest Committee unanimously replaced him with Charlie Bruce as the leader of the follow-up 1922 expedition. Everest, however, had made him a public figure and Howard-Bury turned away from the mountains to pursue a political career, first as Conservative parliamentarian for Wolverhampton – becoming Private Secretary to the Secretary of State for War from 1922 to 1924 – and for some years as Member for Chelmsford. Much of his later life was split between his inherited estate at Mullingar in Ireland and a citrus farm in Tunisia. In Ireland he kept a bear he had befriended as a cub while travelling through Kazakhstan in 1913 with which he conducted wrestling matches, even though it was now over seven foot tall. In Tunisia, by way of contrast, he passed the time more indolently with his live-in actor friend Rex Beaumont, a man said to possess a 'hell-raising exterior' with whom he was said to have shared 'a passion for wild and exotic places'.

Given these distractions, Howard-Bury's remaining mountaineering activity was understandably mostly conducted from his armchair. He never lost his interest in Everest, however, retaining a London flat in order to be close to the headquarters of the Alpine Club. More lucratively, he bred racehorses in Ireland and one that was born in May 1953 was promptly named 'Everest' and went on to win several races.

CUMBRIA, 2011
JULIAN COOPER 1947 -

Julian Cooper stands before his giant canvas of sacred Tibetan peak Mount Kailash. The son of William Heaton Cooper – often considered to be the quintessential English Lake District watercolour painter – and sculptor Ophelia Gordon Bell, Julian was born in the heart of the Lakes and went to Lancaster Art School, before heading for London and Goldsmith's College. Julian has since made his name exploring the relationship between figures and landscapes and his work has ranged widely, from narrative images based on Malcolm Lowry's novel *Under the Volcano* to a series of paintings about the assassination of the Brazilian environmentalist Chico Mendes in Amazonia in 1989.

Yet, it is the mountains that keep calling. In 2001 his *Mind has Mountains* exhibition at the Wordsworth Trust showed work created after an expedition to the Kangchenjunga region. This theme continued with his 2007 solo exhibition *Earthly Powers*, which contrasted work based on a pilgrimage trek through the foothills of Kailash, alongside paintings of abandoned Cumbrian quarries. A major retrospective was held at Museo Nazionale Della Montagna, Turin and Cooper's work was also included in *A Picture of Britain* at Tate Britain. Recently, he began working on a series of Italian paintings based on and inside the marble quarries of Carrara.

But, it is the Kailash canvas that proves the most special. Said to be the abode of Lord Shiva and a place of eternal bliss and rebirth, the mountain is a sacred place for Buddhist and Hindu alike – in Tibetan its name literally means 'the precious jewel of the snows'. But Kailash defies written word or paint. It lies near the source of some of the longest rivers in Asia, the Indus, the Brahmaputra and the Karnali, a tributary of that life-source of so many millions of people, the mighty Ganges. It is considered off limits to climbers, in respect of these religious beliefs, and is certainly the most significant mountain in the world whose summit has not seen the footprint of man.

The great alpinist Reinhold Messner was given the opportunity by the Chinese government to climb the mountain in the 1980s but he declined. In 2001 permission was given to a Spanish team to scale the peak, but in the face of international disapproval the Chinese decided to ban all attempts. Messner said at the time: 'If we conquer this mountain, then we conquer something in people's souls ... I would suggest they go and climb something a little harder'. In 1926, British explorer Hugh Ruttledge studied the North Face from the valley below. 'Utterly unclimable' was his verdict.

Cooper is one of today's brilliant mountain artists, inspired as so many others – like Albert Gos, William Keith, Ruskin or Waterlow – to create works honouring the hills in their wonder and beauty. 'I love the mountains because they remind me that I'm part of something much bigger than myself, which produces a sense of freedom and elation', he tells me. 'As a painter they represent an abundance of new forms, colours and spaces, with layers of meaning as rich as their history, and yet more that I'm still discovering'.

STANAGE, 2011
RAB CARRINGTON 1947 -

During the 1960s and 1970s Rab Carrington was one of the leading rock climbers in Britain, making outstanding extreme climbs throughout the Scottish Highlands. His personal legend began to grow following his 1968 ascent of *The Pinch* (E2 5b) in Glen Etive. This was probably the most serious route in Scotland at the time, tackling blank granite slabs and necessitating Carrington and his partner to move together – a tactic more normally associated with Scottish winter routes than cutting-edge technical summer rock of the time. After moving to North Wales, Carrington struck up a friendship with the charismatic Al Rouse. The result was an electric partnership that resulted in the second ascents of the hardest routes of the day and major new routes whether they be on rock, ice or in the Alps.

In 1977 they spread their wings and headed off to South America and the first ascent of the West Face of Patagonia's Aiguille Poincenot, along with three other pioneering Andean climbs. A previous attempt to get to the Andes, which had been stymied by a dockers' strike, inadvertently started Carrington off on what would later become his livelihood. While waiting in Buenos Aires for their strike-bound kit to arrive, Carrington cadged free lodgings with the Argentine climber and sleeping bag manufacturer Hector Vieytes. By way of repaying his host's generosity, he helped out in the machine shop, acquiring the skills to manufacture down equipment, which he would later put to good use building a business in his own name.

Carrington spent the remainder of the 1970s in the vanguard of the new wave of alpine-style climbing in the Greater Ranges including the highly influential ascent of Jannu's South-East Ridge with Brian Hall and Roger Baxter-Jones in 1978. Following a job working as a rigger on Fred Zinnemann's final film *Five Days One Summer,* he saved enough collateral to start up what was to become the most coveted down clothing brand in the UK.

In 2005 Rab sold the company, which allowed him to spend more time climbing. As a result, although in his sixties, he is now climbing technically harder than ever before. He became President of the British Mountaineering Council in 2010. 'I climb because I love the movement, and the ability to solve the problem of getting from one hold to the next', he tells me. 'Plus, when I was a young man, I found I was also very good at it! I have always stated that there are three requirements for climbing; the people you climb with, the movement of climbing, and the environment in which you climb. If you can get two out of the three you will have a good day out. If all three come together it is fantastic!'

EL CAPITAN, 1970
WARREN HARDING 1924-2002

When California State government's pioneering geologists – hard-bitten field surveyors normally inured to the sight of wildly configured mountains in a continent of geological wonder – first clapped eyes on Yosemite's dramatic peak of Half Dome they were amazed: 'It is a crest of granite rising above the valley, perfectly inaccessible, and probably the only one of all the prominent points about Yosemite which never has been, and never will be, trodden by human foot'.

Such a statement might have been calculated to provoke a five-foot tall climbing dynamo called Warren Harding. In the 1950s he was one of a new breed of determined and technically innovative Californian climbers whose exploits expanded the limits of rock climbing possibility, changing the sport forever. In 1957, Harding lost the race to ascend the alluring Half Dome to his great rival Royal Robbins. The effect was to provoke Harding to engage in battle with an even greater challenge: the soaring 1,000m granite cliff of El Capitan, and its most direct line, known as *The Nose*. Harding devised a siege tactic based on a series of provisioned 'camps' linked together by fixed ropes, running back to a ground-level supply camp. When criticized as unsporting, Harding, never a man unduly concerned with what others thought, said: 'You do it your way, and I'll do it mine'.

'Harding was a devilish fellow', described Yosemite historian Steve Roper: 'Looking at his flashing eyes, his wild black hair, his jet black pants, I was fascinated. Other climbers I knew were bespectacled scientists, staid folks who would never have dreamed of wheeling up to a rock with a sports car and a beer and a flashy dame'. Harding and an interchangeable team of climbing friends were to pull off the groundbreaking climb after forty-seven days spread over almost eighteen months. It had been an exhausting undertaking, during which Harding had come close to death when one of the threadbare fixed manilla ropes snapped, pitching him on to a ledge, miraculously just a few feet below. 'I do recall that El Cap seemed to be in much better condition than I was', Harding noted laconically after reaching the summit.

In this action portrait by Glen Denny, Harding is in the middle of the last pitch of his brilliant new line on El Capitan, the *Dawn Wall*. He had spent twenty-seven nights on the extreme face, living mostly in a tented hammock and consuming prodigious quantities of cheap red wine. Later that day he emerged over the top of the cliff, to meet a throng of press reporters, well-wishes and some furious Park Service rangers who had threatened both to arrest and to rescue him at various points in his epic ascent.

Showmanship was an integral part of Harding's iconoclastically wacky character. Dubbed 'Batso' – after the character 'Ratso Rizzo', the diminutive misfit in the film *Midnight Cowboy* – Harding certainly had a style all of his own. Unlike many of his beatnik climbing peers, who eschewed regular work to climb full-time, Harding remained a weekender, wedded to a conventional career as a land surveyor. This did not stop his leading a high life of drinking, partying, fast cars and, frankly, some pretty fast women. Beryl Knauth, a beautiful San Francisco debutante, was one of Harding's long-term companions whom he jokingly referred to as 'one of my many formerly fine girlfriends'. To the end his scurrilous humour was incorrigible. 'Climbing is no better or worse than anything else in life,' he said when asked to reflect on his achievements. 'It's just another asshole-ish, self-centred thing to do'. In case the listener might mistake him for a nihilist, however, he added, 'but if I could do it all over again, I'd like to be taller and smarter'.

MATTERHORN, 1963
HAMISH MACINNES 1930 -

Dr Hamish MacInnes is nothing if not a mountaineering Renaissance Man: a pioneering alpinist, mountain rescue innovator, equipment designer, ice-tool entrepreneur, photographer and film-maker, he is famed as a climber of legendary resourcefulness who possessed a mind attuned to solving mountaineering problems by a unique brand of lateral thinking.

MacInnes initially achieved notoriety of sorts for his use of aided climbing techniques in the early 1950s at a time when it was frowned upon in Scotland, earning him the unfairly derisive nickname 'MacPiton'. But his exploits and innovations were soon to garner his detractors' deep respect. In 1953 he instigated a celebrated 'alternative' expedition to Everest – comprising only two members, himself and the great Clydebank climber John Cunningham. They set forth carrying the entire expedition supplies on their backs in two 140-pound rucksacks. Meanwhile, the British and Commonwealth Everest Expedition of ten climbers, thirty-four Sherpas and some three hundred porters was already amassing its ranks in Kathmandu. It was an unequal contest of course, and the big guns beat the cocksure Scots to the summit.

Nevertheless, the fact that the shoe-string tartan team not only managed to get to Everest base camp, but succeeded in ascending an unclimbed 6,000m rock spire spoke volumes for the pair's ambition and drive.

MacInnes' hard climbing and challenging winter routes alone would qualify him for a place in a mountaineering Hall of Fame (*Zero Gully* V 4; *Raven's Gully* VI 5; *Agag's Groove* VII 6; *Crowberry Ridge Direct* VII 6), not to mention the first British ascent of the *Bonatti Pillar*, and numerous expeditions all over the world including Everest's South-West Face. But his influence is tangible in many other related spheres as well. He introduced the first all-metal ice-axes and developed the inclined pick to produce the 'Terrordactyl' – the grandfather of all modern steep ice tools. He also pioneered the use of rescue dogs in Britain's hills, redesigned mountain rescue stretchers, and wrote the first proper compilation guides to Scottish climbs in 1971. As if all this wasn't enough he zoomed around the world working as cameraman on Hollywood films, hunting the Yeti in the Himalaya and gold in South America, while simultaneously writing entertaining semi-autobiographical books about his adventures.

DEVILS TOWER, 1991
CATHERINE DESTIVELLE 1960-

During the late 1980s and early 90s Catherine Destivelle was probably the most famous female climber in the world, her striking good looks and ground-breaking climbing achievements ensuring that she was a darling of the media. But she was more than just a poster girl for women's climbing – her reputation was firmly based on world-class ascents on pure rock and an array of tough alpine routes. Destivelle cut her climbing teeth on the hard technical boulder problems of Fontainebleau when she was fourteen, before rapidly graduating to rock climbing on the huge limestone cliffs of the Verdon Gorge. She was soon mastering major Alpine climbs, astonishing her peers by leading every pitch on the hard *American Direct* route on the Dru in seven hours when she was just seventeen.

Originally destined for a life as a physiotherapist, Destivelle changed career to professional climber after winning the very first climbing competition that she entered in 1985. Just ten days later, she fell into a crevasse and broke her back and hip. Showing remarkable strength of will, she recovered quickly and would dominate world competition climbing for the next four years, her fierce competition with leading American competition climber Lynn Hill providing a grand rivalry that helped to popularize the fledging competitive wing of the sport.

In the world of real climbing Destivelle continued to impress. In 1988 she achieved the hardest technical rock climb then made by a woman with her ascent of the F8a/b route *Chouca* at the French crag of Boux. In the 'on-face' action portrait chosen here, Destivelle works her way up the distinctive igneous columns of the Devils Tower in Wyoming's Black Hills. She was training for what became a spectacular solo ascent of the *El Matador* line. But it was arguably in the mountain arena that Destivelle showed her true mettle. In 1990 she achieved what was then the hardest solo Alpine ascent with her lone climb of the *Bonatti Pillar* in just over four hours. She followed this up in 1991 with a new route on the Aiguille du Dru and in 1992 a solo winter ascent of the Eiger's North Face – the first woman to do so – in just sixteen and a half hours. More first female solos followed, such as the *Walker Spur* in 1993, the North Face of the Matterhorn in 1994, and a North Face direct route on the Cima Grande di Lavaredo in 1999. The subject of numerous films and books, Destivelle chose to reduce the amount of solo climbing after becoming a mother and now concentrates on a career as lecturer and writer.

YOSEMITE, 1969
ROYAL ROBBINS 1935-

Royal Robbins was one of the most influential rock climbers of the late twentieth century. Together with Yvon Chouinard he became a vocal advocate for 'clean' climbing ethics, encouraging the maximum use and preservation of natural rock features on routes, in opposition to the increasing use of artificial aids that were becoming prevalent in late 1950s and 60s Yosemite climbing. His books *Rockcraft* and *Advanced Rockcraft* were a major influence in moving the climbing world towards the use of removable protection, placed on the lead, rather than fixed pitons and bolts. The detail, and the philosophy, contained within them struck a chord with the climbing community, selling over 400,000 copies. 'A first ascent is a creation in the same sense as is a painting or a song', he wrote, and 'choosing the right climbing line should be an act of brilliant creativity'. In Robbins' view, the decision to place a single piton could be a matter of enormous importance, because 'like a single word in a poem, it can affect the entire composition'.

Robbins also became a proponent of single-push ascents, as opposed to the multi-day 'sieges' which had been common on the biggest routes up to that time, and he was able to argue from a position of pronounced credibility. He had under his belt the ascents of many iconic big-wall hard-granite routes, among them the first line on the North-West Face of the iconic Half Dome (the first climb in the US to be graded VI), and the *Salathé Wall* and the *North America Wall* on El Capitan. His importance to the development of Yosemite climbing is illustrated by the fact that of the six major El Cap routes established during that period, Robbins made either the first or second ascent, except for *Muir Wall*, of which he made the first solo ascent in 1968. In this brilliant portrait by his friend and frequent climbing partner Glen Denny, Robbins relaxes on the trail back to camp after the first ascent of *Tis-sa-ack*, another new route on the North-West Face of Half Dome, in the long summer of 1969.

Outside America, Robbins created important climbs in Canada and in the Alps, where he completed hard variants to established lines on the West Face of the Dru, including the *American Direct*, then considered to be the hardest technical climb in the Alps. When arthritis curtailed his extreme climbing in the late 1970s, he turned to extreme kayaking, and made the first descents of many challenging rivers in western US mountain states. In addition to his profound legacy of inspiring ascents, these days Robbins' name is just as familiar to the current generation of climbers through his outdoor clothing company, which he still runs with his wife Liz.

DUDLEY, 1990
BERT BISSELL 1902-1998

Bert Bissell could fairly be described as that most unusual of mountaineers: a 'mountain mono-centric'. For over half a century he ascended hundreds of thousands of feet – but it was nearly all on Britain's highest peak, Ben Nevis. Between 1945 and 1995, by the time Bert was ninety-three, he had climbed 'The Ben' over a hundred times.

A Dudley man to the core, Bissell was a deeply committed Methodist and avowed pacifist. In 1925 he founded the Young Men's Bible Class at Vicar Street Methodist Church in the Worcestershire town, and began visiting the Lochaber region of Scotland in 1937 with his young charges to meet with Scottish Methodists. During their visits they would invariably climb Ben Nevis. In 1945, overjoyed at the end of the terrible war, he led a party up the mountain on 'Victory in Japan Day' to commemorate the cessation of hostilities. There they constructed a 'Peace Cairn', comprising a large pile of stones, which would eventually acquire a large plaque stating boldly: 'Blessed are the peacemakers'.

These 'spiritual pilgrimages' as he described them were repeated for a further fifty years and over the ensuing decades they were accompanied by hundreds of people on the anniversary of VJ Day and Remembrance Sunday. Bissell built such a rapport between Dudley and Fort William, with annual reciprocal visits, that the towns were effectively 'twinned' fifteen years ago and he was made a Freeman of Lochaber. He appears in this charming portrait for a local press photographer who came to his house one afternoon, shortly after Bissell had returned from Scotland completing a century of treks up the mountain. He was pleased to pose for a portrait, though was careful not to get too much mud from his boots on his carpet.

After his death in 1998, the pilgrimages ended; and sadly nobody has followed in his footsteps. His peace cairn remains as the highest war memorial in the land, despite calls for it to be re-sited in a garden at the foot of the mountain in Glen Nevis, close to where Bissell himself is now buried.

ZERMATT, 1900
JOHN NORMAN COLLIE 1859-1942

Professor of Organic Chemistry, Norman Collie was a talented scientist whose achievements included playing a part in the discovery of Neon, and making the first X-ray photograph for medical purposes. But Collie's genius extended to mountaineering too, where he excelled both on rock and ice.

In the late-Victorian period he helped pioneer climbing both in the English Lake District –where he achieved the first Grade V winter climb in the world, *Steep Gill,* in 1891 – and Skye's Cuillin. Together with local Gael John Mackenzie he climbed every peak in the range between 1888 and 1896, including the last unclimbed summit in Britain. His climbs in Glencoe and on Ben Nevis in 1894 are often taken as the beginning of serious mountaineering on the Scottish mainland. In the Alps he was part of an elite band of alpinists led by Fred Mummery, and was involved in several of the latter's ground-breaking guideless ascents. Collie also helped initiate climbing exploration in Norway's Lofoten Islands and the Canadian Rockies. In 1895, Collie, Mummery and fellow alpinist Geoffrey Hastings, went to the Himalayas, for the world's first major attempt at an 8,000m peak, Nanga Parbat. They were years ahead of their time, and that terrible mountain was to claim the first of its numerous victims: Mummery and their two Gurkha companions, Ragobir and Singh, were engulfed in an avalanche and never seen again.

A few years later, Collie was back in the high mountains, proving particularly energetic in the Rockies, making a clutch of first ascents and discovering the giant Columbia Icefield. He would make expeditions to Canada five more times over the years, garnering twenty-one first ascents and naming more than thirty peaks. But, the hills were not the only attractions there it would seem. On top of this climbing prowess, he was both tall and good-looking, as an envious friend noted on a trip to Canada: 'The ladies spied him. Next moment his person reclined in a low chair, the centre of an admiring circle, while two fair dames, each supporting on high one of his neatly bandaged legs, tested with dainty fingers the sharpness of his Mummery screws'. Collie also had a reputation as an aesthete, wore sharp tweeds, smoked a Meerschaum pipe and was an expert on oriental art, wine, food and cigars. Perhaps unsurprisingly when he went to Norway, 'crowds flocked to see him under the impression that he was Sherlock Holmes'.

As befits his enigmatic reputation, he retired to live alone on the Isle of Skye, taking rooms at the Sligachan Hotel within sight of his beloved Cuillin. Just before his death in 1942, he was observed by the young RAF pilot Richard Hillary on leave in Skye: 'We were alone in the inn, save for one old man who had returned there to die. His hair was white but his face and bearing were still those of a great mountaineer, though he must have been a great age. He never spoke, but appeared regularly at meals to take his place at a table, tight-pressed against the windows, alone with his wine and his memories. We thought him rather fine'.

CAIRNGORMS, 2011
ADAM WATSON 1930-

As a professional ecologist, mountaineer and environmental campaigner, Adam Watson has combined a lifetime's scientific study of Scotland's Cairngorms with a passionate devotion to the hills, their wildlife and their people. Raised in Scotland, he was inspired by the great Scottish naturalist Seton Gordon to take to the Highlands, where he became entranced by the natural history and mountain landscapes he found there. From the age of eight Watson began making systematic records of various natural phenomena, such as the size and longevity of snow beds – data that has become evermore valuable in helping to chart the effects of climate change.

Watson turned his passion into his profession, working for Britain's government nature conservation agency for forty years, and undertaking influential studies of animal population dynamics and behaviour, particularly on red grouse and ptarmigan. During this time he has contributed to fifteen books and over five hundred other publications, together with nearly two hundred technical reports relating to his scientific research. Watson's commitment to the Cairngorms reaches far beyond science though. In the 1950s he was part of a 'Golden Age' of Cairngorms mountaineering and rock-climbing with such luminaries as Tom Patey. He played a major role in checking routes for the very first climbers' guidebook to the Cairngorms and was a pioneer of Cairngorm langlauf skiing, making the first ski traverse of the six biggest peaks in the range.

Watson's name is now synonymous with Cairngorm conservation. His active involvement as a campaigner stretches back over thirty years. He played a crucial role in the fight to restrict damaging ski developments in the 1980s; his stature and gravitas as a mountain ecologist turning the tide in the conservationists' favour at the Public Inquiry. 'I have travelled the globe widely', he says, 'but every time I return I still think that the Cairngorms are the most wonderful place on earth. They are certainly not the most impressive peaks but they have a beauty and mystery all of their own and I feel truly at peace among them'.

TINGRI DZONG, 1922
GEORGE INGLE FINCH 1888-1970

George Finch was a maverick Australian alpinist who spent a great deal of time fighting skirmishes with the British climbing establishment while on the fringes of selection for the early Everest expeditions. Partnered by his brother Max, George had an exceptional record of climbing in the Alps, which included routes such as the North Face of Castor, the South-West Ridge of the Midi and the West Ridge of the Bifertenstock. He ought to have been an automatic choice for the first Everest reconnaissance in 1921. But Finch was neither a member of the Alpine Club, nor had he been to a public school or a British university (though he had attended a Technical University in Zurich, and is said to have spoken better German than he did English). He was an individual and wonderful because of it, but not everyone saw it that way. More in tune with the 1960s than the 1920s, he grew his hair long and rarely wore a hat, unless specifically forced to, as he was here in this official expedition photograph. On seeing another photograph of Finch mending his own boots (rather than letting a servant do it), Edward Strutt, deputy leader of the 1922 Everest expedition felt moved to remark, 'I always knew the fellow was a shit'. As far as most of the Establishment was concerned, the uncouth Aussie was quite simply 'not one of us'. As a result, he was unfairly overlooked.

By way of a riposte, Finch immediately took off to the Alps and made a series of stylish first ascents, including the difficult North Face of the Dent d'Hérens. So when it came to selecting the team for the 1922 attempt, there was realistically no way he could be denied. Finch was also technically precocious: he made the first climbers' down jacket from thin balloon material and goose down. As a consequence he was officially selected as a 'scientist', in charge of the new-fangled oxygen apparatus, which would be trialled fully for the first time. The equipment was heavy and unreliable, and there was considerable resistance to the idea from many climbers on the grounds that it constituted 'cheating'. The Everest climbers and committee split into pro-oxygen and anti-oxygen factions. Nevertheless, Finch was proved right when, with novice Geoffrey Bruce, he reached 8,320m before a broken glass valve in Bruce's fragile and temperamental oxygen set forced them to abandon a summit bid.

Their climb may be reckoned a hugely important one in the history of the mountain. They pioneered a new route and established a new altitude record. As Reinhold Messner was to do almost sixty years later, Finch cut stylishly across the North Face, heading for the deep cleft of the Great Couloir. It is 'just conceivable that if he had been alone he might have reached the summit', says Stephen Venables, so too a brilliant alpinist and something of an Everest authority these days. They had also established a new high Camp V, some 150m higher than Mallory's, before a storm pinned them down in their tiny tent. That evening, in 'one of the many extraordinary displays of generous loyalty', a team of Sherpas climbed all the way up from the North Col with thermos flasks of hot tea and Bovril. Meanwhile, Finch had been staving off the effects of altitude with regular gasps of oxygen, between puffs on a cigarette!

Despite his bravura performance Finch was not invited onto the 1924 expedition following his refusal to comply with demands that expeditioners should not give lectures without permission. The impasse ensured it was the end of his association with Everest. Finch continued to climb, but in 1931 he suffered an accident on the Jungfrau in which one of his partners died. He never climbed seriously again, instead putting all his energy into his burgeoning scientific career. He became Professor of Applied Physical Chemistry at Imperial College, a scientific adviser to the Home Secretary and also the Director of the National Chemical Laboratory of India. With such a weight of respectable achievement, the climbing Establishment came to accept him in the end, eventually awarding him the Presidency of the Alpine Club in 1959. He returned the favour by becoming as cantankerous and reactionary as the old timers who resented him in the 1920s. When the great debate was held in the mid-1960s as to whether to amalgamate the Climbing Group with the Alpine Club itself, Finch staunchly opposed the idea of letting youngsters in, saying they 'should all be flogged instead'.

EVEREST, 1953
TENZING NORGAY 1914-1986

The early life story of Tenzing Norgay is one of remarkable determination and self-belief. Starting off a simple porter and ending up as a lead climber, over a period of nearly twenty years he made sure he was part of every expedition that tried to climb Everest. His eventual success and fame is all the more impressive when you consider that Tenzing came from just about the lowliest 'caste' of the Sherpa diaspora, that of a *Bhotia*, or Tibetan 'incomer' to the Sherpa homeland of Khumbu.

The ambitious Tenzing left his disapproving parents after his eighteenth birthday and journeyed to Darjeeling, where he hoped to be able to join one of the British expeditions to Everest as a porter. Tenzing's performance on Eric Shipton's 1935 expedition was such that he had no trouble in being hired on the following expeditions of 1936 and 1938. Unlike most of his fellow Sherpas for whom, by and large, climbing was just a challenging way of making a living, Tenzing desperately wanted to get to the summit of the mountain: 'For in my heart,' he later wrote, 'I needed to go ... the pull of Everest was stronger for me than any force on earth'. His obsession was so great that he even participated in a clandestine 1947 trip to the mountain through Tibet, with solitary Anglo-Canadian climber Earl Denman. He was back on a more conventional expedition in 1952 as climber with the Swiss, reaching just 237m short of the summit with Raymond Lambert.

By 1953, Tenzing had spent more time on Everest than any other human being, a fact of which the British were well aware. He was therefore one of the mainstays of their attack on the mountain, and crucial to the success of the expedition as a whole. This famous photograph by George Band shows Tenzing enjoying a mug of warm lemonade at Camp IV in the Western Cwm, after his successful push for the summit.

After Everest, Tenzing received many honours though became a bit of a political football. The Nepalis claimed him as one of their own, as did the newly independent Indians, and he was much in demand by a world public hungry for post-war heroes. He was invited everywhere and did much travelling. The tug-of-war over his 'nationality' was eventually won by the Indians, predominantly thanks to charismatic Prime Minister Nehru who took Tenzing under his wing and offered him a salaried position as the first Field Director of the newly-established Himalayan Mountaineering Institute in Darjeeling, a post that he held for twenty-two years. The move partially alienated him from many Nepalese and Sherpa, who had previously regarded him as a local hero. Eventually Tenzing also fell out with the Indian Civil Service who piled increasingly bureaucratic restrictions on his activities. The last years of his life were marked by some doubt and a loss of direction, but the mountain people of Asia still revered him; when Tenzing died, the procession that followed his funeral bier was more than half a mile long.

CHAMONIX, 2010
ANDY PARKIN 1954 -

Andy Parkin was one of Britain's leading rock and ice climbers when he suffered a catastrophic accident while climbing in the Swiss Alps. The way in which he came to terms with his injuries and adapted in order to climb at the highest standards once more has been nothing short of inspirational to succeeding generations. In the 1970s Parkin made ascents of Lobsang Spire and Broad Peak in the Karakoram, and almost pulled off a new route on K2 with Doug Scott before making the first solo winter ascent of the difficult and serious *Walker Spur* on the Grandes Jorasses. The future seemed limitless, but in 1984 he was pulled from a belay on the Riffelhorn after some rocks collapsed. His injuries required numerous emergency operations on heart, spleen, liver, hip, elbow and pelvis – which was broken in thirteen different places. He spent a year in hospital.

Assuming that he would never climb again, Parkin took up painting and spent several years perfecting a unique style. Then 'a few years later', he relates, 'I just woke up one day and knew I was better ... first I was a climber, then I was a painter, and now I need both'. Since then, both facets of his creativity have been given full reign. On his 'comeback' expedition to Makalu he undertook full-scale canvasses on the spot. Back in his adopted home of Chamonix he started scouring the Boissons Glacier for aeroplane wreckage and rubbish left by climbers and skiers from which he made sculptures to raise awareness of the effects of humans on the alpine environment.

But it was Parkin's return to elite alpinism that most astonished the climbing community. Despite his fused hip and right elbow he went on to put up routes such as the revered *Beyond Good and Evil*, with fellow alpinist Mark Twight; a route so difficult it went many years without a repeat. In 1993 he made the first ascent, solo, of *Vol de Nuit* on the East Face of the Mermoz in Patagonia, a climb with thin vertical ice and irreversible moves. The following year high on a new route on Cerro Torre with François Marsigny, the pair were engulfed by a ferocious storm, forcing them to retreat down the other side of the mountain onto the Patagonian ice cap. With no food and no map, they began a desperate hunger march back to basecamp, finally stumbling onto the pampas days later, eating dandelions to keep themselves alive. In recognition of this amazing experience Parkin became the first Briton to be awarded the prestigious French *Piolet d'Or, tu 'Golden Ice-Axe'*. 'Obviously, if I could get my body whole again, that would be marvellous, I'd sacrifice almost anything for that', Andy has said. 'But at the same time, if I could have it all back again, would I be willing to lose what I've gained? I've got a richness of life now. I'm no longer that tunnel-vision climber I used to be. I'd like to think I'm a better person'.

GASHERBRUM II, 2011
SIMONE MORO 1967-

Italian Simone Moro has made his name as an elite mountaineer, especially through his daring ascents of Himalayan peaks in the most inhospitable season possible: winter. Moro is now a veteran of ten such expeditions and in January 2005 he became the first non-Polish mountaineer to make a winter ascent of an 8,000m mountain, reaching the summit of Shish Pangma (8,027m), together with his Polish team-mate Piotr Morawski. In February 2009 he made the first winter ascent of 8,463m Makalu with his friend Denis Urubko in true 'alpine-style', going fast and light, without supplementary oxygen or the assistance of high-altitude porters. His most recent winter 'eight-thousander' is Gasherbrum II, climbed in February 2011 with Urubko and new kid on the block, innovative alpinist-photographer Cory Richards.

Moro doesn't just climb in the winter months of course, and in 2006 he made the first solo traverse of Everest, climbing the South-East Ridge and descending the North-East Ridge. While attempting to make the challenging high-altitude traverse between Everest and Lhotse in 2001 he abandoned the climb to come to the aid of a young British climber in trouble on Lhotse. Quite rightly he was praised highly by the climbing community around the world, for a selfless act true to the spirit of fellowship that still shines among many in the mountains. As a result he was awarded the 'International Fair Play' award from UNESCO, the Civilian Gold Medal from Italian President Carlo Azeglio Ciampi and the David Sowles Memorial Award, the highest award for valour from the American Alpine Club. For Simone, 'climbing the world's mountains is a way of discovering not only one's own strengths and weaknesses, but also the cultures, peoples and problems of the world'. But he's no doubt at his happiest, goggles on, ice-axe in hand, in the midst of some good, 'honest', winter weather. He turns his face toward the summit, shoulders his pack, and gets on with it.

MOUNT ASGARD, 2009
LEO HOULDING 1980-

Lake District lad Leo Houlding burst onto the climbing scene in 1996 when, as a sixteen year-old stripling, he made an audacious ascent of the fearsome E7 Welsh climb *Master's Wall*. What made the feat even more startling was the fact that the cocksure teenager wore a pair of borrowed rock boots which were a size and a half too big for him. This eccentric devotion to baggy footwear was not new; Houlding had also climbed the impressive E6 Welsh sea-cliff climb *Conon the Librarian*, in a friend's re-soled pair of trainers that were *three* sizes too big.

Another ascent, which had climbing's greybeards shaking their heads, was his torchlight midnight succes on the daunting E6 Llanberis climb *Lord of the Flies*. Houlding's battery failed during the climb, necessitating a downclimb from the middle of the crux sequence to better holds from where he could lower a rope for a replacement battery and finish the route. At the same time, the young Houlding was accomplishing more conventional repeats of the cutting-edge E8 rock climbs of the day. Although such nonchalance was interpreted by many as youthful hubris, others suspected that an unorthodox rock-genius might be in the making, testing the boundaries of his ability in an unplanned, haphazard manner. This indeed proved to be the case.

In 1998 Houlding's reputation went global after he and partner Jason Pickles achieved a free ascent of the West Face of the Leaning Tower, one of Yosemite's uncompromisingly arid big walls. He followed this by a seven-hour speed climb of El Capitan's *Nose*, deliberately setting off after mid day with no head-torches after a morning's boozing. They made it back down just before dark, Houlding having narrowly avoided a big fall. While solo, trailing 40m of slack rope, he slipped, making a reflex to catch the four-inch wide belay ledge as he began the plummet, saving the day. To prove his newly-found mastery of big-wall climbing, Houlding then repeated on-sight *El Nino* on the *North America Wall* which had only just been completed by the expert Huber brothers the previous day. The cocky 'have a go' attitude charmed the Americans.

In 2002, however, there was a set back, when he fell from high on the *Maestri-Egger* route on the Patagonia's Cerro Torre, slamming his right foot into a ledge and shattering his ankle. A nightmare descent involving eight diagonal abseils, four hours crawling over glaciers and six hours painful hobbling down jagged scree slopes ensued. 'I used to say that I only ever got hurt, never injured', he reflected ruefully after months of physiotherapy. Houlding bounced back quickly and over the past decade he has become a top BASE-jumper, summited Everest and pursued a busy TV presenting career. Hard climbing remains at the centre of his life, however, with recent highlights including the first free ascent of the 5.13d El Capitan epic *The Prophet*.

'A few vertical steps take you far from the oppressive order of horizontal life. On the wall you are free, governed only by your own fear and desire', he later explains to me. 'There is nobody to answer to, nobody to blame and nobody to bail you out. Nature provides the set, the ambition of your imagination creates the scene. Anyone can do anything, you just have to tune in', he says, with a confidence only granted to those with supreme amounts of talent.

Houlding created this self-portrait after the ninth day on his new route *Inukshuk*, hanging on a precarious sky-hook on pitch thirteen, high on the North West Face of Baffin Island's Mount Asgard. Feeling, in his words, 'very alone and extremely committed', Leo leads the way 800m up the wall, a hundred miles from anywhere. Freezing conditions here, deep in the Canadian Arctic, and desperate, perilous terrain pushed Houlding and his team right to their limit. On reaching the top, a quick handshake and a moment to soak in the view, Houlding turns on his heels and launches himself into the abyss, making the first wing-suit BASE-jump from the summit. In a matter of minutes he was standing, safe, on the glacier far below.

MOUNT LOUIS, 1961
HANS GMOSER 1932-2006

In one of the gentle ironies that riddle mountaineering history, the man who arguably helped promote Canadian mountain sports more than any other was in fact an Austrian. Hans Gmoser emigrated to Canada in 1951 and from then on threw himself into climbing and skiing, in the process effectively creating Canada's modern guiding and commercial mountaineering industry. Gmoser was far from just a businessman, of course. In the 1950s and 60s he pioneered new climbs in the Rockies, notably the *Grillmair Chimney*, the first route to breach the great limestone cliffs of Yamnuska in the Bow Valley. This introduced a new standard of technical climbing to the Rockies and it is widely regarded as marking the beginning of the modern era in Canadian rock climbing.

In the high mountains, Gmoser made the third ascents of Mount Alberta and Brussels Peak and, further afield, the first ascent of Alaska's Mount Blackburn. In 1959 Gmoser led an expedition through the wilderness of the Rockies to climb Mount Logan's East Ridge and followed this in 1961 with a continuous ski traverse along the icefields of the continental divide. He also climbed Denali via a new route up the enormous Wickersham Wall in 1963. He retired in the early 1990s but remained extremely active in Nordic skiing and road cycling. Energetic to the last, he died after falling from his bike while engaged in a 150km day trip through the Rockies.

Despite his distinguished exploratory mountaineering and skiing record, it is probably as a guide and founder of the Association of Canadian Mountain Guides and Canadian Mountain Holidays – which grew to become the largest provider of adventurous travel in the country – that Gmoser is best known. In the process he pioneered the practice of heli-skiing, which has remained a blessing or a curse in the mountains ever since, depending on your perspective. In the words of the impressive Canadian mountaineer Chic Scott: 'Everyone working in the mountain adventure business in western Canada today owes their job to Hans'.

LONDON, 1910
ELIZABETH HAWKINS-WHITSHED 1861-1934

At the tender age of eighteen Lizzie Hawkins-Whitshed, 'a delicate child of wealthy parents', married a much older Guards officer and became one of 'The Prince of Wales Set', renowned for their glamorous social life. The partying exerted a price however; Lizzie's health declined, and suffering from consumption, she was sent to Switzerland to recuperate. Initially, this was quite a shock to the system. 'I knew nothing about mountains and cared less' she said, remembering her initial reaction to the concept of an Alpine exile. But the magic of the mountains quickly captured her imagination and within a year, somewhat predictably, she set her sights on Mont Blanc, though poor weather repulsed her first attempts. The setback was followed by word that her husband had died a hero at the Battle of Abu Klea in the Sudan, with a spear through the throat. Recovering remarkably quickly from the news, she bagged Mont Blanc on the rebound – and added the Grandes Jorasses for good measure.

Such behaviour appalled her family. Her parents were said to be horrified, while a great-aunt was not amused. 'Stop her climbing the mountains! She is scandalising all London and looks like a Red Indian'. But it was too late. In the hills Lizzie found freedom from the conventional stuffiness of London society. Being 'the personification of elegance' as one gushing admirer wrote, she initially employed maids. The first eloped with a courier, while the next had a fit of hysteria when her mistress was back late from a difficult climb. Lizzie quickly dropped the maids and began taking her own boots off.

After making summer ascents of most of the main peaks in the Alps she became one of the very first women to brave winter climbs, undertaking first ascents of the Aiguille du Tour, Col du Tacul, Col du Chardonnet and the Col d'Argentiere. After climbing the Aiguille du Midi canons were fired in celebration in Chamonix. She also made a winter attempt on Monte Rosa, accompanied by the dashing Italian explorer and photographer Vittorio Sella, though they were defeated by storm at 4,200m. Lizzie's domestic life was just as hectic. Following the death of her husband she married again, to a Mr Main, with whom she made some adventurous trips to China, but he, too, was soon dead. Next up was the exotically named Aubrey Le Blond who managed to keep up with her – and survived. All the while, the winter ascents kept coming; Piz Sella and Piz Zugö both fell, as well as one of the most arduous winter climbs attempted to that point, to the summit of Monte Disgrazia.

Lizzie was smashing social as well as altitude barriers. Her ascent of Piz Palü in 1900 was probably the very first *cordée féminine*, climbed with the equally feisty Lady Evelyn McDonnell, and she was the first woman to lead guideless parties up alpine routes in both summer and winter. Lizzie also wrote several best-selling books about her adventures and was a prime mover behind the formation of the Ladies' Alpine Club in 1907. She became its first President ('one of the nicest things that ever happened to me') and served until her death in 1934. 'I owe a supreme debt of gratitude to the mountains for knocking from me the shackles of conventionality', she said.

1ST PRESIDENT LADIES ALPINE CLUB.

CHAMONIX, 1918

WANDA RUTKIEWICZ 1943-1992

Lithuanian-born Wanda Rutkiewicz was arguably the finest female high-altitude mountaineer of the twentieth century. During her action-packed life she led or participated in some twenty-two expeditions to the Himalaya and Pamirs and climbed extensively in the Andes. She reached the summit of eight 8,000m peaks.

Raised in Warsaw and educated as a computer engineer, Rutkiewicz was a talented skier, swimmer and gymnast who was introduced to climbing in 1961 while she was training for the Tokyo Olympics with the Polish women's volleyball team. She recalled her first climbs as having been made with 'much emotion but bad style'. Rutkiewicz soon improved and began undertaking difficult alpine climbs in Austria and Norway. Her first high-altitude success came in 1970 when she climbed Peak Lenin in the Pamirs and from then on an endless series of expeditions began, during which Rutkiewicz began pioneering the concept of all-female teams. Her winter ascent of the North Face of the Matterhorn with Irena Kesa, Anna Czerwinska and Krystyna Plamowska was especially influential. Rutkiewicz also made strides for women's climbing in terms of expedition leadership of mixed teams, being the co-leader of the expedition that made the first ascent of Gasherbrum III in 1975.

As if all this wasn't enough, Rutkiewicz even took up rally driving after becoming the first European woman to climb Everest in 1978. Her steely approach to the challenges of life was further proven in 1981 when a skier crashed into her on Mount Elbrus, fracturing her leg. Despite having to use crutches for two years, she nevertheless led a successful expedition to K2. She was the first woman to climb and descend that merciless mountain, though her success was undoubtedly marred as her companions Liliane and Maurice Barrard were separated in a blizzard and both fell to their deaths. In this now infamous 'Black Summer' of 1986, some thirteen people lost their lives in pursuit of this most challenging of 8,000m summits. Rutkiewicz went on to achieve more big peak success, such as the isolated Shishapangma and the 'Turquoise Goddess' Cho Oyu, but her ambitions finally caught up with her. She disappeared high on Kangchenjunga, hoping to make a solo bid for the summit, in pursuing her declared mission to try to become the first woman to climb all the 8,000m mountains. Her body has never been recovered.

BEN NEVIS, 2011
DAVE MACLEOD 1979 -

In this professional era top climbers typically focus on one or two areas of the sport, thanks to the time and effort taken to be the best at any one aspect. But the remarkable Glaswegian climber Dave MacLeod appears to have never heard of this 'rule', excelling in all facets of the game, including traditional rock climbing, bouldering, sport-climbing and winter routes. 'I feel sorry for those who specialise', he says, 'because I always see people go through months of down time, low motivation and no climbing'.

Remarkably, MacLeod did not gain his enviable portfolio of abilities through some kind of sports science hothousing – but by a completely understated and self-taught climbing regime on his local urban crag of Dumbarton Rock. From the age of seventeen he became such a familiar presence, performing his rock callisthenics over its graffitoed routes, that he attracted the moniker 'Dumbie Dave'. MacLeod solved some of Dumbarton's trickiest boulder problems and, armed with his newly-honed technical skills – but still no driving licence – began travelling further afield by means of thumb and bus, surprising the English by climbing four E7s on Peak District gritstone in one week during an early border raid. At the same time MacLeod had begun winter climbing in earnest, overcome by keenness despite a lack of equipment. He didn't let a small thing like that hold him back – he was soon leading Grade VI.

With his rapid apprenticeship well and truly over, MacLeod began repeating and then creating the hardest rock and ice climbs in the country.

His breakthrough climb, as far as the wider climbing world was concerned, came back at Dumbarton Rock where he succeeded, after many spectacular falls, on the route *Rhapsody,* the first to be given the grade E11. The campaign was captured on film and led to the wider recognition of his status. After MacLeod and his wife Claire relocated to Fort William he made an even harder climb, *Echo Wall,* up the fearsomely overhanging cliffs of Ben Nevis. Since then he has complemented the hardest rock climbs in the country with the hardest winter climbs, in the form of *The Hurting* in the Cairngorms (the first winter climb to be graded XI, 11) and *Don't Die of Ignorance* (XI, 11) on Ben Nevis, climbed after an epic ascent during which his second fell off and dangled in space for two hours and MacLeod became hypothermic.

MacLeod has featured regularly on television, most recently climbing a desperately hard new route live up the immense overhanging crag of Sron Ulladale on the remote Isle of Lewis, despite heavy rain and winds and a serious injury to his ankle caused by a falling rock. He has also become a leading expert and innovator in the field of training for climbing. Away from his beloved Scottish Highlands, he has achieved sport climbs up to a grade of French 9a (*A Muerte* at Siurana), bouldering problems up to a grade of Font 8b (*Pressure*, Dumbarton Rock) as well as solo climbs up to grade 8c (*Darwin Dixit* in Margalef). Not bad for a man who has very recently become a dad, and is not pushing his climbing as hard as he'd like.

HAMILTON GORGE, 1925
NORMAN CLYDE 1885-1972

Originally from Philadelphia, Norman Clyde migrated to California to become a schoolteacher in his mid-twenties. After the sudden death of his wife in 1919 he went to live alone in the Eastern Sierras and became wedded instead to the mountains, devoting most of the rest of his long life to pioneering climbs there. Renowned for his fitness and stamina – his peer David Brower dubbed him, 'the pack who walks like a man' – Clyde threw himself into extended mountaineering journeys, once climbing thirty-six peaks in thirty-six days, many of them first ascents. During the 1920s he would make as many as 160 first ascents, many climbed solo. Fittingly, in 1931, he ascended the last unclimbed 14,000ft (4,268m) mountain in the Sierras, Thunderbird Peak, so named after an electrical storm engulfed his summit party.

Clyde was far more than a peak-bagger however. His participation in the first ascent of the East Face of Mount Whitney, for example, was one of the first big walls to be climbed in the range and pointed the way towards higher technical standards in Californian rock climbing. Other advanced climbs by Clyde included the U-Notch Couloir, Clyde Couloir on East Palisade and the East Arête of Mount Humphreys in 1935. In this rather painful-looking portrait Clyde performs a dulfersitz rappel before the waiting camera, some way above Hamilton Lake, deep in Sequoia National Park. Usually sporting a wide-brimmed 'campaign hat', Clyde became a notably eccentric character of the region. His famed rucksack was described by a contemporary as an 'especially picturesque enormity of skyscraper architecture'. This was because it often contained many items including as many as five cameras and, when guiding a client, a hammer and cobbler's anvil in order to make repairs to boots while on the move.

His legacy is literally writ large across the Sierras with landmarks such as the Clyde Minaret, Norman Clyde Peak and the Clyde Spires. In addition, he was a prolific writer with over thirty articles published recounting his climbs and travels. A true mountain man and always a fresh-air fiend, he still often slept outside his ranch house in a sleeping bag when over eighty years old. He said that to be closer to nature was to be closer to the meaning of everything.

CHUGACH, 2006
CANDIDE THOVEX 1982-

Candide Thovex is one of the world's most outstanding extreme skiers, a star of numerous cult ski films and the perpetrator of some of the most audacious ski jumps recorded. The Frenchman, who is often cited as 'the best freestyler in the world', was born in the Haute Savoie in the heart of the Alps. Living close to numerous ski resorts he was able to practise endlessly and perfect his famed 'big air' technique.

In ski competitions he has displayed an amazing versatility of talent, becoming three times winner of the Winter X Games in several disciplines: big air, slopestyle and superpipe. He has also been involved in documenting his skills on camera throughout his career, his films being known for their stylish aesthetic as well as being spectacular.

This portrait was created by celebrated Swedish photographer Christoffer Sjöström, who has spent over ten years shooting with this French freesking superstar. On this occasion they were on location not far from Girdwood, Alaska, deep in the Chugach Mountains; an area renowned both for remote winter-skiing on its seven nearby glaciers and for the northernmost rainforest in the world.

Thovex received a setback in 2007 when he broke his back but made a blistering comeback, winning the 2010 World Freeride Championship – mastering this most taxing of ski disciplines in his very first season. Now, after nearly a decade and a half of touring and competing in every corner of the world (and usually winning), Thovex is taking time off from the competition circuit to make a feature-length movie. 'I've always been passionate about directing, and I've been waiting for this opportunity for a long time', he says. 'It wasn't an easy decision to take time out from competition and particularly the Freeride World Tour, especially after I had such a good season in 2010. I'll be concentrating on the film for two seasons, but I haven't ruled out returning to competition when it's finished'.

ASPEN, 1968
JEAN-CLAUDE KILLY 1943 -

A legend in the 'old world' of skiing, Jean-Claude Killy dominated the sport in the late 1960s. Born in Paris, Killy's family relocated to Val d'Isère in the Alps when he was still a child and it was here that he learned to ski, helped by the fact that his father, an ex-fighter pilot, had opened a ski shop. Unhappy at school, and by now obsessed with the exciting new sport, Killy dropped out aged fifteen to become a member of the French National junior ski team. He was not an immediate success, however, and had to wait until he was eighteen before he won his first race, but when he did, it was spectacular – winning the giant slalom in his home village of Val d'Isère despite the fact he had started off back in thirty-ninth place.

A daredevil style characterized his performances. In a race in Cortina in 1962 Killy skidded and fell on ice 180m from the finish. Instinctively recovering and bouncing back up immediately, he crossed the line still the fastest competitor; and on just one ski, with his other leg broken in the fall. Victory came at a cost, as it meant he missed his chance to represent France in the skiing World Championships three weeks later. Killy's bad luck continued when he picked up dysentery and hepatitis in Algeria during his Army National Service, ruining his chances in the 1964 Winter Olympics. Things finally began to go right after 1966 in World Championship competitions and he came to truly dominate the sport, winning the 'Triple Crown' of Alpine Skiing with a clean sweep of all three gold medals at the 1968 Winter Olympics, in the slalom, giant slalom and downhill events.

In this portrait, Killy greets his fans after the Roch Cup downhill events in Aspen, Colorado's fashionable resort. Though he retired from top flight competition in 1969, he remained a familiar public figure, being associated with several ski companies and acting as the face of luxury champagne and automobile brands, whilst also presenting two ski-related TV shows and appearing in a number of forgettable feature films. Killy briefly came out of retirement in 1972 for one season, to win the US Pro Circuit much to the delight of his admirers. He also tried his hand as a racing driver, participating in major events such as the Paris-Dakar Rally, before serving on many sports councils related to skiing, cycling and the International Olympic Committee, using his considerable charm, and winning smile, to great effect. He became a Grand Officer of the *Légion d'honneur* in 2000, for his skiing achievements and for the service of his sport.

KHUMBU, 2006
KIT DESLAURIERS 1969-

Kit DesLauriers was the first person to ski down from the top of all the so-called 'Seven Summits' – the highest points of the seven continents. Along the way, she has also garnered a multitude of women's ski 'firsts': the first woman to ski from the summit of Everest, the first female ski descent of Mount Vincent in Antarctica and the first female ski descent down the North Face of Mount Elbrus, to name but a few. This beautiful photograph by Jimmy Chin shows DesLauriers making her way through the Khumbu Icefall, in the shadow of Everest, at the beginning of her climb there.

DesLauriers inherited a family history steeped in skiing achievements – her grandfather pioneered building chairlifts in Vermont – and she has been hitting the pistes since she was a girl. Her skills set was strengthened still further with ski mountaineering techniques learnt during a spell living near Telluride, Colorado, where she worked as part of the San Miguel County Search and Rescue Team on many rescue operations and as a professional ski patroller.

And, as if to prove she was not just an 'expedition skier', in the midst of her Seven Summits challenge, DesLauriers also won back-to-back Free Skiing World Championship titles in 2004 and 2005, in addition to being the US. Freeskiing Women's Champion. She has also made other notable descents in Siberia, the French Alps, New Zealand, Alaska, the Tetons, the Sierra Nevada and Colorado. Aside these skiing feats, Kit is also an experienced rock climber and mountain biker. Perhaps, unsurprisingly, she reckons her biggest weakness is: 'Wanting to do everything, really well, all at once!'

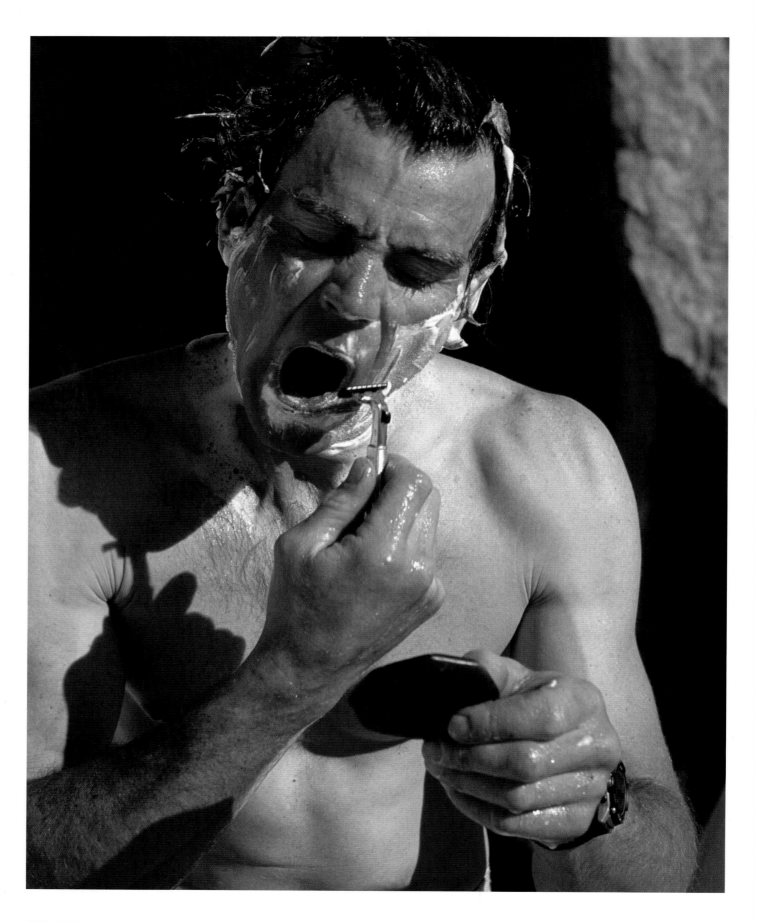

BAFFIN ISLAND, 1998
ALEX LOWE 1958-1999

With nicknames such as 'the Lung with Legs', and 'the Mutant' it comes as no surprise that American Alex Lowe had a reputation as one of the fittest and strongest mountaineers who ever lived. Lowe's exceptional upper body strength was developed through a fanatical exercise regime that regularly included four hundred chin-ups and hundreds of dips. But Lowe's fame arose not so much from his possession of such enviable physical attributes, but the application of them. His reputation began in his adopted state of Montana where he made numerous hard rock and ice climbs and ski descents and where his strength and fortitude became legendary.

In one famous incident a free-standing icicle he was climbing broke free, carrying him 30m down before he hit a ledge, smashing his forehead into his ice-axe. Lowe, however, promptly stood up and proclaimed himself 'OK'. But his friends could see he wasn't: a large section of his scalp was draped over one eye, exposing his skull. Undeterred, Lowe later recalled what followed: 'We ... kinda taped the scalp back into place, and put a hat on, and taped around the hat, and started skiing out. [We] kinda knew it was time to go to the ER. But we also knew it was going to be a long evening there, so we stopped down at the coffee shop and got lattes. It was great. My clothes were saturated with blood. We parked in the handicap spot in front of the coffee shop, marched right in, and then headed for the hospital'.

Other notable incidents included his part in helping to rescue some Spanish climbers trapped by a storm high on Denali. He srtuggled up steep ice slopes at high altitude while carrying a frost-bitten climber on his back, so he could be evacuated by helicopter. 'He literally, single-handedly saved several people', announced the chief mountaineering ranger for the National Park Service at the time.

Lowe's climbing achievements were just as impressive: he led the first ascent of the North-West Face of the Great Trango Tower, in the Karakoram, despite a 35m fall and injured elbow, a solo ascent of the North Face of the Matterhorn, the first solo ascent in winter of the North Face of the Grand Teton in Wyoming, and no fewer than sixteen routes up Yosemite's El Capitan. Lowe also summited Everest twice, as well as climbing in Antarctica, Baffin Island in the Canadian Arctic, Indonesia's Carstenz Pyramid and the Cordillera Blanca in Peru. In this candid portrait, by Gordon Wiltsie, Alex celebrates his successful climb of Great Sail Peak, by taking a shave in base camp and then washing his hair. Job done, he wanders back into his tent to open a cold beer.

'We're all at this one level,' the top alpinist Conrad Anker once remarked, 'and then there's Alex'. Lowe was tragically lost in an avalanche while climbing Shishapangma in 1999. Often named in magazines and by his peers as the best climber in the world, he had shrugged off the unwanted label with typical diffidence, responding: 'The best climber is the one having the most fun'.

NORTH TWIN, 2004
STEVE HOUSE 1970-

Dubbed 'the best high-altitude climber in the world today' by no less a luminary than the legendary mountaineer Reinhold Messner, American Steve House has made his name in the uncompromisingly tough and dangerous sphere of elite alpinism. Eschewing the security of fixed ropes and large teams, he has pursued the art of lightweight and fast 'alpine-style' assaults on huge mountains such as Nanga Parbat, in an intense approach that is physically and mentally demanding and which leaves very little room for error. A big mistake at this level of extreme mountaineering almost certainly leads to injury, and frequently to death.

House has therefore achieved some of the most audacious big mountain climbs of the past fifteen years. His startling solo climbs of Alaskan mixed routes and Himalayan peaks such as K7 quickly entered climbing legend, as did his and Marko Prezelj's *tour de force* on the forbidding North Face of Canada's remote North Twin Tower. They succeeded here despite House dropping one of his outer boots from halfway up the rock face, precipitating an epic battle to escape from the mountain. Prezelj took this photograph the following day, when House simply had to adapt to survive. Night was falling and the storm clouds were brewing. Lacking the gear to rappel all the way down the wall to search for an outer boot shell they would likely never find deep in the snow, they were left with little choice. Do or die. Unable to go down, they had to continue up. Lashing his crampon directly to his taped up foam inner boot and sock (foot wrapped in a plastic bag, 'the kind you'd put apples in at the grocery store'), and later unable to use his skis, with considerable effort and skill they pushed on to the summit, then fought their way home through the crevassed labyrinth of the Columbia Icefield. And all in a whiteout, they eventually reached a road head. They were safe.

Arguably House's most impressive achievement to date has been his and Vince Andersen's phenomenal ascent of the massive Rupal Face of Nanga Parbat – a line long sought-after but which had frustrated generations of elite mountaineers. None of this has come without a price: House has lost many friends and climbing partners and he himself narrowly escaped entombment within a French crevasse. House has proved as adept with a pen as an ice-axe. His autobiography *Beyond the Mountain* achieved the rare mountain literature double, grabbing top prizes on both sides of the Atlantic with victory at the Banff Mountain Book Festival and the Boardman-Tasker Award. He remains modest nevertheless. 'Being called the best', he says, 'makes me very uncomfortable ... my intention is purely to climb well, to be as good as I can be. The simpler you make things, the richer the experience becomes'.

Messner is clear about House's talents. 'I admire Steve for his approach to the mountains. Step by step he has become the best alpinist he can become. In my view he is at the top of mountaineering. He climbs the right routes on the right mountains in a time when everyone is climbing Everest. He is also a great storyteller: he tells about doing, not about morals or lessons. Steve says his most rewarding days are when he cuts away everything. And with these few words he holds the same line as Mummery, Bonatti and Robbins. It's the style that makes the difference'. House does not celebrate a battle with the elements, no hollow words of victory. Instead, he shares the suffering and challenges of freezing cold bivouacs, the discomfort of altitude, yet too the simple joy of being out on the hills – for the embrace of nature, its beauty, and the solitude. For his innovation, his boldness, and for his honesty, House really deserves his place among these great names of mountaineering.

BAFFIN ISLAND, 2008
STEFAN GLOWACZ 1965 -

Stefan Glowacz became a familiar name in European climbing in the 1980s thanks to his dominance of the first professional competitions. In 1985 he won Sport Roccia in Bardoneccia, Italy – the first sport climbing competition ever held. Initially, he was taken aback by its seriousness: 'I thought the event would be a good time like many of the traditional meets', he remembers. 'We were wrong. We entered the climbers camp and saw the sombre faces of contestants. Laughs and socializing were replaced by sidelong glances and nervous chatter. Many serious young lizards just spent the time cleaning their sticky-rubber soles to a squeak'.

Despite misgivings Glowacz went on to become the three-time winner of Italy's most prestigious event, the Arco Rock Masters. He 'won gold' when competition climbing was tested as an Olympic demonstration sport during the Albertville Winter Olympics, also becoming a frequent sight in climbing media – and in the movies – starring in Werner Hertzog's film, *Cerro Torre: Scream of Stone*. He retired from competition in 1993 to concentrate on 'natural' climbing. A final nod to his 'artificial' origins came in his creation of the multi-pitch bolted route *Des Kaisers Neue Kleider* in Austria. At the grade of 5.14c it was one of the technically most difficult routes in the Alps and not repeated for nine years.

Since then Glowacz has radically changed direction, specializing in traditional adventurous climbing on big walls in very remote areas, trying, where possible, to avoid mechanical means and eschewing bolts. Using canoes, he approached the daunting 'Cirque of the Unclimbables' in Canada's Yukon to make the first ascent of the 5.12 *Fitzcarraldo* on Mount Harrison Smith. Other expeditions include sailing to Antarctica to climb the 900m Renard Tower, and using sea kayaks to explore the cliffs of Baffin Island and Greenland. In this striking portrait by Klaus Fengler, Glowacz takes time to chill out in his portaledge tent, high up on an extreme Arctic wall, overlooking Buchan Gulf. He was halfway through a monster 700m twenty-one-pitch route up a formation called 'The Bastion'. With difficulties up to F8a+ and A4 it is likely the hardest route on Baffin Island. Some time later, he named their route – *Take the Long Way Home* – after a fairly epic journey back to civilization that followed the climb. They travelled for sixteen days on foot and skis to reach Clyde River, a small settlement over two hundred miles from their starting point.

More adventures are on the horizon. Glowacz has recently become internationally respected for his climbs in Patagonia with Robert Jasper where they tackled the remote 1,000m North Face of Cerro Murallòn, an ascent that earned a *Piolet d'Or* nomination. 'I see rock climbing not just as sport, but a way of life. Sometimes I can just sit at the bottom of a cliff, look around and feel good. I don't even have to climb', he says. 'Quite often, I will take in the view half-way up a mountain, and that really is one of the best things in life'.

LES BOSSONS, 2010
ZOE HART 1978 -

We're sitting in the backyard of a house, tucked into the mountainside not far from Chamonix. Our host, Zoe Hart, is enjoying a little time off. Cups of tea and reading. An unusual Saturday afternoon, perhaps, for a Patagonia-sponsored athlete with a string of major climbs to her credit. The self-styled 'Alpine Princess' – or, more candidly, she says, 'a Jersey girl gone wild' – Hart represents a still-rare species of climber: a fully fledged female mountain guide. Now based here in the French Alps, Hart is only the fourth American woman to gain International Federation of Mountain Guides Association status – the highest level of credential available to a professional mountain guide anywhere in the world. Needless to say, it's pretty tough to make the grade.

More remarkably, she gained the qualification only ten years after taking up climbing. In that decade she packed in more intense mountain experiences than most climbers manage in a lifetime, scaling fearsome alpine routes in Alaska and Europe, steep ice in Colorado and Canada, big walls in Yosemite and Oman, ski descents in the Karakoram and, arguably the ultimate test of keenness in any mountaineer, enduring the Scottish winter, where she made a new route in the Cairngorms.

She describes herself as a 'perpetual transient', a gentle soul who hasn't lived in the same place for more than three months over the past eight years. 'It was nice, you know', she tells me later, 'to have a portrait created in my backyard in the sunshine, in a summer dress. I guess, kind of a dichotomy between the life I live, the harsh mountain life, and the part of me that likes to be home, and write in my journal and bake cakes – the pull between the two aspects of who I am. I relish the days I can sit in comfy clothes, feet bare on the cold stone of my terrace, sitting back, being still a while, beneath the splendor of the mountains. These days allow me to remember my soft, vulnerable, feminine traits that harsh alpine routes don't allow for. A North Face doesn't care if I'm a man or a woman, it just asks me to be tough, to suffer with or without grace, and to keep moving upwards at times when going down is not an option. I love the mountains because they make you find strength that you wouldn't otherwise know you had, they allow you to share experiences with others that are very real and they push me out of a comfort zone in a way you can't do on a daily basis in our safe Western world. They make you *present*, they urge you to embrace the here and now, and for that alone we can all be blessed'.

MOUNT ROBSON, 1913
CONRAD KAIN 1883-1934

The Austrian Conrad Kain represented a new breed of turn-of-the century mountain guide, who cut their teeth in traditional European Alpine climbing before taking their skills to other ranges abroad. He began guiding aged nineteen and such was his skill and daring that his services were sought for expeditions to places as varied as Spitsbergen in 1901, Egypt in 1902 and the Altai in 1912.

In 1909, his talents were procured by the Alpine Club of Canada and the following year he joined Canadian Arthur Wheeler and British climber Tom Longstaff on an exploratory expedition to what became known as the Bugaboos. It marked the start of a love affair with the Canadian Rockies that would lead to Kain becoming the pre-eminent pioneer climber in the range. In 1911, while supporting another survey expedition, he climbed Mount Whitehorn and then, in 1913, shortly after this photograph was taken, the highest peak in the Rockies, the 3,954m Mount Robson. His route up the North-East Face, climbed with two ACC members, remained unrepeated for eleven years – until Kain climbed it again.

He proved a popular man with clients. J. Monroe Thorington said that Kain was '...endowed with a gift of laughter and a sense that the world was quite mad'. Between 1913 and 1916 Kain guided in the mountains of New Zealand where he made twenty-nine first ascents, including the first traverse of the country's highest mountain, Mount Cook. But in 1916, he returned to Canada, married a British Columbia girl and worked as a farmhand, trapper and horsepacker.

Despite the pressures of earning a living, now having to be a respectable and considerate husband, he climbed hard when he could find the time. The year of his return he made the first ascent of Mount Louis, a winter solo of Jumbo Mountain in the Purcells and made first summer ascents of several of the Bugaboos including Howser Tower and Bugaboo Spire. The rock climbing on the latter remained the hardest in Canada for some time. 'Life is so short, and I think one should make a good time of it if one can', he wrote. 'The only thing I enjoy now is Nature, especially spring in the mountains, and letters from friends. Sometimes I think I have seen too much for a poor man. There are things that make a man unhappy if he sees the wrongs and can't change them'. But after looking across to some beautiful Rockies landscape he added: 'It occurred to me that after all I was a rich man, even if I had no money'.

MOUNT WELLINGTON, 2011
PAUL PRITCHARD 1967-

To many, the appearance on the climbing scene in the 1980s of Bolton back-street boy Paul Liam Pritchard came as a breath of fresh air. Here was someone who appeared to be recapturing the romantic adventurousness of British climbing, bucking a trend towards micro-routes and sport climbing, climbing in a traditional manner while at the same time not sacrificing technical challenge. On Welsh slate, a combination of sheer neck and ability helped him to play a major role in the new-routing boom. His reputation was cemented when he transferred his skills to the loose, dangerous terrain of Anglesey's sea-cliffs, where he made some extraordinarily worrying, hard routes in crumbling situations of alpine seriousness.

Unlike many of his peers, who sought the benefits of career-plan sponsorship, Pritchard seemed happy to accept any remunerative crumbs that came his way as a bonus by-product of his amateur activities. Instead he felt impelled to put adventure pure and simple at the top of his personal agenda, and it is this, as well as his ability and laid back personality, which has maintained such a high regard and respect towards him amongst the sometimes hypercritical community of climbers. Consequently, he began to embrace Scottish winter climbing and made a rare transition from high-standard crag climbing to the big mountains, leading expeditions to big walls in Patagonia, Baffin Island, the Karakoram and Himalaya, as well as outlandish parts of Britain such as the Hebrides.

All this hectic activity was not without a price. Accidents and poor health dogged Pritchard, making his achievements and continuing enthusiasm all the more remarkable. First, he took a huge ground fall at Wen Zawn, surviving the drop but almost drowning in a rock pool. Then came another massive fall while winter climbing on Creag Meagaidh, which resulted in more hospitalization. There followed a bout of a mysterious ME-type disease and on top of all this, he continued to suffer from mountain sickness on most of his high-altitude expeditions.

Sadly, there was to be an even greater trial to come. After a blue riband year which had seen him make a full recovery and emerge triumphant with the Boardman-Tasker prize for his brilliant autobiographical first book *Deep Play*, a breeze block sized lump of rock detached itself from a Tasmanian sea-stack while he was at its base, directly hitting him on the head, removing part of his brain and leaving him hemiplegic. The terrible injury he sustained provided him with the biggest challenge of his life yet, but his reaction to the calamity, and his powerful second book written in response, demonstrated he is one of the few people capable of rising to it. Now resident in Tasmania after marrying one of the nurses who initially helped him recover, Paul is a dad and full-time writer.

Despite selling all his climbing gear after his accident in a symbolic boat-burning act, he has now returned to the rock face, seconding friends up routes, as well as climbing Mount Kenya and Kilimanjaro and becoming a demon recumbent bicycle rider and sea-going peddle kayaker. His portrait was created specially for this book by British photographer James Bowden on Tasmania's Mount Wellington. Pritchard lives on its lower slopes and he trains here most days. 'Why I keep going to the mountains, even now', he tells me, 'is very clear – when I climb I feel alive. There is a certain meditative aspect to climbing. As soon as you step off the ground you are forced to live in the moment. When you are in danger you become hyper-aware: the texture of the rock, the colour of the lichen in front of your nose or the grain of sand as it is crushed beneath your slipper sole. It's like yoga for cheats! It is life to me, pure and simple'.

BANFF, 1975
BRUNO ENGLER 1915-2001

Bruno Engler's life marked the end of an era in the development of Canadian outdoor recreation. He was the last of the 'Swiss Guides' that played such an important early role in mountain exploration in this vast nation. Engler was born in Lugano and was already established as a ski-racing champion and mountaineer when he arrived from Switzerland in 1939. He spent the next sixty years in western Canada as a mountain guide, ski instructor, photographer and cinematographer. His stunning black-and-white photos capture the magnificence and grandeur of the Canadian alpine landscape, from the smallest plant to the highest peak. He became renowned as one of the Canadian Rockies' great characters.

Engler first worked as a ski instructor in Alberta before helping to teach the Canadian Army in survival and mountain warfare skills during the war. In his forty-year guiding career Engler's clients included such luminaries as Frank Smythe, former Canadian Premier Pierre Trudeau and Canada's Governor-General Roland Michener. Climbing, however, was merely one strand of a multi-faceted mountain career. Engler's other impact came through his photography and filming. Over sixty years he compiled a collection of striking photographs, which are now regarded as a definitive archive covering a period of intense change in Canadian outdoor sports and its national parks.

In the mid-1950s he established a company offering cinematography, location spotting and mountain safety consulting to the film industry. As a result he worked with Disney, the National Film Board of Canada and Canadian and American television networks and became friends with Hollywood stars, among them James Stewart, Paul Newman and Charles Bronson who came to make films on location in the Rockies. Bruno remained a well-grounded man, despite national praise and a dizzying circle of admirers. 'I always used to run into the mountains for peace. I found peace and I found myself. I got out of the confusion. I became myself again. The mountains are a living thing to me. When folk say I'm a legend, well, I just tell them I've been here too long'.

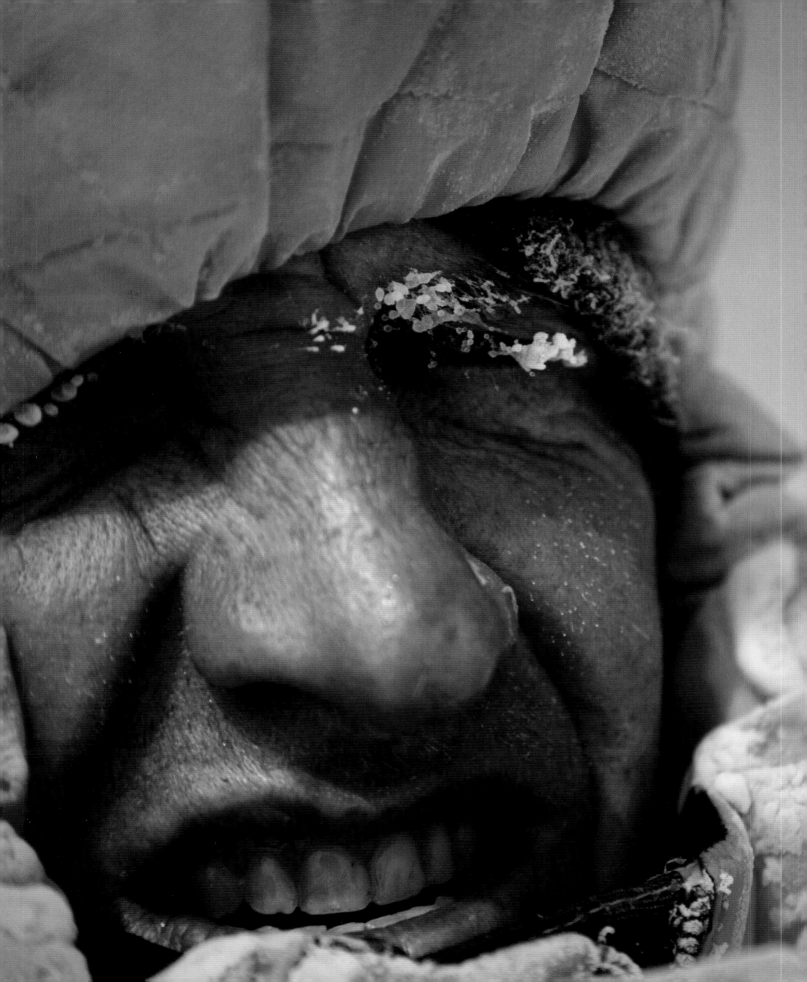

GASHERBRUM II, 2011
DENIS URUBKO 1973-

Moscow-based Kazakhstani mountaineer Denis Urubko is one of a new generation of extreme alpinists who are pushing the athletic boundaries of performance at high altitude without the use of artificial oxygen. In 2009 he became the fifteenth person to have climbed all fourteen 8,000m peaks in the world, and just the eighth to complete the feat without bottled oxygen. The achievement is all the more remarkable given that as a boy Urubko suffered from allergic asthma – indeed his Russian parents deliberately moved east to Sakhalin, in what is now Kazakhstan, in order to be closer to the cleaner air of the taiga and the sea.

There he developed a love of wild places and began mountain climbing in his teens in Kamchatka. During the 1990s he began a series of notable climbs in the Pamirs, including climbing all five 7,000m peaks in this range and the Tian Shan in just thirty-nine days. He was honoured with awards as a Soviet 'Snow Leopard' for his efforts. At the beginning of the new millennium, Urubko began his campaign to climb the world's 8,000m peaks, completing the task in less than nine years and including the first winter ascents of Makalu and Gasherbrum II. This portrait was created by the irrepressible Cory Richards during their recent expedition there. Perhaps unsurprisingly, Urubko also holds several mountaineering speed records, including the most rapid ascent of Gasherbrum II from Camp 1 to the summit in just seven hours and the fastest ascent of Elbrus, climbing 3,242m in under four hours!

Urubko is also notable for the number of high-altitude rescues he has been involved with. Between 2001 and 2008 he came to the assistance of several mountaineers in difficulties, including such famous names as the Polish mountaineer Anna Czerwinska on Lhotse and French alpinist Jean-Christophe Lafaille on Broad Peak, who Urubko pulled from the bottom of a crevasse. He is a genuinely a 'great' mountaineer, and a hero to many, in an age when words like these are so easily bandied around they lose their currency and true meaning. Urubko is the real deal.

EVEREST, 1938

BILL TILMAN 1898-1977

Often cited as one of the originators of the stylish 'lightweight' approach to mountaineering, Major Harold William 'Bill' Tilman was a remarkable man of action who continues to inspire generations of adventurers. Not only did he succeed in climbing Nanda Devi, the highest peak climbed before the Second World War – despite suffering from debilitating altitude sickness for much of his climbing life – he also fought in two World Wars and was parachuted behind enemy lines in the Balkans at the age of forty-five to organize resistance to the Nazis. As he got older, rather than retiring to a well earned pipe-and-slippers rest, he turned to exploring the more remote mountains of the world using ancient sea-going barques and pilot cutters, several of which sunk amongst ice-floes leading to major epics. To top it all, he was a wonderful, understated writer, describing his adventures 'with a wit so dry sparrows could bathe in it'.

'He was one of the toughest guys I ever knew', said US climber Charlie Houston. 'One sometimes felt that he courted disaster, longed for trauma, and he never did things the easy way if with a little effort they could be made to be impossible'. Tilman was born the youngest son of a prosperous Liverpool merchant and saw plenty of action as a teenager in the Great War, fighting at the Somme and winning the Military Cross by the time he was eighteen. Following the danger and excitement of war service, Tilman spent ten years farming in Kenya. But when he was thirty-one he bumped into Eric Shipton who was looking for someone to go mountaineering with – and his life changed in an instant.

Together they made some now legendary mountaineering trips including the first traverse of the exposed ridge between Mount Kenya's highest summits, the first traverse of the mighty Rishi Ganga Gorge in the Indian Himalaya, and the first exploration of the Nanda Devi 'Sanctuary' at its head, as well as two expeditions to Everest and a four-month trip across one of the wildest and most uncharted ranges of the world, the Karakoram. Despite the adventures and risks they shared, the pair couldn't help retaining a high degree of middle-class English reserve. 'As we had done in Africa', wrote Shipton, 'we continued to address one another as *Tilman* and *Shipton*; and when, after another seven months continuously together, I suggested that it was time he called me Eric he became acutely embarrassed, hung his head and muttered, 'It sounds so damned silly.'

After an eventful war, Tilman acquired a barque, which he named *Mischief*, and for his first serious attempt at sailing he headed out into the Atlantic with a view to making for Patagonia. This first voyage tended to set the tone for many others to follow – he had trouble with his cautious crew from the start. They mutinied in Gibraltar. A replacement crew proved a much happier one, in fact many of Tilman's crews seemed to be capricious like this; they either couldn't stand the old curmudgeon or they were fiercely loyal to his eccentric ways. Without further ado, Tilman then voyaged to South America and made the first crossing of the Patagonian icecap.

It was the beginning of a whole new sea-going mountaineering career at an age when most people would be thinking of easing up. Over the next decade and a half he would sail and climb in Greenland, Iceland, Baffin Island, South Georgia, the South Shetlands, and Spitsbergen, losing two ships in the process, but always coming back with renewed enthusiasm. Many climbers have recently been pioneering remote new routes, in places like Greenland and the Antarctic Peninsula, literally steeping off the deck of their yachts to begin a pitch. They owe this clarity of purpose much to a fellow like Tilman. As befitted a lifelong man of action, sadly, it all ended abruptly. Dying with his sea boots on, Tilman disappeared in a fierce storm off the Falklands in 1977.

LAKE TAHOE, 2004
FRED BECKEY 1923 -

Fred Beckey started as he meant to go on, making a first ascent of Washington State's Mount Despair when just sixteen in 1939. From then on he never thought of pursuing any life other than that of a mountaineer. He has now made over a thousand first ascents in America alone, 'although I've never bothered to count 'em', he chuckles.

Beckey was born in Düsseldorf but moved to Washington with his family when he was three. He first made national news when, joined by his sixteen-year old brother, he made the second ascent of the difficult and remote Mount Waddington in 1942. This was a peak that had repelled sixteen attempts by the leading alpinists of the day before it was finally climbed by the legendary mountaineer Fritz Weissner in 1936. The shoe-string tyro mountaineers trekked for days through forest and climbed the difficult South Face, showing remarkable prescience for their age by swapping mountain boots for tennis shoes to scramble up it's wet summit rocks. The American climbing establishment collectively dropped its jaw – it seemed as if a couple of children had pulled off the climb of one of the hardest mountains in the land.

Since then Beckey's name has been writ large over the Cascade Range of America's Pacific North-West, with myriad first ascents including Liberty Bell, Mount Slesse's North Buttress and Mount Rainer's Mowich Face, all climbed when the area was much less developed and harder to access than now. In Canada Beckey has made classic routes such as Snowpatch Spire's East Face in the Bugaboos, the North Face of Mount Edith Cavell, the first ascent of the Devil's Thumb and the first winter ascent of Mount Robson. In Alaska Beckey bagged the first ascents of Mount Hunter and Mount Deborah and Denali's North-West Buttress. He has also has a long association with the Himalaya, attempting Lhotse as early as 1955 and organizing a successful expedition to the 6,540m Jiazi in China when he was spritely sixty-one years old.

Nonetheless, most of his activity has been restricted to North America, due to the simple fact that, as his friend Eric Bjornstad notes, 'Fred was always poor, living out of his car, eating out of cans. He lives very inexpensively. He likes McDonald's because he saves the coffee cup and reuses it for months and gets free coffee'. Not for nothing has Fred been dubbed 'the climbing hobo's climbing hobo'. He is proud of this moniker, too, posing for celebrated photographer Corey Rich in this charismatic shot, thumbing a lift to the local cliffs near Lake Tahoe. Beckey remains rich in climbing experience, however. Although holding the record for making the most first ascents of anyone on earth he is, incredibly, still climbing. 'How old am I? We're not gonna talk about that', he says to anyone with the cheek to ask. 'It's a secret – they can find it on the Internet. I tell the girls I'm thirty-nine and let it go at that'.

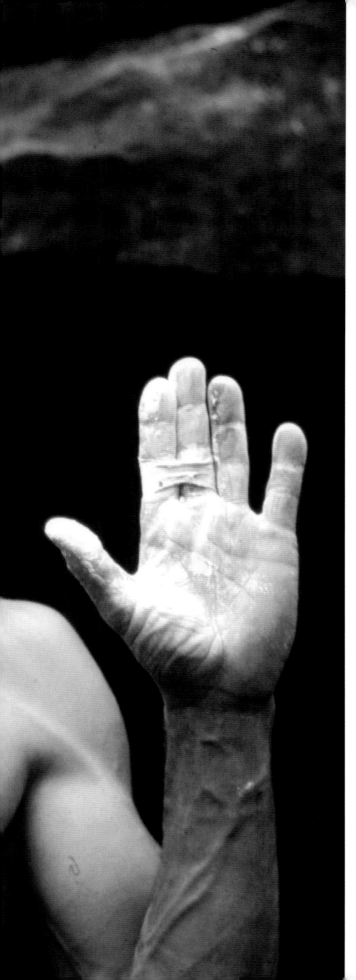

WILDER KAISER, 1979
REINHARD KARL 1946-1982

In the early 1980s Reinhard Karl was one of the rising stars of German climbing, famous for scaling Everest and lauded for his mountain books and photography. It seemed he was destined to become one of the leading high-altitude mountaineers, but, like so many before him, his life was cut tragically short while pursuing this high-risk passion.

Karl left school in Heidelberg when he was just fourteen and began an apprenticeship as a motor mechanic, 'really the dirtiest and most rotten of all dream jobs', he later wrote. Seeking escape he became fascinated by mountaineering literature and his mother encouraged him to join the local chapter of the German Alpine Club. Weekend climbing gave him the release he craved and Karl progressed rapidly. During the 1960s and 1970s he climbed many major alpine routes, including what was then the fastest ascent of the Eiger's North Face in a day and a half.

In the 1970s, Karl was among the first Europeans to visit the Yosemite Valley and he would climb many of the classic hard routes on El Capitan and Half Dome such as *The Nose, Salathé Wall, West Face, Son of Heart, The Shield* and *Separate Reality*. Influenced by the vibrant Californian free-climbing scene he promulgated the same ideas back home in Germany and Austria. As a result, in 1977, together with Helmut Kiene, he made the free ascent of a climb in the Kaisergebirge, the *Pumprisse*, which was the first to be recognized as Grade VII on the UIAA scale in the Alps.

At the same time Karl was making a reputation for himself as an energetic photographer and writer and this would lead, inadvertently, to his becoming the first German to stand on the summit of Everest in 1978. He was commissioned by a magazine to cover Reinhold Messner's upcoming oxygen-less attempt on the mountain. Following the failure of Messner and climbing partner Peter Habeler's first attempt, Karl and expedition doctor Oswald Oelz made for the top using bottled oxygen. In recognition, he was honoured with the 'Silver Laurel Leaf' award for sporting prowess by the German government. Karl followed up his success on Everest by climbing Gasherbrum II in 1979. A flurry of expeditions to several mountain ranges ensued, including the Patagonian Andes and other difficult routes on Himalayan peaks, though they were mostly dogged by bad luck with weather or illness. His great adventure came to an end in 1982 when he was engulfed in an avalanche while attempting Cho Oyu. Wiped out in his climbing prime, he was just thirty-five years old.

MOUNT KENYA, 2010
TORMOD GRANHEIM 1974-

Tormod Granheim is the latest in a long line of Norwegian adventurers who have pushed the limits on mountains and the oceans. His particular contribution to this legacy is pioneering ski descents of some of the highest peaks in the world. In 2002 Granheim reached the summit of Aconcagua and skied the Polish Glacier and later tackled the Chinese peaks Muztagh Ata and Kuksay within a week. He went on to make ski descents of Cho Oyu and Shishapangma and in 2006 he startled the world by daring the first ski descent of Everest by the Norton Couloir. He ascended the mountain from an advanced camp, covering 2,500m of altitude gain in a continuous twenty-four-hour climb. Together with his Swedish partner Tomas Olsson, they skied onto the North Face by the Norton Couloir, the 3,000m-long, fifty-five-degree gully line that bisects the upper part of the mountain. Tragedy struck during an abseil over a cliff, when Olsson's anchor failed. He fell to his death. Granheim had to ski on alone to the North Col.

In 2010 Tormod headed to East Africa in the off season, with his good friend photographer Fredrik Schenholm, in their bid to ski down Kilimanjaro's glacial flanks. It is part of a current project, attempting to climb and ski the prized 'Seven Summits' and the seven highest volcanoes. 'We call our collection of mountains, the Super Seven', he tells me. This is just a framework, an excuse of course, for a lot of climbing, skiing and adventure! We went to Mount Kenya to acclimatize. From the Austrian hut we got up a few hours before daylight. Having negotiated an equatorial glacier, some 4,500m above sea level, we found ourselves in a boulder-field near the bottom of the 400m wall we intended to climb, where this picture was taken'.

'In climbing, for me, *light is right*. We carried next to nothing, only a light rack, two thin ropes, water and cameras. This is the moment I love most in the mountains, as the sun rises and a new day begins. This is also usually a turning point where everything becomes a little bit warmer and easier. Soon after Fredrik took this shot, we were surprized by torrential, freezing rain and given the lightweight concept we'd committed to, it really cooled us down. It took us many pitches of climbing to warm up'. 'I suppose', Tormod says, 'a part of me is very analytical, asking questions like: *Is it possible? Is it safe? How little gear can it be done with?* But another part of me is more poetic, especially when I have a chance to live in the mountains. They mirror our hopes and reflect our joy. They represent friendship, challenge, fear, fun and endless beauty. To me Everest was the ultimate challenge, others climb it, we could ski it. Traversing onto the North Face at 8,700m was dream-like. A moment I will never forget'.

LLANBERIS, 2008
JOE SIMPSON 1960-

The author of the internationally best-selling *Touching the Void* began his climbing career with an accident. He fell 25m from the Glencoe ice climb *The Screen* following a guileless beginner's attempt to climb it with a leashless ice-hammer. Displaying a remarkable physical resilience that would become his trademark, he managed to stagger back down to the Clachaig Inn despite broken rips, cracked femur and internal injuries. This incident was a mere primer for a whole series of hair-raising near misses and direct hits. Following a successful season in the Alps, Simpson survived a spectacular descent when an avalanche hurled him 2,000ft down the Courtes. Amazingly, he emerged with just cuts and concussion. Equally amazingly, the experience didn't put him off.

Returning to Chamonix, Simpson became one of the famous early-1980s group of 'alpine bin-men': young British climbers who eked out a living removing the trash of a chalet complex in order to finance their fix of climbing. Simpson's next near-death spectacular involved Lancashire climber Ian Whitaker with whom he attempted the famed *Bonatti Pillar*. A rock ledge they were bivouacking on collapsed, leaving them hanging in their sleeping bangs from a frayed rope on a single loose peg. Suspended above a 1,000m drop for almost twelve hours, they were eventually plucked from the face by winch operated from the summit by a rescue team. Undeterred, together with fellow bin-man Simon Yates, Joe decided to extend their mountaineering experience further than the crowded Alps, and in 1985 embarked on a two-person assault of the West Face of the 6,344m Suila Grande in Peru. The expedition was a great climbing success – the pair accomplished a hard new route up an intricate face to the summit – but what happened on the descent would make the story world famous.

Simpson fell and broke his leg and had to be lowered slowly and painfully by Yates. During a storm that suddenly overwhelmed the mountain, they lost contact in the maelstrom and Yates unwittingly lowered him into a crevasse,

leading to a much-debated moment in British climbing history. Yates – bucket seat collapsing in soft snow and being dragged to certain death by the dead-weight of his injured partner – managed to grab hold of his Swiss army knife, and cut the rope. With no sign of him following a break in the weather, Yates assumed the worst and soloed back to camp, where he prepared to leave. Meanwhile, Simpson was still alive. From the hidden snow bridge that had arrested his plunge into darkness, he somehow managed to crawl out of the crevasse to make his way back to camp, dragging himself across glaciers and moraine over several days despite his severe injuries.

While recuperating he wrote his account of what had happened. *Touching the Void* was a mesmerizing story of a life-or-death struggle that seemed to strike an emotional chord with virtually everyone who read it, and it was most recently made into an award-winning film. Following a long and painful series of operations and intensive physiotherapy Simpson would return to climbing; and further close calls, enduring a huge fall on the Nepalese peak Pachermo with Mal Duff. Simpson had to be lowered down a mountainside again, except this time Duff handed over his pocket knife before commencing. Yet more operations and therapy followed, but Simpson has managed once again to return to climbing and to pen more best-selling accounts of his ordeals. He has now sold over a million books and is translated into more than fourteen languages. Yet it's Simpson's writings on the spirit and ethics of mountaineering that stand out, in particular his feelings for the shadows he sees falling on famous mountains like Everest; reduced at times to a commercial circus on the now-familiar routes, guided and fixed-roped for the ants slowly trudging uphill bedecked in their sponsor's logos. The mountains endure, however, it's just man's approach that changes. Real mountaineering challenges lie waiting all over the world, ready for those dangerous men who 'act their dreams with open eyes'.

NASSER BRAKK, 2007
MARKO PREZELJ 1965 -

If you were to poll the world's top mountaineers, the chances are that they would nominate wedding photographer turned climbing phenomenon Marko Prezelj as best in the game. The Slovenian describes himself as 'an honest, old-school climber'. 'But, for those that don't think style matters, let me say style matters', he tells me, as we chat awhile about this motivations in the mountains. It's this openness, together with a puckish sense of humour which has endeared him to so many of the world's great climbers; that and a fearsome record for pulling out all the stops to climb insanely difficult routes in pure alpine style.

Prezelj began impressing his peers with audacious ascents in the late 1980s. A 'professional amateur', he was studying for a degree in chemical engineering while pulling off world-class climbs like his new route on Cho Oyu, the first ascent of Menglungtse (7,181m) and winning the inaugural *Piolet d'Or* with Andrej Sternfelj for their new line up Kangchenjunga. All the while, Prezelj prefers to let his climbing do the talking: in 2007 he won another *Piolet d'Or* for his ascent of the North-West Pillar of Chomo Lhari with Boris Lorencic – and promptly used the awards ceremony to denounce climbing awards in general, cheerfully stating that: 'Fame is a cheap trap set by the media in which the complacent are quickly caught and exploited'.

He's as eloquent to speak with, as his climbs are visionary in their clarity. 'The decision-making process is the challenge. Doubt and uncertainty are the essence; trying to balance them with my choices is the passion. No regrets is the rule. When I know the outcome, the game is different and in the end less fun'. A climb that amply demonstrated Prezelj's commitment to the purest form of ascent possible was his route *Light Traveler*, on Denali's South-West Face. Prezelj and American extreme snowboarder Stephen Koch pushed the parameters of alpine style, completing the 2,000m free on-sight M8 mixed route in a continuous climb of fifty-one hours. 'We both found ourselves falling asleep while belaying', Prezelj admits. 'It took me a month to recover'. The ascent prompted yet another nomination for the *Piolet d'Or*. Koch is effusive in his praise for Prezelj: 'I basically learned what I was capable of from him', he says. It's no small praise coming as it does from one of the most talented of the new-wave American mountain athletes.

In 2004 Prezelj joined forces with yet another outstanding alpinist, Steve House, to pull off one of the most dazzling North American alpine climbs of the last decade: the first repeat, with a variation, of the *Lowe-Jones Route* on the North Face of North Twin. The route – described by Canadian mountain man Barry Blanchard as making 'the North Face of the Eiger look like a kiddie's sandbox' – is the hardest in the range, comprising 5,000ft of sheer, black, north-facing limestone, steeper than the Eiger, higher than El Cap, prone to raking stonefall and overhung by huge seracs.

Prezelj and House's ascent was incident-packed. While committed high on the face House dropped one of his plastic boot shells, then shredded a rope when taking a swing trying to follow a traverse. He hobbled up the final ten pitches with his crampon lashed to his inner boot. Prezelj describes topping out above the last of the technical difficulties after four days of stressful climbing with almost Tilmanesque understatement: 'We shook hands even though it was still a long way home. I thought this is unusual. Never before had I shaken hands with my partner in the middle of a climb'. House himself honours Prezelj above all others. On the final desperate pitches up the ice-glazed exit chimneys on North Twin, he delivered this tribute. Reduced to total dependence on Prezelj he simply said: 'You're the man – I'm just the belay jacket'.

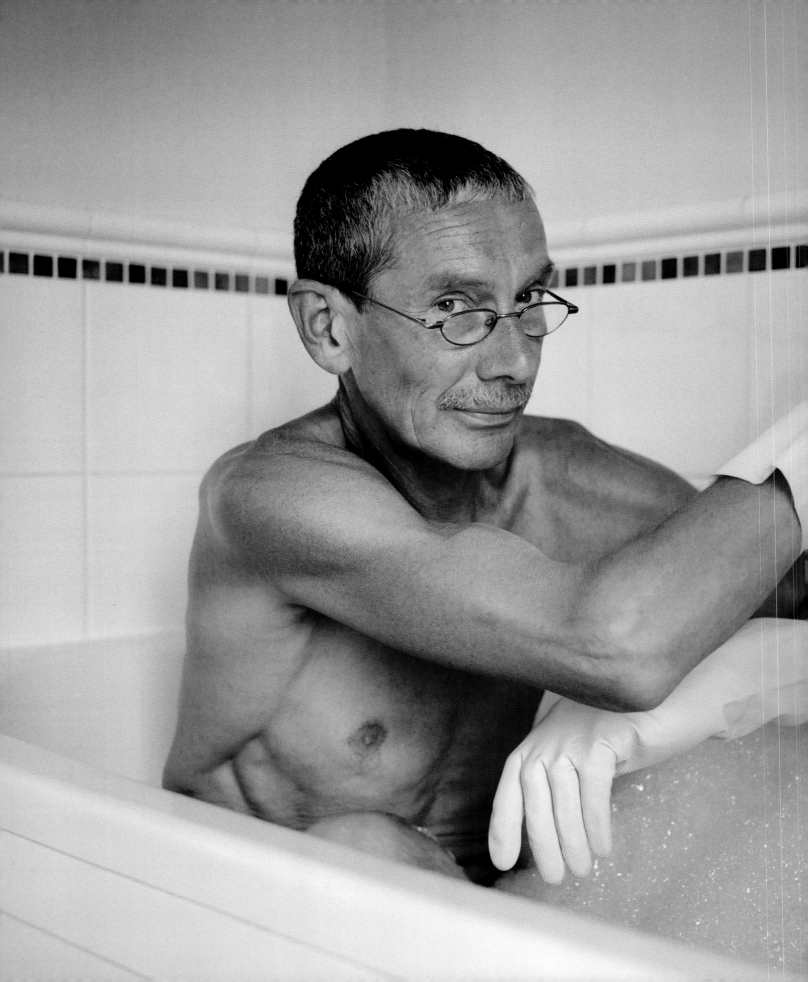

HATHERSAGE, 2009
RON FAWCETT 1955-

'Big Ron' Fawcett, an amiable moustachioed Yorkshireman, cut an unlikely figure as a leading rock climber and pioneer of corporate sponsorship. Unlike his continental peers of the era though, he eschewed brash posturing on the covers of glossy magazines. Instead, despite his prodigious climbing genius, he somehow projected an air of unaffected modesty. As a consequence, although he was a climbing superstar, British climbers still felt he was always 'one of them'.

Nevertheless, Fawcett was one of the key players that transformed climbing in the 1970s from an almost completely amateur activity into one with a significant professional component. His first major new climb, *Mulatto Wall* (E3) at Malham Cove, was completed when he was just fifteen. By the middle of the 1970s he was smashing mental and physical barriers with his routes and high standards of athleticism. From then on he dominated top-end climbing throughout the country. In those years, Ron was so dedicated to his climbing that he used to wear rubber washing-up gloves in the bath to avoid losing the tough skin he had built up. He kindly recreated the scene for us at home, courtesy of a cracking new shot by Ed Luke.

During the late 1970s there was no one who could touch him, but by the mid-1980s a chasing pack of young climbers were closing in, inspired by Fawcett's own training-honed power climbing regime. The likes of Jerry Moffatt were soon snapping at his heels. 'The Body Machine', as Ron had been dubbed by the media, wasn't finished yet, however, and after the pretender to the throne top-roped an almost holdless arête at Derbyshire's Millstone Edge and proclaimed that whoever led it clean (i.e. himself one day) would be 'the true Master', Big Ron promptly beat him to it. He gave his brilliant gritstone climb the then-startling grade of E7 6b, and with it the perfect name, *The Master's Edge*.

Although this marked the peak of Fawcett's rock climbing career, he would go on to create many more cutting-edge routes and boulder problems, and amazed the climbing world by soloing a hundred extreme-graded climbs in a day. He later took up paragliding and fell-running, and is a leading 'veteran', competing regularly. He still climbs nearly every day.

KENDAL, 2009
UELI STECK 1976 -

'I like to push my personal limits. It doesn't matter what the result is afterwards ... for me it's most important to push my body to its full potential'. So says Ueli Steck, whose staggering mountaineering achievements include solo climbing the Eiger's North Face in an unbelievable two hours forty-seven minutes. The first ascent in 1938 took three harrowing days. Not only that, Steck has polished off the North Face of the Matterhorn in one hour fifty-six minutes and the North Face of the Grandes Jorasses in just a little over two hours. Reading these bare statistics it seems hard to believe that these are still alpine climbs with mean reputations, on the tick-lists of many elite climbers, and routes which continue to claim the lives of many would-be suitors. Not for nothing has Ueli Steck been dubbed 'The Swiss Machine'.

'Steck is simply running up the thing', remarked mountaineering commentator Ed Douglas on seeing footage of his record Eiger climb. 'And to be honest I was shocked by how sketchy some of it looked. I would assume that a climber several thousand feet off the ground without a rope would want to make sure each placement is solid. Not Ueli. He is the ultimate man in a hurry'. The clock certainly ticks loudly, but Steck is far more than simply a speed merchant. The thirty-five-year-old former carpenter has now excelled in just about every climbing discipline, whether it be Yosemite big-wall free climbs, first ascents of Alaskan mountains, 8,000m peaks or 5.13 rock climbing solos.

Originally a competitive hockey player, Steck became drawn to climbing because of its simplicity. 'The rules were so clear. You get to the top or not. There is no maybe, no doubts ... sometimes just to be out there is so simple. You're happy as soon as you are lying in your sleeping bag with a warm meal'. Steck claims that his days of speed records are now behind him and he is focusing on transferring his exceptional skill, stamina and mental control to challenges in the Greater Ranges. He has made solo first ascents of Cholatse's North Face (6,640m), the East Face of Tawoche (6,505m), and in 2008 completed the first alpine-style ascent of the North Face of Tengkampoche (6,500m) with Simon Anthamatten, which won a *Piolet d'Or* award. In 2009 he reached the summits of two 8,000m peaks. Steck himself remains circumspect about his mountaineering achievements. 'To climb something very difficult you need to be at the right time in the right place', he says. 'And you also need to remember, the mountain is always stronger than you'.

GOLDEN, 2011
ERIK WEIHENMAYER 1968 -

Erik Weihenmayer was born with the eye disease retinoschisis, so that by the age of thirteen he had become completely blind. 'I wasn't afraid to go blind and see nothing but darkness', he remembered. 'I was afraid to be swept to the sidelines and be forgotten, to be obsolete'. Determined not to let his blindness get in the way of his ambition to achieve sporting success, he became a champion student wrestler before taking up mountain trekking. This quickly led on to mountaineering and he was soon climbing major peaks such as Denali.

In 2001 he became the first blind person to climb Everest. 'I refused to be the weak link of the team', he says. 'I wanted them to put their lives in my hands as I would put mine in theirs. I would carry my share. I would contribute as any other team member. I would not be carried up to the mountain and spiked on top like a football. If I were to reach the summit, I would reach it with dignity'. The following year he crowned this remarkable feat by completing the 'Seven Summits'; an incomparable achievement when one considers the effort and will he must have had to summon in overcoming these challenges, not to mention the mountains encountered in everyday life, even before he began his inspirational journey.

Not content with just high-altitude mountaineering, the resoundingly positive Erik is also a skydiver, long-distance biker, marathon runner, skier, and climber of rock and ice. Now closely associated with the organization 'Braille Without Borders', which aims to empower blind people in developing countries, Erik has visited Tibet to climb with teenagers from a school for the blind and has also led a team of visually-impaired students on a mountain trek across the Andes. 'You don't just deal with adversity', he says. 'You use it to propel yourself forward'.

LONDON, 1922
GEORGE MALLORY 1886-1924

George Mallory and Everest became inseparable in the public imagination during the first attempts to climb the mountain in the early 1920s. Both became icons; the latter as a symbol of the terrible might of nature, and the former as the idealized, romantic Englishman rising to its challenge in giving his all, before meeting a glorious death. The poetic alpinist Geoffrey Winthrop-Young was wont to describe him, 'our Sir Galahad'.

Mallory was born into a Cheshire church family and sent to boarding school at Winchester where he was introduced to alpine climbing by one of his masters, Graham Irving. He displayed an aptitude for it, his natural athleticism compensating for a sometimes cavalier approach and a chronic disorganization. This forgetfulness never left him; General Bruce, leader of the 1922 and 1924 Everest expeditions remarked that 'he is a great dear, but forgets his boots on all occasions'. Fellow climber John Morris went further. 'He was the most absent-minded man I have ever known,' he wrote. 'We took turns to see that none of his kit was left behind'.

At Cambridge in 1905 he moved in exalted circles. Among his acquaintances were Bohemian intellectuals including the lascivious literary critic Lytton Strachey, who was instantly smitten by Mallory's physique. Strachey famously wrote to a friend in admiration: 'Mon Dieu! – George Mallory! When that's been written, what more need be said?' Mallory developed a politically liberal world-view during his time at Cambridge and also developed influential contacts, such as Winthrop-Young, which would lead to his automatic selection for the early Everest expeditions following the First World War in which Mallory served with distinction. By this stage Mallory was married with two children, but Winthrop-Young persuaded him that his future could be even more secure as a writer if he achieved the celebrity status assured by being the first person to climb the world's highest peak. In between expeditions, Mallory gave lectures in Britain and North America and it was during the US tour of 1923 that he is alleged to have made his famous reply 'because it is there' when asked the question 'Why climb Everest?' Mallory and Irvine's disappearance high on it's North-East Ridge in 1924 resulted in one of the longest-running mountaineering mysteries of all time, and the question of whether the duo may have summited and what happened to them has continued to excite the passions of historians ever since. The sensational discovery of his body by an American expedition in 1999 reignited the debate and merely reinforced Mallory's position as probably the best-known mountaineer in the world.

It is right to give Mallory the final word here. He speaks in 1922, the year this portrait was created: 'The first question which you will always ask and which I must try to answer is this, "What is the use of climbing Mount Everest?" and my answer must at once be, "It is no use". There is not the slightest prospect of any gain whatsoever. Oh, we may learn a little about the behaviour of the human body at high altitudes, and possibly medical men may turn our observation to some account for the purposes of aviation. But otherwise nothing will come of it. We shall not bring back a single bit of gold or silver, not a gem, nor any coal or iron. We shall not find a single foot of earth that can be planted with crops to raise food. It's no use. So, if you cannot understand that there is something in man which responds to the challenge of this mountain and goes out to meet it, that the struggle is the struggle of life itself upward and forever upward, then you won't see why we go. What we get from this adventure is just sheer joy. And joy is, after all, the end of life'.

CUMBRIA, 2011
DOUG SCOTT 1941 -

Nottingham-born Doug Scott first became prominent in the climbing world tackling outrageously overhanging pieces of rock in Derbyshire, the Hebrides and Anglesey with the aid of pitons and étriers. He would later put his expertise to good use on the 'Big Walls' of the Dolomites, Yosemite, Norway and Baffin Island, but he would soon disavow the use of such artificial aids to climbing. His real *métier* proved to be expedition mountaineering, an arena he entered in 1967 with a trip to Afghanistan. It resulted in a new route up Koh-i-Bandaka, which opened his eyes to the wide horizons of possibility for lightweight trips to the big mountains. Further shoe-string expeditions to Chad and Kurdistan followed. He swapped a teaching career for a life of climbing during which he has pioneered new routes on peaks in the Alps, the Karakoram and Hindu Kush, within Africa, Alaska, Russia and Arabia, from Iceland to Antarctica. It has, in so many ways, been a phenomenal mountain life.

Yet it is for his ascents in the Himalaya that Doug well deserves his acclaim. He became a public figure when he and Dougal Haston became the first Britons to stand atop Everest in 1975 and survived what was then the highest recorded bivouac at 8,760m. His preference, however, has always been for unobtrusive small-scale 'alpine-style' expeditions, and he has spent most of the last thirty years pursuing this passion reaching the summit of more than forty peaks, of which half were climbed by new routes or for the first time in this style. Amongst myriad climbing adventures, some of the more influential have included his 1979 success on Kangchenjunga and the 1977 ascent of the West Ridge of the Karakoram's Baintha Brakk, 'The Ogre', with Chris Bonington. It was a stunning ascent that involved the hardest technical rock climbing then achieved at high altitude, to be followed by an epic descent with both of his legs broken at the ankle.

Having recovered, the route Doug later created on Shivling's East Pillar in 1981 – with his companions Rick White, Georges Bettembourg and Greg Child – is still recognized as one of the most accomplished and audacious in the world. It is legendary for its difficulty, beauty, and for the style in which it was climbed. A past President of the Alpine Club, a CBE, and a Patron's Gold Medallist of the Royal Geographical Society, among countless other accolades, in 2011 Scott was honoured with the *Piolet d'Or* 'Lifetime Contribution Award'. Following revered alpinists Walter Bonatti and Reinhold Messner in collecting this most special of prizes, it is Scott's style and vision for some of the finest routes in the world that has rightly earned him a place among the very best of this, and former, generations of mountain men. But for Scott, as for so many of these great climbers, it is not about the public acclaim, the shouts or the applause, but rather for the freedom and the solace that these wild and wonderful places can genuinely offer, rewarding anyone willing to step off the beaten path and to look at the world in a new way.

Perhaps the distinguishing feature of Scott's approach all told has been his modesty and his genuine concern for the mountain environment and its inhabitants. He has been heavily involved in securing hygienic water supplies for villages in the Karakoram and Himalayas founding Community Action Nepal, a charity with the aim of supporting the mountain people, and Community Action Treks, a cooperative ensuring porters receive fair wages and reasonable working conditions. Scott is renowned for his laid-back, philosophical approach to mountaineering. 'In order to climb properly on a big peak', he has said, 'you must free yourself of fear. This means you must say to yourself, "I may die here"'. Despite the risks of high-altitude climbing, he still feels strongly that the life one can experience in the hills makes any suffering worth bearing. 'You'll never find enlightenment on a full stomach', he says with a warm smile.

PHOTOGRAPHY NOW

Thousands of tired, nerve-shaken, over-civilized people are beginning to find out that going to the mountains is going home: that wilderness is a necessity; and that mountain parks and reservations are useful not only as fountains of timber and irrigating rivers, but as fountains of life.

JOHN MUIR, 1901

Men go back to the mountains, as they go back to sailing ships at sea, because in the mountains and on the sea they must face up, as did men of another age, to the challenge of nature. Modern man lives in a highly synthetic kind of existence. He specializes in this and that. Rarely does he test all his powers or find himself whole. But in the hills and on the water the character of a man comes out.

ABRAM T. COLLIER, 1964

The virtue of the camera is not the power it has to transform the photographer into an artist, but the impulse it gives him to keep on looking.　BROOKS ANDERSON, 1990

DISCUSSION
PHOTOGRAPHY NOW
HUW LEWIS-JONES with GORDON WILTSIE, GLEN DENNY AND CORY RICHARDS

Gordon Wiltsie: I was called to cover an expedition to a mountain range south of the Patagonian Ice Cap. It was a region where the weather was so terrible it had never been accurately mapped or visited by modern-day explorers. It was my first *National Geographic* assignment. Over fifty-five days we enjoyed only five that could be called good. We endured 160kmph winds, weeks of rain, snow or complete whiteout, and long stays in snow caves that constantly dripped, soaking us to the bone. Then one day, while we were at a high camp, the weather cleared and we raced for whatever summits we could climb. We wanted the highest in the range but were stymied by the approach, but did tackle a beast nearby. The summit view was magnificent, with dozens of snow peaks, filigreed with rime and rising above a seemingly infinite sea of fog.

Almost instantly my mind pictured a scene, and once we'd celebrated a few minutes I asked four of my companions – Tyler Van Arsdell, Peter Garber, Rob Hart and Phillip Lloyd – whether they would like to climb the mountain we named 'Gremlin's Cap', right in the sweet spot of my frame. They were off in moments. But then, to my dismay, I realized that moisture had fogged the

interior of my only telephoto and then frozen solid. Hoping against all odds, I propped it in such a way that sunlight focused through the glass, and just as the climbers approached their summit, it thawed. Perhaps the picture was meant to be. Over the next ten minutes I shot wide, medium and close-up shots that would later become the signature pictures of the trip. Looking back, I realize that our suffering was the biggest part of its production. It's a picture that has huge significance for me now. Rob was recently killed skiing in Montana and, just a year after the expedition, Phillip fell off the nearby Towers of Paine. The mountains can lift our spirits. But they can also be devastatingly cruel.

Huw Lewis-Jones: Where did your life as a photographer begin?

GW: My parents gave me a Kodak Brownie on my eighth birthday. I raced my way through several of my father's models too, learning the basics of f-stop and shutter speed as I went. I grew up with a closet stuffed with old issues of *National Geographic* and poured over page after page of exciting images. I became a photographer

PREVIOUS PAGE: After a rare break in the weather, and now high above the clouds, four climbers make their way up 'Gremlin's Cap', one of the higher peaks in the previously unexplored Cordillera Sarmiento range in the remote Chilean Patagonia, 1992. It was Gordon Wiltsie's 'first really famous *National Geographic* picture' and it remains one of his favourites.

LEFT: Great Sail Peak and saxifrage flowers after the spring thaw, Baffin Island, by Gordon Wiltsie, 1998.

NEPAL, Himalaya AN 510d
80 year old rice farmer of
Magnar tribe.
DUPLICATE SLIDE
(Original Available)
© GORDON WILTSIE 1977

CL 4850
MOUNTAINEERING CL 4850
Jan-Marc Baker in windblown
snow above Palisade Glacier
(Sierra) John Muir Wild.
© GORDON WILTSIE 1989

SN103
MT. Whitney
(14,495')
dawn before a storm
Sierra Nevada
© GORDON WILTSIE 1976

CL 7297
ROCK CLIMBING CL 7297
Alex Lowe ice climbing in
Hyalite Canyon, Montana.
GORDON WILTSIE 1996
HYALITE CYN. MT.
RDP 25

CL 3307ad
ROCK CLIMBING CL 3307a
Eichorn's Pinnacle,
Cathedral Peak, Yosemite NP
DUPLICATE SLIDE
(Original Available)
© GORDON WILTSIE 1986

BP 6521-d1
RUNNING, Kris Erickson at Bridger Bowl,
MT.
© GORDON WILTSIE 19

COPYRIGHT 1993
GORDON WILTSIE
CL6455
ROCK CLIMBING CL 6455
Climbers on spire in
Gallatin Canyon, Montana.

CORD. SARMIENTO EXP. CE 4869
Rob Hart (MR) descends steep
ice on Fickle Finger of Fate
Patagonia, Chile.
GORDON WILTSIE
CORDILLERA SARMIENTO
195 RVP 11/92 05924
NG. 05924-5-07b

ROCK CLIMBING CL 2495
Climber ascending rope to
Glacier Point, Yosemite NP
Half Dome bkg. (MR)
© GORDON WILTSIE 198

for my high-school newspaper, using better equipment and processing hundreds of rolls of black and white film – which, gleefully, I didn't have to pay for. After years of being a bookish nerd photography gave me a respectable identity. I began taking photographs in the hills and shooting climbing pictures as soon as I learned how to tie into a rope. Needless to say, my first camera was quickly dented. Others were completely wrecked.

When I was still in high school, I chanced to go climbing with Galen Rowell, who was then still a car mechanic but also a rising star in mountaineering photography, mostly because of images he shot with a pocket-sized Kodak Instamatic. He had graduated to Nikons and his work seemed to be getting better with every roll he shot. We remained friends and just a few years later he shot his first cover story for *National Geographic*. I thought – quite unrealistically – that if Galen could do it, so could I! Little did I realize how hard he worked to earn that opportunity, and how many years of obsessive energy it would take for me to reach a similar milestone.

HLJ: What is it about the mountains, do you think, that draws people?

GW: There are probably as many reasons as there are people who go there. Some of these are conflicting. A hiker looks at an alpine setting far differently than a miner, a logger or a developer. I think that most people though are drawn to mountains because they feel inspired there. Just being in the mountains is an elixir – a clear example of something bigger and more powerful than ourselves. The time I've spent in the mountains has brought me as close to God as I've ever felt anywhere else. Yet another reason that many – including myself – go into the mountains is to test our mettle in very real, and sometimes very dangerous, situations. I can think of few places where I've been as frightened or close to death as on the faces of mountains – especially during storms – and yet so often by the time we're back to the tent we're already laughing about one of the greatest experiences of our lives. A friend once said that the only reason most people go climbing *twice* is that the 'golden sieve of memory' filters out all the bad and leaves only glowing reflections.

Glen Denny: I drove to Yosemite in September 1958 to learn to climb. I ran into a traffic jam of people watching the first ascent of El Capitan. Through binoculars I could see tiny climbers inching up a magnificent wall.

Nowadays I suppose there are jams of climbers on the big faces themselves, but back then it was a brave new world. I knew I had come to the right place. All around was inspiration. When I saw what Ansel Adams had achieved I knew that, with a little patience and a lot of hard work, photography could be a medium of genuine expression for me. I started taking landscapes that year, following his example. If I had to pick one image back then, that really did change my life, it would be his *Winter Sunrise, the Sierra Nevada, from Lone Pine*. I remember Ansel talking about the suspense and joy he felt when he saw a patch of sunlight moving across the valley floor.

After Adams, I discovered Edward Weston and Henri Cartier-Bresson. I learned a lot from Weston's seeming simplicity and Bresson's ability to find balance in complex situations. Their photos were of ordinary things, but their selectivity made the images mysterious. When I settled on using a 35mm camera, Robert Frank became a big influence too. I was overwhelmed, visually, by countless things in those years. But then you have to start selecting; otherwise you'll be too dazzled to function. And I started taking photos on climbs. At first these were simple snapshots that said, 'look where I've been', but soon I was learning to cope with the special problem of getting shots when living in a vertical world, where there was usually nothing to stand on but air.

HLJ: One of the many challenges building such a memorable body of work?

GD: Yes indeed, but securing the shot all depends on the situation. Some chances are fleeting – you're lucky to get one good frame. Others are static – you can shoot all you want. Patience is the key factor. At a fun party there may be nothing photographic happening for hours. Then suddenly a whole load of intense images dance before your lens. One of my well-known landscape shots, a view of Yosemite Valley from Wawona Tunnel, was born through patience. For many days, whenever I saw a thunderstorm approaching from the High Sierra, I would drive up to the tunnel and wait for hours until the clouds were composed to my liking, casting shadows where I hoped they would fall, making a receding sequence of light and dark.

GW: Patience is nine tenths of the job. Still another form of patience is not going nuts when you've been stuck in a tent or a snow cave for a week, unable to shoot anything but boredom and misery! There is an old adage that says for a great photo, 'f/8 and be there!' While there is some truth to this, simply because many adventures are naturally photogenic, I disagree with the idea. To my mind, a strong photograph requires straightforward mastery of your camera but also a clear aesthetic sense and attention to pictures of all scales. Even with the fanciest digital camera you can't just point it at a climber ascending something difficult and expect to get a great image.

GD: The best way to get climbing shots is to jumar along on fixed ropes, independent of the climbing team, but I didn't do that. The climbs you see in my book, *Yosemite in the Sixties*, were not done for the camera. I just grabbed what I could on the way up. This led to some interesting situations because it's hard to climb, or belay, and take photographs at the same time. Often I was so smashed by the heat or shaking from the cold that I didn't give a damn about the camera. I just wanted to survive.

Camp 4 was the launch pad for our adventures; sometimes it was a refuge from them. Here plans were made, teams were formed, and the rest of life was lived. An odd kind of history was happening each day, and every night the quicksilver of our experience slipped through the cracks in the tabletops and disappeared into the grimy dust below. In the 1960s life in Camp 4 was free. You could survive on a dollar a day. I wanted to capture moments that kept our experience from disappearing. I looked for images that would show what it was like and why we were there. I started talking less and seeing more, watching conversations, parties and gear sortouts through my viewfinder, waiting for the images to appear. I caught some, but many got away. If I could bring just one scene back it would be Chuck Pratt conducting with an oil dipstick from an abandoned car. He was usually shy about such things, but sometimes you could find him listening to Tchaikovsky or Mahler on a portable record player, waving his improvised baton vigorously, a beatific smile on his face. I once saw him standing on a boulder at the edge of camp, conducting the trees and meadows, the cliffs and waterfalls of the Yosemite Philharmonic. He said that each section of the orchestra played beautifully.

HLJ: Can you share some thoughts on a couple of your *favourite* mountain shots?

GD: That's so hard. One of my climbing photos I like most was created on the first ascent of *The Dihedral*

FOLLOWING PAGE:
Glen Denny's vision of Yosemite Valley, with an afternoon thunderstorm approaching from the high country. The 'Great Rocks of the Valley', from left to right: El Capitan, Cloud's Rest in the far distance, Half Dome, Sentinel Rock, the three Cathedral Rocks with Bridalveil Fall beneath them, and the Leaning Tower, 1964.

LEFT: A selection of Gordon's Wiltsise's duplicate slides from mountain adventures all over the world, still a valuable back up despite the rapid advance of digital. Long gone are the days that these little 'hard copy' gems are sent out to clients, who now 'mostly want things at high resolution, and they want it yesterday'. 'For tamer shooting', he says, 'I can't imagine ever going back to film. Digital is just so much cheaper, you can instantly see how you are doing and can usually fix things up in post-production in ways that would be impossible with film. My lecture presentations, which are still mostly built from my scanned slides, actually look much better than if I showed the slides themselves and – better still – I no longer have to drag around projectors and carousels. I can stuff a dozen programs into my tiny little laptop, or even just a memory stick. I'll never go back'.

Wall. We were 500m off the ground. It was a dramatic, exposed situation, and I wanted to capture it on film. As we climbed I kept looking for the right composition. I saw a central triangle of rock pointing down and thought it could be a strong visual element. I moved up and left until the triangle was the right size in the frame, leaving room to show the valley floor far below us. I took a few frames as my partner moved up the rope. The narrowing triangle of rock creates a plunging effect that enhances the feeling of great exposure. This makes it look like the photo was taken with a wide-angle, but it was just a normal 50mm lens.

On another occasion I was taking photos from various places as climbers moved up the early pitches of *The Nose*. For such scenes, telephoto lenses usually produce a flattening effect, but I became intrigued with this framing. The first part of the route is relatively low angle, but the upper part is very steep. The 200mm lens enhanced these differences, creating an effect that corresponds to how it is to be on a wall like that. The upper wall billows out, as if an endless sea of granite, and it looks like the climbers are at the start of a long voyage. That's what climbing El Cap felt like in the early 1960s.

GW: Near the end of my last polar big-wall climb, during which we spent six weeks finding a route up a 1,200m overhanging cliff on Great Sail Peak in the High Arctic, I wanted a picture that really showed the perspective of the horrifying place where we had been sleeping. The only way to do this effectively was to suspend myself out from the wall on a bipod that I had chanced to bring along, dangling from our fixed rope anchors 60m above. I lowered myself down, knowing that if it collapsed I would pendulum, slamming into the wall, or worse, drop into the abyss below. I could touch nothing solid and remained in constant, slow rotation. I would twist myself around and fire as many frames as I could until I was facing the other way. I would have loved a stiff drink when it was over.

Only a few days after capturing that shot we were descending treacherous talus bearing heavy loads. I'm not sure why I glanced back, but suddenly the mountain looked like a goddess, bathed in midnight sun and wreathed with clearing mist. My very first thought was 'damn, I really should take a picture, but I'm just too tired and it's too hard to take off my pack'. Then I thought about my job, saw the flowers at my feet and realized I had no choice. It took me at least an hour and a lot of technique to get what I wanted.

I had no idea whether it would work or not, but as is so often the case, the best pictures happen when you take a chance.

GD: And at other times, it all seems to magically click into place. One of my favourite portraits is the one we chose to illustrate Royal Robbins in this book. He had just made the arduous eight-day first ascent of *Tis-sa-ack* on the North-west Face of Half Dome. As we walked down the trail, I noticed that the shape of his sagging, overstuffed pack seemed to echo how he was feeling after such an ordeal. When we came to a smooth slab, I suggested we take a break. Royal leaned against the rock and we talked about the climb. His expression varied as I took half-a-dozen frames; I think this one conveyed his experience best. The blood on his leg is from a sharp-edged jam crack. There is a tiny rib of rock that seems to be emerging from the thumb of his right hand, as if a connection between flesh and stone. In his exhausted state, it suggests to me a final spark of energy.

GW: Although I do enjoy shooting landscapes, at heart I've always been a people photographer. I would guess that at least ninety percent of my images include humans somehow. Even tiny figures add scale and accessibility to a landscape, and as an expedition photographer my whole job is about shooting people doing things in the wilderness. I've reached a point in mountaineering photography where I feel like I've already pushed both my luck and my creative abilities about as far as I can go. I really don't know how I could do better work of big-wall climbing, say, than the stuff I shot in Antarctica or Baffin Island. I think that I have set

LEFT: A selection of Glen Denny's favourite images. Clockwise from top left: Charlie Raymond in a squeeze chimney on the *Remnant*, 1968; Ed Cooper, bivouac on the *Dihedral Wall*, 1962; *Dihedral Wall*, on the first ascent, El Capitan, 1962; Royal Robbins and Tom Frost bivouacking on the *North America Wall* reconnaissance, 1964. They were famous for their seamless teamwork and warm friendship, inspiring many around them, and a generation who followed; Camp 4, listening to music, 1968; Camp 4, sorting out the 'tools of the trade', a Yosemite ritual, 1969.

ABOVE: Gordon Wiltsie dangles into position to shoot Alex Lowe's Arctic big-wall climbing camp, Great Sail Peak, Baffin Island, 1998.

the bar high enough that it's tough for me to clear it any more. It's now up to younger, fitter people like Cory to raise it again.

Cory Richards: I began creating photographs when I was about eighteen, though I had always been into art. When I was a child, I found it a healthy way to get attention from my folks – better than breaking stuff anyway. My first camera was a heinous 1984 Ricoh point-and-shoot, manufactured just three years after I was born. It was the only camera I could get my hands on at the time. I began taking shots of the mountains as I was learning to climb. I was living with family in Seattle and my uncle was strict with a plan for my meagre savings, to make my dreams happen. I was a high-school dropout and I badly needed his help. He monitored every penny I brought in from my three jobs. If I hadn't been living under his roof I'm sure I wouldn't be a photographer today.

HLJ: Photography is anything but straightforward, but what makes a *great* photograph?

CR: As you know, *great* is so subjective. So much of the avant-garde is considered great, and yet to most people it's just too abstract to care about. A lot is crap fluffed up by words in the art circles: snapshots printed big and thrown under the umbrella of contemporary art are still just snapshots. Great photography is anything but straightforward not because it is so difficult to create, but because it's hard to define what's great. A lot of what we do as outdoor photographers could be criticized as too literal, too obvious. For me good photography is emotionally stimulating. That can be created two feet from your front door, or a thousand miles in the backcountry. The art is in the developed anticipation: knowing when and where those moments exist, seeing them before they happen, and capturing that moment on film. There are other pieces of the puzzle – light, subject, context, technicality – but a truly beautiful photograph can break all the rules of what a great photograph is by pulling at the heartstrings.

GW: A powerful portrait is more than just an engaging image of a face too. It's a communication of something vital about that person, their life, or even their culture that instantly grabs us. Think of all of the movie stars and politicians that have been etched into our minds by photographers like Yousuf Karsh, Leibowitz or Avedon. Those portraits, however, are usually set up to the nth degree. In terms of real life portraiture I can think of few photographers to rival Steve McCurry, most famous for his picture of an Afghan girl. Not only did this one riveting image communicate volumes about the horrors of war there, it went on to symbolize an entire magazine, *National Geographic*. Now there are so many professional outdoor photographers that it's hard to distinguish the really innovative work. For peers close to my own age – who have survived – I really respect Norway's Børge Ousland and the adventurer Tommy Ulrich.

CR: We're all inspired by the human element. By that I mean the rawness of what makes us people; the emotions felt every day. Adventure photography, because it's an observation of voluntary struggle, emphasizes those moments and condenses them. In portraiture there is that 'decisive moment', instantaneous and fleeting, which reveals so much about the person being photographed. Getting it is rare and special, and I think I've only really cracked it a few times. If I look through *National Geographic* now I see inspirational images in all sorts of contexts. I've been energized by the work of Jimmy Chin, Boone Speed, and Keith Ladzinski. These guys, like Gordon and Glen before them, understand the climbing subject.

GD: These days I am still inspired but I don't shoot often. And to paraphrase Plato: the life spent doing emails is not worth living! For a few years I did freelance photography as a source of income. I worked hard at it but didn't care about what I was shooting. I was using my visual skills to produce junk, and I didn't like it. I worked at other jobs, making pictures only when I felt a strong personal urge. We'd all like to shoot in landscapes that no one has seen. These days, that's quite a challenge, but I still have some photo projects in mind. Even our busiest places can be interesting for outdoor photographers. I'd like to return to the surreal landscape of San Francisco's Financial District. I spent several years there doing street photography while working on a Masters degree. It has austere vertical forms, like Yosemite, with strange varieties of human life below. The huge granite-sheathed towers are almost as impressive as mountains but, of course, they won't last as long.

HLJ: What camera equipment are you now using?

GD: I've always kept my photography kit simple. In the early 1960s, I used a Kodak Retina IIa. This was a small, folding 35mm camera with a fixed 50mm high-quality

LEFT: And the shot that Wiltsie secured. The big-wall hanging camp, many hundreds of metres above the glacier floor, on expedition deep in the Arctic, Great Sail Peak, 1998. An overhang protects the portaledge tents from falling rock and ice, but life here is still extremely precarious.

lens. It had no light meter; I guessed the exposures. Its size made it ideal for climbing as I could wear it while leading difficult pitches. In 1965 I bought a Nikon F and four lenses: 35, 50, 105, and 200mm. I used the 200 on a tripod for long shots that showed climbers as small specks on the wall. In Camp 4 I would stroll about with three lenses. I didn't use flash, lights, reflectors, or other paraphernalia – that seemed too artificial. At night I used the tripod and long exposures, taking photos by the fireside, lampglow, or candlelight. The film was Kodak Plus-X. In dim light I used Tri-X pushed to ASA 1200.

CR: I always take too much. My kit-list runs long. Expedition climbing, I use a Canon 5D mark II with a 24-105mm f.4 and a 16-35mm f.28. I usually take three bodies, two 5Ds and one mark IV 1D, 50mm 1.2, 24mm 1.4, the two previously mentioned, a 70-200mm 2.8 with doubler, two speedlite external flashes, one softbox, one umbrella, pocket wizards, light meter ... you are probably bored by now? I take all of it to base camp, plus what I need for video. But only one body and two lenses come with me on a big climb.

GW: I'm also now shooting fully digital, but for all of my mountaineering work I shot film. No matter what, I always took at least one Nikon FM2, which will work in almost all weather conditions. I carry flashes, gels, filters, a monopod (tripods are too heavy), and homemade cases to hold everything individually so I can stash gear throughout my luggage and sneak equipment into countries where journalists might be suspect, and avoid having camera cases that scream 'steal me!' Once I'm shooting, my needs for the day go into a regular knapsack, with my main camera nestled into a waist-level case that I designed both for rapid access and heavy-duty protection when the weather turns nasty. To a waistband I attach the padded cases containing whatever lens or flashes I may want to grab in a hurry: everything handy, even when I'm dangling on a rope.

HLJ: How often do you shoot?

GW: I try to shoot at least one picture every day, even if it's only of my family's moody cat. Whenever I'm on a job – whether it takes a day, a week or a month – I'm at work even before I'm out my sleeping bag. I'm envisioning what is likely to happen in the coming hours and what lenses and gear I will need. I peer out at the weather to plan my lighting equipment and – in extreme cases – honestly worry whether I will survive the day. It's a justifiable fear. This is a dangerous business and way too many of my companions have been killed. I consider it no less than a miracle that so far I have substantially outlived my own nine lives.

Once I get to work my fears usually fade, as if looking through the viewfinder somehow shields me from falling rocks or an avalanche. I may already have dreamt up specific images I want to shoot and then struggle to get ahead of my companions so that I am ready when they appear. When I shot one of my pictures from Queen Maud Land in Antarctica – with three tiny skiers dragging sleds up a slope with distant, fang-like peaks behind – I left camp hours early so I would be in position when Alex Lowe, Conrad Anker and Jon Krakauer started towards the climb. Nothing is really set up in the picture, except that I asked them to stick close together.

CR: I'd like to say I create everyday, but that just isn't true. The photographer's life is so punctuated. But when I'm on projects in the field it's total work. My last shoot was documenting the first winter ascent of Gasherbrum II, with Simone Moro and Denis Urubko earlier this year. It was a six-week job in the middle of Pakistan in winter, certainly the hardest I've done. I struggled in that environment, struggled with the cameras, my own condition, and the conditions around me. It was exhausting – climbing, shooting, getting video and cutting dispatches from base camp. I don't think I'll recover for months. All of the adventure shoots are like that though – it's just constant work. Up early, in bed late, managing yourself as well as your assets: taxing, stressful, a world away from holiday. Though it's extremely rewarding to come back with work you are proud of, on this expedition, well, I was just happy to come home alive.

One of my favourite shots is a self-portrait. I can already hear the jokes I'm going to get for saying that, but it's true. I don't enjoy it because it's me – it hardly looks like me. In fact, my own mother asked who it was. On our descent from GII we were hit by an enormous avalanche. We saw it coming, but couldn't outrun it. I thought there'd be no way to survive. Somehow however, we did. While I was still half-buried, I turned the camera on myself and cracked through a couple of frames. I hardly remember taking them. It was like my arm was controlling itself. The image exposes me in a way that I still find disturbing. I feel 'it' – the gift of having survived – every time I look at the shot. Maybe its too personal and other people don't see it. But I would be lying if I said it wasn't one of my favourite images.

LEFT: Cory Richards 'after the avalanche' and lucky to be alive, Gasherbrum II, 2011.

GW: I have many mountain heroes. Shackleton's photographer Frank Hurley was a great. Sir Ed Hillary, who I encountered during my first trip to Nepal, obviously stands out too. I've always regretted not taking his picture while we sat round a campfire, laughing with his friends. Tilman and Shipton, the quintessential mountain vagabonds, are here, as are renegades Whillans and Haston. Fred Beckey, America's ultimate mountain hobo is another longstanding hero of mine. Doug Scott deserves universal respect for his breadth of experience and for the sheer *will* that enabled him to survive a disaster on the Ogre that would have killed almost anyone else. Reinhold Messner, with whom I travelled in the Arctic, was an inspiration the moment I met him.

If I had to choose one climber that I was luckiest to befriend, it would have to be Alex Lowe, who was not only the toughest, hardest-working person I have ever met, but also one of the kindest – a shining spirit who touched the lives of many people. I was blessed to travel with him, experiencing his boundless energy, all fuelled by his credo that *the best climber was really the one having the most fun.* Nor would I have become a mountain photographer without the guidance of Doug Robinson. He was also the first hippy I ever met and, like a pied piper, he led me into a mountain world I couldn't have imagined. Some climbers are hailed by the public as heroes, yet to those close to them they are just wonderful, humble companions – just so much more than headlines and celebrity.

HLJ: I find *hero* an uncomfortable word, especially when talking about people who go into the mountains for all the right reasons: for joy and challenge, not seeking fame or notoriety. But, certainly, there are people whose skills and approach to life makes them heroic in my eyes. I owe my first introductions to the hills to my friend John McCarthy, at that time a perfectly rebellious – and to my mind therefore, a totally inspirational – Outward Bound tutor. Respect extends to a wide bunch of people I've only read about, of course. I think of the visionary John Muir, pioneer Cecil Slingsby, raconteur Tom Patey, or superlative Polish mountaineer Jerzy Kukuczka. All would have been welcome additions. I'm pleased to have included my all-time favourites though: Noyce, Boardman, Shipton and Tilman. The list of impressive climbers quickly becomes many pages long, so it was always going to be tough with this modest project. Even Bonatti didn't make it into the main gallery, though he probably should have. But it's not a full stop. Another book, another time I hope.

HLJ: Maybe you were lucky that day, but crucially you had the skill, and the great guys around you, to pull through. The poet Al Alvarez, sometime climbing partner of brilliant mountaineer Mo Anthoine, summed it up well: 'The pleasure of risk is in the control needed to ride it with assurance so that what appears dangerous to the outsider is, to the participant, simply a matter of intelligence, skill, intuition, coordination ... in a word, *experience*. For a brief period I am directly responsible for my actions. In that beautiful, silent, world of mountains, it seems to me worth a little risk'. Mo, in fact, once saved Al's life when they were caught out in a snowstorm high on the North Face of Cima Grande de Lavaredo. Hugely experienced, he remained calm, pumelling Alvarez all night to keep him awake and get his circulation going. They escaped the ordeal with mild frostbite, and both came down alive. Clearly, experiences in the mountains form bonds of friendship that transcend the everyday.

GD: I've made my best friends in hard times on the mountain face. I'm fortunate to have climbed with people like Harding, Robbins, Frost, and others you see in this book. What a group of characters! I would give anything though to have photographed Whymper and Carrel racing to ascend the Matterhorn, or Vittorio Sella making his classic images in the Karakoram. In more modern times, other heroes stand out: Buhl during his Nanga Parbat ascent, Bonatti climbing the pillar of the Dru, Peter Croft making the first unroped ascent of the East Face of Yosemite's Washington Column. And, in the future, the first person to climb El Cap completely unroped?

CR: I agree. Though we include many good folks, the list always goes on. My father naturally heads my list of mountain heroes. George Lowe comes in a strong second. Big praise to Steve House, Simone and Denis, but also guys we didn't feature here, like Sonnie Trotter, Barry Blanchard, Conrad Anker and Pete Athans. I'm so privileged now to call these people friends. I love them all tremendously. Their accomplishments are incredible, but it's their personalities that make them special. None of us are defined by our accomplishments – those are just things that come and go – but it's the manner in which we treat others and the way we respect our world that is important.

HLJ: What excites you most about adventure photography?

CR: The fame and fast women – and by that I mean spending way too much time in tents with smelly dudes who have a lot of angst. Really, what excites me most is where it takes me, and where it can take us.

GD: For me, it's still the hunt and the unanswered questions. Searching for the frame that captures the experience. Sometimes I discover things I didn't realize I was looking for. That's when photography gets really interesting – the simultaneity of what's out there and what's in your head, and getting them into the same frame. I think that the good photographs challenge and inspire us. As a photographer this means *really* seeing what's in front of you and knowing what to do with it. By looking at familiar things in new ways, the possibilities can be endless.

CR: I had a client recently who wanted in-the-moment photojournalistic images for an advertising campaign. In fact, the whole photo brief was a homage to your photography Glen. I had a client saying 'this is what we want', and it's basically a collection of some of the most iconic climbing shots ever taken! Years of great work and you're asked to get it in a month. And of course you can't. Other clients want the whole story in a single 'iconic' image. Perfect light, perfect composition, *perfect perfect perfect*. Sometimes that happens. But it's rare. The problem with looking for the big shot is that you are so overtaken by that task you miss the side moments, and often those are the best for the rich storytelling that defines good photojournalism.

GW: Most sponsors ask me to shoot because they like my style and know that I'll work hard to create images that showcase their products without looking faked. On expedition this can be a challenge when working both for a magazine and for the sponsors. Most magazines prefer not to have company logos splashed all over their pages, while the sponsors are providing money and equipment specifically in hope that they *will* get that kind of imagery. The trick is to create enough work to meet everyone's needs. This gets down to niggling details, like whether or not a sponsored climber shaves, how cleanly a tent is pitched or the perfect fit of a jacket. When shooting strictly for commercial purposes that's all fine with me, but it gets in the way when you're hoping to shoot a gritty story and sponsored athletes are trying to look like Adonis.

HLJ: What advice would you give a young photographer?

CR: Set your alarm.

GD: Watch out and read carefully before signing! And, when you're on a big face, the more you get involved with the shot, the more you need to check that you're still tied in…

GW: I feel guilty encouraging anyone to go into adventure photography as a bonafide profession. There are now so many wannabe journalists with expensive digital tools who are happy just to give their work away for free gear, or their name in print, that many clients who used to keep us going no longer want to pay. I encourage students to study for a 'real' career that helps them to be in places they want to be – such as geology, biology, mountain guiding – and then pursue photography just because they love it. If they have real passion, they'll master their cameras, create opportunities and build a body of work that may eventually chime with an editor. Bottom line, to really succeed you have to be passionate to the point of obsession, and that can take a heavy toll on the rest of your life, as well as your body.

HLJ: What is the future for image making and where do you think photography is headed?

GD: People have spent hundreds of years grappling with the question of 'what is art', and 'which way are we going'? Art painted itself into a corner in the twentieth century. Someone said, 'art is whatever you can get away with'. For me, the true test of any artwork is wanting to see it again. There's always been something magical about

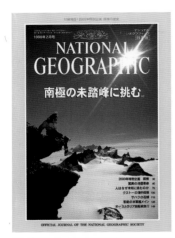

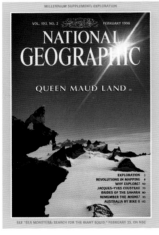

RIGHT: Perched near the summit of Kubus (2,985m) in Antarctica, climber Conrad Anker looks out over the mile-thick ice cap that buries lesser peaks of Queen Maud Land, shot by Gordon Wiltsie, 1997. Owned by the elements, Queen Maud Land still beckons that new breed of climber who comes to witness and wonder, not conquer and claim. 'This really is no-man's-land', Conrad said at the time. 'We are very much guests on this continent'. This image graced the cover of the February 1998 issue of *National Geographic* and countless international editions.

photography. I would have been excited to work with it at any stage in its evolution, since Daguerre's revelations in 1839; that said, I'm happy with what amazing things can be done now. It's unlikely film will still be able to compete within this overwhelming digital world.

GW: From some perspectives the future for photography is grim – 'a planet full of monkeys with point-and-shoot cameras and mobile-phones', posting whatever comes out of their memory cards into the internet's nearly infinite maw. Already this has taken a toll on the quality of photography we see being published, but I hope that will change. Innovative visual artists who can keep a jump ahead will always be vital. Some will continue to use traditional techniques but with an ever-more creative blending of the real and surreal, fuelled by digital technology. There is no going back from the trashy imagery cluttering almost everywhere we look, but that only makes the pictures made by people who really work at them all the more special. A great photograph is one that communicates something important to a very broad audience – one that lingers in the mind and may even change the way that people think about things. Those rare pictures are the ones I think we can safely call *art*.

HLJ: Just as photography touched, but didn't overwhelm, painting the digital era will make photography *more* of an art, not less. Yet as things progress, more images will be taken from video. As the resolution and technology increases, the still frame may become less regarded commercially. We will just film and pull high-res stills exactly where we want them; we can already do it with some cameras. But that doesn't bother me so much as the *art* of taking photographs will become more special and unique. I look forward to the evolution. But, what of the future for the mountains of our world?

GW: We can safely assume that whatever happens to human civilization, mountains will survive. We may melt the glaciers, cut down forests and decimate wildlife, but mountain environments will endure. Human history is but a momentary blip. I do worry very deeply though. Although rock is indifferent, both the beauty of craggy landscapes and the things that grow upon them are a vital, but fragile, part of our spirit. With so many human forces that care little about anything but money, these places are being irreparably harmed for future generations. It's long overdue for mountaineers to help to protect what

little wilderness remains, and keep it thriving for as long as we can. It's our responsibility to heed the warning of the times and make sure that we act as stewards of the planet – not the owners.

HLJ: When William Murray caught his first glimpse of the Himalaya from Ranikhet he called it 'a great continent of the heavens, wholly apart from Earth'. Shelley, when finally taking in the view of Mont Blanc, declared he felt 'a sentiment of ecstatic wonder, not unallied to madness'. Generations since have described in so many different ways the joy of seeing – and experiencing – the hills. Do you think that photography can capture that magic for us?

CR: I hope it can. There is an underlying vulnerability that the mountains draw out in most of us: at times it is subtle, at others it's an emphatic reminder of just how fragile we are. But that is all pretty deep in the recesses, more immediately I think the raw beauty of wild places resonates with the hunter and gatherer in us all. The mountains are a primal sanctuary. They show us we're part of a bigger system and what it truly *feels* like to be alive.

GD: We go to the mountains to escape from the ordinary. Perhaps this is cliché, but it is true. Compared to daily life, especially in cities and suburbs, the mountains are new and different; they are beautiful, exhilarating, and awesome. This is why painters and photographers love them. For walkers, they offer healthful exercise. To explorers, they offered mysteries and challenges – sometimes fatal. To climbers, they can offer a day of moderately adventurous exercise, or the ultimate test of physical and mental toughness – frequently fatal.

CR: I'll trade you my favourite quote. Ansel Adams once said 'no matter how sophisticated you may be, a large granite mountain cannot be denied – it speaks in silence to the very core of your being'. Mountains, and the experiences they bring, offer us a chance to evolve. For me, the artistic challenge is in creating what I can in the knowledge that I'll never be able to really capture the whole soul. It's too big and too wild; plus, some things just aren't there to be understood. The challenge is in being adventurous enough to find yourself in situations that expose those rare and raw moments, slipping into that world as a quiet guest, and walking away with an image that escapes words.

London and Washington, 2011

WHERE THE SPIRIT SOARS

I live not in myself, but I become
Portion of that around me; and to me,
High mountains are a feeling, but the hum
Of human cities torture.

GEORGE BYRON, *Childe Harold's Pilgrimage,* 1818

For, to myself, mountains are the beginning and end of all natural scenery.

JOHN RUSKIN, 1843

In these days of upheaval and violent change, when the basic values of today
are the vain and shattered dreams of tomorrow, there is much to be said for a
philosophy which aims at living a full life while the opportunity offers. There
are few treasures of more lasting worth than the experience of a way of life
that is in itself wholly satisfying. Such, after all, are the only possessions of
which no fate, no cosmic catastrophe, can deprive us; nothing can alter the
fact if for one moment in eternity we have really lived.

ERIC SHIPTON, *Upon That Mountain,* 1943

COMMENTARY
WHERE THE SPIRIT SOARS
STEPHEN VENABLES

I grew up amongst the gentle fields and woods of southern England, and there I have spent most of my life. Mountains are a place of escape – foreign, different, exotic. Few experiences have equalled the excitement of setting off, aged nine, on my first skiing trip to the Alps. The idea that one might actually *climb* up those mountains came later. There was no blinding Damascene moment, but I do remember standing at the Langflue cable car station, above Saas-Fee, when I was fifteen, staring up at the Täschhorn and wondering idly what it would be like to pick one's way up that whiter-than-white fluted face. I had no idea how to use an ice-axe, no way of gauging the steepness of the apparently vertical precipice soaring so enticingly beyond the crevassed undulations of the glacier. I was just very curious.

Perhaps it is that curiosity that sets mountaineers apart. Faced with a sublimely beautiful vertical landscape, we are not content simply to look: we have to touch it, feel its texture, probe its secrets. And, although we are often reluctant to admit this, experience its dangers, or at least its difficulties. So it's a double curiosity: not just, 'what is that mountain like?' but also, 'how will I cope?'

The most memorable, intensely lived, climbs are the ones where you feel that you are setting off on a great journey into the unknown. It doesn't matter whether you are a rock climber unravelling the subtle intricacies of a 10m section of unclimbed granite, or Eric Shipton trying to see over yet another unexplored pass in the vast wilds of Central Asia: the motivation is just the same; they are just two extremes of a gloriously wide spectrum. For myself, a mountain jack-of-all-trades, it is the unlimited variety of mountaineering that is so appealing. I love the tactile indulgence of pure rock climbing; I love the speed and rhythm of skiing; I love the complexity of a huge mixed mountain face. And I love the infinite variety of the landscape, from the temperate rainforest of Tierra del Fuego to the luminous high altitude desert of the Karakoram.

What I also like is the sense of narrative. For all its wildness, the mountain landscape is rarely a blank canvas. Trek through almost any area of the Himalaya and you meet farmers, shepherds, millers, traders, nomads, porters, nuns, monks and more, all living and working on the margin. For us mountain tourists there isn't the

Charnaux frères & Cⁱᵉ   GENÈVE

ABOVE: Highly-collectible Player's Navy Cut Cigarettes Mount Everest card. The back reads: 'This remarkable photograph was taken by Dr Somervell at a height of 20,000 feet. The picture shows the final pyramid of Everest, and in the foreground is Norton who staggered on alone and reached eighty feet higher than Somervell did. The climbers were doing only one step forward to every ten or twelve breaths, and the air had become so thin that it was impossible to progress another step'. 'Ladies and their Guides', the Mer de Glace, Mont Blanc, by Charnaux Frères, 1886

RIGHT: Sean Villanueva works pitch eighteen on the East Face of the Central Tower, Torres del Paine, Chilean Patagonia, 2009. This epic shot is by American Ben Ditto who joined Belgian Villanueva and Nico Favresse's pioneering first free ascent of the 1974 South African route, spending over thirteen days working their way up the granite wall. In 2011, Villanueva, the Favresse brothers, and Ditto were awarded the *Piolet d'Or* for the style and spirit of their enterprising big-wall climbs in Greenland.

same deadly serious eking out of a subsistence living, and if there is hardship it is self-imposed, gratuitously. Nevertheless we have our own traditions, our own story,

Even if you don't deliberately go out seeking an epic, you can't help wondering what it would be like should you find yourself in that situation.

particularly in the European Alps, where it all started. My two most memorable alpine climbs are the ones most steeped in history.

One was the North Face of the Eiger. I dreamed about this gigantic wall for years before finally setting foot on it with Luke Hughes in 1986. Every ledge was layered with the sediment of history, every feature redolent with the tales of the brave young men who had first dared to trespass here fifty years earlier. The other, less clichéd, more remote, was the North-East Face of the Finsteraarhorn, which I climbed in the winter of 1983 with one of Britain's very best alpinists Dick Renshaw. What was so startling about this wall was the fact that it had first been climbed in 1904, and first *attempted* – almost successfully – two years earlier by that remarkable archaeologist, scholar and mountaineer, Gertrude Bell. The climb had a raw, untamed quality that left you marvelling at the boldness of Bell and her two local guides. Climbing it in winter reduced the risk of rockfall, but it intensified the sense of remoteness. Just getting to the foot of the face took two days on skis; the whole round trip lasted a week. On the seventh day, when we finally took off our skis to hobble down through the first spring flowers to the Rhône valley, the glow of fulfilment was palpable.

It was the same, four years later, arriving with Phil Bartlett and Duncan Tunstall amongst the ripening barley fields of Shimshal, after a long, committing journey through the Karakoram range. Our journey over the remote, barely known, Khurdopin Pass, had been filled with adventure and surprise, new vistas unfolding, fresh problems to solve round every corner. But, as so often happens, we were not the first to come this way. In fact the whole exercise had been inspired by those doyens of exploration, Shipton and Tilman, whose journey through this same range fifty years earlier was immortalized in Shipton's eloquent *Blank on the Map*. What emerges again and again from Shipton's books is a sense of serendipitous enchantment. His planning was competent but gloriously simple – almost haphazard – leaving plenty of scope for spontaneity. Likewise ours. Hence our delight at stumbling across a cluster of granite spires that would have made St Exupery proud. They were so beautiful, so compelling, that we just had to have a look at the pointiest one. And I was so niggled by our failure to reach the top a month later – determined to escape the tyranny of regret – I returned to complete the ascent, alone.

That first ascent, solo, of the Solu Tower, was very fulfilling. But perhaps my most satisfying first ascent was of another peak of about the same height, 6,000m, in Kashmir, called Kishtwar-Shivling. On that occasion I was again climbing with my friend Dick Renshaw. Neither of us is a great conversationalist, so it was a fairly silent expedition, but it was probably the most perfect I have been on. It was partly the anticipation, as I had dreamed about this peak for four years – again that wondering, that curiosity. It was also the approach, through the scented cedar forests of the Chenab gorge. And the base camp, in a birch glade shared with local Gujah nomadic shepherds, seemed an Arcadian idyll. And the climb? Well, the climb had everything from vertical walls of blue ice, to immaculate sheets of fine-grained granite, to outrageous Baroque fantasies of snow sculpture. Every pitch was beautiful, absorbing, intricate; each day brought fresh surprises, each bivouac a more unlikely ledge, as we trespassed higher and higher into the sky. There were moments of pure intense enjoyment, when I felt, genuinely, that there was nowhere else on earth I would rather be. But of course, there were also moments of fear and anxiety, particularly on the fifth, summit, day, when we didn't get back to our bivouac until midnight.

We returned to base camp on the evening of the seventh day. As Reinhold Messner has often observed – in his case of greater, more gruelling climbs – that is the most exquisite moment: that moment when you return safely to earth, journey complete. Reading accounts by other extreme pioneers, such as Hermann Buhl or Walter Bonatti, most of us are inevitably fascinated by the climbs

where they were pushed closest to the edge of survival. Because, even though mountaineering is essentially a hedonistic pursuit of pleasure, it does occasionally need the frisson of risk. Even if you don't deliberately go out seeking an epic, you can't help wondering what it would be like should you find yourself in that situation.

My opportunity to find out came on Everest. Like most of the best things in life, it was unplanned. A chance meeting in a pub with John Hunt led indirectly to my being invited out of the blue to join an American-Canadian team on the 'Thirty-Fifth Anniversary' expedition to Everest. By the time we assembled in Tibet, it was obvious that this was going to be the perfect synthesis of everything a climb should be. There was a growing sense of anticipation, as we journeyed slowly, with many delays, over the Langma La, wondering what on earth our proposed new route up the great East Face would be like – wondering whether it would even be possible. We were following in the steps of the earliest Everest pioneers, who came to look at this face in 1921. We laughed brazenly at Mallory's famously dismissive verdict – 'other men, less wise, might attempt this way if they would, but, emphatically, it was not for us'. We looked up at the impossibly remote North-East Ridge, where Mallory had disappeared three years later, and where Dick's friends, Boardman and Tasker, had died in 1982. Like them, we were going without oxygen, taking a leaf out of the book of Bill Tilman, who wrote in 1938: 'My own opinion is that the mountain could and should be climbed without, and I think there is a cogent reason for not climbing it at all rather than climb it with the help of oxygen ... If man wishes gratuitously to fight nature, not for existence or the means of existence but for fun, or at the worst self-aggrandisement, it should be done with the natural weapons'.

Uncompromising words from a man who can seem unduly austere to the modern adventurer. But for all his apparent gruffness, Tilman had a brilliant sense of humour and a profound talent for enjoyment. And *enjoyment* was the keynote of our Everest adventure, as we surprised and delighted ourselves, writing our own chapter, drawing our own crazy improbable line up the mountain, going to work each day in one of the most dazzling mountain panoramas on earth. I was blessed with excellent companions – Robert Anderson, Paul Teare and Ed Webster – but that didn't stop me from leaving them behind on the final journey to the summit. For all the teamwork and camaraderie, it has always seemed to me that mountaineering can be an intensely personal, egotistical business. And one with a considerable element of luck. Success or failure at extreme altitude depends a

good deal on physiological fortune and on the big day my body just managed to go slightly faster than the rest. And perhaps, like Edmund Hillary thirty-five years earlier, I just wanted it more strongly than the others.

Whatever the reason, I was the lucky one who got the icing on the cake, the gift of standing briefly on top of the world. But the icing came at a price. Descending late in the day, slower than I had intended, unwilling to risk a mistake in the dark, I stopped at nightfall to bivouac in the open. Lying out alone, without shelter, at just over 8,600m above sea level, was a long, shivering vigil. At the time no-one had survived such a high bivouac alone, but I wasn't really alone. Apart from the imaginary people, who came and went during the night, cluttering my hypoxic, hallucinatory brain, there was also the real, rational knowledge of others – like Scott and Haston, Bishop, Hornbein, Jerstad and Unsoeld – who had also survived the night up here. We were, after all, just another chapter in the story.

Anderson and Webster, who both made it to the South Summit, had an almost equally bad night, without sleeping bags, in an abandoned tent at about 8,400m. For all three of us, eventually descending to rejoin Paul at Advance Base on the Kangshung Glacier, the return journey took on a whole new dimension. We didn't plan it that way, but I almost felt glad to find myself *having* to dig deeper and deeper each day, dredging up new reserves of determination, just to keep going. Having read all those accounts of other people struggling through similar epics, there was an almost childish satisfaction in realizing, 'I can do this too'. And this time, of course, that moment of return was more deliciously sweet than ever before.

There are mountaineers in this book who seem to have the ability and the drive to keep on seeking extremes, almost as if addicted. Others of us are lazier, or our circumstances change. For myself, lower, gentler, warmer hills are increasingly seductive. So too are the pleasures of pure rock, unsullied by snow and ice. And scale, contrary to popular perception, is often irrelevant. My most satisfying recent mountain days were spent in an obscure Welsh valley, exploring new routes up cliffs no more than 10m high. As the American writer, Gretel Ehrlich observed so eloquently, there is a 'solace' in wild places. In that Welsh valley, alone with the guttural chatter of the ravens and the sweet scents of peat and heather, absorbed totally in the intricate pattern and texture of ancient gritstone sculpted by the last Ice Age, I was very content.

Kathmandu, 2011

ABOVE: 'The Longest Night'. Exhausted but alive, Stephen Venables tries to force a smile through frozen lips after his night out in the open at about 8,560m on Everest, portrait by his team-mate Ed Webster, 1988.

LEFT: Norway's Eidfjord is an ice-climbers' paradise, a frozen Yosemite of rich new climbing possibility, home to huge waterfalls like this, and most are previously unclimbed. In this remarkable shot by Christian Pondella, legendary Canadian Will Gadd leads his new route on the Skrikjofossen in 2010, which he calls 'the classiest, the cleanest, the most stellar' waterfall line he has ever done. He left the 500m route ungraded. 'Grade it whatever you need to feel good about the grade,' Gadd said afterwords. 'Ice-climbing is all about wild experience and this gives you everything you need'.

AS IT WAS IN THE BEGINNING

> If adventure has a final and all-embracing motive, it is surely this: we go out because it is our nature to go out, to climb mountains, and to paddle rivers, to fly to the planets and plunge into the depths of the oceans ... when man ceases to do these things, he is no longer man. **WILFRID NOYCE, 1962**

> In the mountains, worldly attachments are left behind, and in the absence of material distractions, we are opened up to spiritual thought ... we should be attempting to carry the spiritual experience of the mountains with us everywhere. **JAMLING TENZING NORGAY, 2011**

> The fleeting hour of life of those who love the hills is quickly spent, but the hills are eternal. Always there will be the lonely ridge, the dancing beck, the silent forest; always there will be the exhilaration of the summits.
> **ALFRED WAINWRIGHT, 1966**

AFTERWORD

AS IT WAS IN THE BEGINNING

DOUG SCOTT

For our distant ancestors, and for the hunter-gathering communities still remaining, hunting was a Holy occupation. In taking the game there is, they say, the obligation to reciprocate by performing prescribed rituals and giving heart-felt thanks.

Since the modern mountaineer symbolically relives the life of our ancestors in terms of facing up to uncertainty and risk on a daily basis, putting life and limb in the lap of the Gods and going for it in the wildest places, far from help, strung out and totally committed, it seems like a good idea to check out those hunters who still live in the most extreme places. One such region is the Labrador Peninsula, at the edge of the Arctic, cold but wet cold being near to the ocean. The most informative book on the subject to my mind is Frank Speck's *Naskapi*. He lived with the Naskapi Indians during the first quarter of the twentieth century. Of many native North Americans, he considered them to follow as pure a path as any that lived so close to the land.

The Naskapi he found have a strong, ethical factor in their soul philosophy. They must keep well-connected with *Mista 'Peo* or *the Great Man* – their 'sixth sense' – through dreams and direct intuitive awareness as to where to go for game and how to catch it. Failure to keep in close touch with the Great One would result in 'the loss of a powerful and far-seeing guide ... and starvation'. The Great Man became ever more helpful in supplying all material needs, providing the individual 'tells no lies, practises no deception on others. In particular he is pleased with generosity, kindness and help to others'.

This resonates completely for me with the deeper aspects of mountaineering, bringing me close to those people and cultures so far away in time and space whose lifestyle has now probably been consumed by Western materialism, except that they have our admiration and thanks for being a reminding factor of deep down where we have to be to survive, not only extreme situations on a mountain-side but also to live our lives to the full in all situations. Those climbing days that have given me greatest satisfaction – where

the memory of them remains strongest, where I surpassed myself and where the climb proved to be the most revealing and transforming – were those in the company of just a few close friends sharing the experience like the Naskapi, looking out for each other in a spirit of 'generosity, kindness and help'.

Of course simply being in the wild, connecting with the natural world, lifts the spirit. It happens when we are immersed in the wilderness. It can happen from a distance too, sometimes a mere glimpse of mountain is enough. It came to me just the other day, when driving to my office one Monday morning, a morning like any other. Feeling down at the thought of being cooped up after a weekend's rock climbing, my route suddenly rose up onto the high ground to reveal the Pennines to the east and the hills of the Lake District on my right and in between huge towering cumulus stretching away south, catching the early morning sun – a most glorious sight that positively affected the rest of my day. Why does this happen, I wondered, why does the human being have this capacity to be so affected by the natural environment? Surely it's not a characteristic essential for our survival – or maybe it is and more so now as many of us, for a large part of the day, are cocooned from 'great nature', locked up in towns and cities. We become extensions of our machines and with so many distractions have little time for reflection to strike a balance with ourselves, and no time to think, or return to our origins and the source of everything. This is understood today by many traditional groups, including the Caribou Inuit who say that 'all true wisdom is only to be found far from the dwellings of men, in the great solitudes, and it can only be obtained through suffering'. Suffering and privation, it is said, are the only things that can open the mind of men to that which is hidden from his fellows. I have to agree that I am most likely to find what is normally hidden after a day in the hills. This is recognized by thousands, hundreds of thousands in fact, who have now taken up hill-walking, mountaineering or even those who have just taken on an allotment on the edge of town.

In 1971 I visited Yosemite Valley, teaming up with Peter Habeler to tackle one of the finest rock climbs in the world: the 1,000m *Salathé Wall*. For both of us it was a step into the unknown. As the first non-American ascent of this 35-pitch route, it was clearly far harder and longer than anything either of us had managed before. Climbing slowly, we were on that vertical desert for almost five days. We were caught out by night between ledges and made a sort of hammock from the ropes, wrapped like two

chrysalis awaiting the dawn. We eventually got onto the head wall that continued to lean out with the climbing still strenuous albeit exhilarating. On the fifth evening we topped out. I wrote about this experience soon after:

As the light faded, we went our separate ways on to the dome of El Cap. My walk slowed to a half pace as I stepped out, feeling my boots sink into the soft, friable earth that had only recently emerged from the melting snows. Heaps of pine cones crackled and crunched loudly in the still evening air as I walked over them. Stopping, I smelt the pine trees with an intensity I had never before experienced. I lifted my head to take in this sensation, like an animal sniffing out its quarry.

I saw for the first time the full range of subtle, mellow colours in that evening light. The wind-scalloped surface of lingering snow patches twinkled like jewels in the fading light and all to the east the peaks of the High Sierra were pink above a purple haze of forested valleys. Something enabled me to discern colours where before I had only seen one. I stood guzzling in these new sensations like a greedy child, hoping this beautiful experience would never end.

Our paths came together and we walked silently along a vague track, finally getting lost in the snow. As we settled down for the night in a forest clearing, I nibbled with relish at my shrunken salami. I can still recall the succulence of each mouthful. Next morning we made our way down towards the Lost Arrow and by a zigzag path to the camp. On any multi-day, big-wall route, the climber will discipline his body and its appetites, in the manner of the ascetics. Like them, he will probably experience hardship through extremes of heat and cold, lie uncomfortable and sleepless on a hard bed, go without washing, remain immobile in certain bodily positions for long periods, wear 'chains or other painful bonds', and go in for a certain amount of self-mutilation.

Any climber will be aware of this list of sufferings and will be able to cite instances in which he was afflicted by some or all of them whilst climbing. Indeed, I have not said much that any climber home from a weekend's cragging doesn't know about. He returns relaxed after escaping the anxieties and pressures of city life. What I am trying to say, however, is that with longer and more demanding climbs there are added ingredients of both suffering and reward.

ABOVE: Edward Whymper in his 'Alpine Rig' and 'Lunchtime on Lock Maree', rare glass lantern slides. Cecil Slingsby, pioneer of many first ascents in Norway, sits beside Norman Collie who is handing a dram to Haskett Smith of Napes Needle fame.

LEFT: A team of climbers begin their ascent of El Capitan's *Nose* in 1965. The route was first climbed by Warren Harding in a mammoth siege-style assault, placing bolts and fixing ropes, over almost fifty days. In 1960 a small team led by Royal Robbins repeated the route in just seven days, in the first continuous climb without such insensitive siege tactics. In more recent years, the climb has become a test-piece and on typical days in the autumn there may be as many as ten different parties strung out along its thirty rope lengths to the top. The first ascent in a day was accomplished by John Long and Jim Bridwell in 1975. In 1993 Lynn Hill managed to free climb the route without using any artificial aid. In 2010 Alex Honnold climbed the route alone in an incredible five hours fifty minutes.

ABOVE: Doug Scott, Martin Boysen and Dougal Haston share a joke at their Changabang Glacier camp prior to their first ascent, while Tashi busies himself with his equipment, 1974.

If big-wall climbing is pursued in a more hostile environment and for longer periods, or if the big-wall climber climbs alone, as Bonatti did on the Dru, then the doors of perception will presumably be opened wider still. The climber who is willing to extend himself to the limit of his technical skill and endurance on any long climb is en route up the profundity trail.

Well above the tree line, beyond the grass and flowers in the region where the land is pristine, untouched by man, and where the air is so clear as to show the mountain tops vibrant against the blue sky, I involuntarily give a huge sigh of relief that I am back – where I belong – reliving a sense of the challenging life of our ancestors that first had the courage to walk out of Africa over those distant mountain ranges and beyond.

It is here where the real transformation takes place, as I found on Everest in 1975. Reaching the summit of Everest is always going to be a significant event in any climber's life, however much we may try to convince ourselves that it's just another summit. Everest is quite simply the mountain with the most history attached to it, as one would expect of the highest, where the air is thinnest, the temperatures lowest and the storms most severe. Every climber known to me that has reached the top has been changed by the experience. Up there with Dougal Haston for an hour or so, on the evening of 24 September 1975, was unforgettable for me: watching the sun set above the valleys of Nepal filling with evening cloud, shining over the peaks poking up from the purple plateau of

Tibet and making out the perfect curve of the earth in a sweep of 400 miles, feeling fulfilled, on top of the game – confident yet aware of being a part of something going on all around, much bigger than myself, like a child lost in wonder – it was in every sense wonderful!

Getting there had not been without its trials and tribulations. Before we ever left home no one seemed to be giving us much of a chance to climb Everest by the South-West Face. There had already been five attempts, which had all failed spectacularly below the rock band and some 600m below the summit. In fact, our attempt remained uncertain until the end and was never a foregone conclusion in our thoughts, never mind the pundits back home who had written us off as a waste of time and money. Yet six of the team had been there before, and three of us twice – we had *experience*. We were well organized and well led by Chris Bonington, who brought the art of large expedition planning to perfection after his experiences on Annapurna, and on the South-West Face of Everest in 1972. He kept the team focussed, motivated and inspired by his own example leading from just behind the front.

We were also well funded enough to afford all the latest equipment including oxygen, a huge team of twelve climbers and sixty sherpas, ably led by their sirdar Pertemba, carrying all the materials into place, employing fixed rope all the way from the Western Cwm up to Camp and beyond. From previous experience we chose the right time to walk in, to be on the mountain just as the monsoon was ending,

and before the onslaught of the westerlies. In the wide scheme of things, climbing the South-West Face was significant, in that it demonstrated once and for all that if enough experienced climbers and high-altitude sherpas are put to work on a big face, well led using oxygen and fixed ropes in reasonable weather, then one can more or less guarantee success on any big face in the Himalaya – end game.

So why was our climb uncertain right to the end, even after all the camps were well stocked, and our friends Paul Braithwaite and Nick Estcourt had put in a brilliant day's climbing up and through the lefthand gully of the rock band, paving the way for Camp 6? Recounting my journey to the summit and back with Dougal, gives some answers.

Dougal and I were the lucky lads chosen to have first crack at the summit, being in the right place, fit, acclimatized and knowing the score. Dougal set off for Camp 5 up the rope left by Nick and Paul, whilst I did some last minute packing. Chris Bonington sat in the next tent loudly talking down the radio. Just as I set off after Dougal, he called out that his back end was collapsing. 'Nasty that, haemorrhoids up here', I thought. Chris went on to explain that he, and therefore us, had worse problems than that. Several of the climbers below were disgruntled and even talking about retiring since they were unhappy with his planning of subsequent attempts. Chris was in the unenviable position of having too many fit and able climbers, all strong characters, looking for the ultimate satisfaction. 'I am not sure we can

keep you supplied', he said forlornly. I caught up Dougal and told him the problem. He wasn't too pleased and cursed the indiscipline of those below. 'We'll manage Youth, it will be all right', I said without knowing just how. Ang Phurba caught us up at the end of Nick's fixed rope and proceeded to belay me up towards a site for Camp 6. At the same time he was taking in Dougal's rope, as Dougal had dropped back since his crampons had come off his spongy over-boots – in other words Ang Phurba was handling the situation like a regular alpinist, not just a beast of burden, even as he was also carrying our tent.

After establishing camp we pushed out 150m of rope across the upper snowfield, returning to find that Chris had rallied the troops and himself made a magnificent carry, along with Mike Thompson, Mick Burke and several sherpas. As one doubt was resolved another took hold. This time, beyond the fixed rope, out on our own, Dougal's oxygen set refused to function. He was all for going back but first I decided to use my Swiss penknife, unscrewing the jubilee clips to find the pipes gunged up with ice. I flailed the pipes and mask against the rock of the yellow band. The ice came pouring out and Dougal again could breathe pure oxygen. He belayed me up the yellow band where I put in three pegs to gain the south summit couloirs. Dougal took up the challenge of unconsolidated snow thigh deep then waist deep and finally with me pushing from behind, chest deep, taking forever, time passing so quickly in that powder – so much so we didn't reach the south summit until 4.00pm late that afternoon.

ABOVE: Guarding the summit of Mount Everest is the Hillary Step, the last obstacle before reaching the top. On the South-West Face expedition in 1975 the normal rock pitch was banked out in monsoon snow with a granular quality, like sugar, that demanded the greatest care, especially for Dougal Haston who had to lead it. At 6.00pm later that day, 24 September, Scott and Haston became the first Brits to attain the summit, and the first to reach it by the new South-West Face route. 'We walked up side by side the last few paces to the top, arriving there together, and the entire world lay before us', Doug describes. 'That summit was everything and more than a summit should be. My usually reticent partner became expansive, his face broke out in a broad, happy smile and we stood there hugging each other and thumping each other's backs'.

Dougal, who had put in such a big effort, was all for bivouacking and going on to the summit in the morning. I knew if I did that I would only want to go down the next day, so after a brew I kept on going along the frontier ridge which was more consolidated right up to the Hillary Step. Dougal led us through in fine style. I led on towards the summit with my mind parting company from my body. I was now looking down upon my physical self from about 20m above my left shoulder from where I gave advice and direction. I watched myself

> No one climbing Everest is ever quite the same thereafter. We all come back a wiser man and in most cases more humble knowing we were one of the lucky ones to survive.

stumbling through the crusty snow and advised that if I didn't slow down and get a good rhythm going I would never make it. I saw I was heading towards the cornices on the right and told myself to keep left. It all seemed very natural at the time. It was only later down at Base Camp reflecting on the climb that this did seem a bit odd. So often these out of body experiences happen at the limit of endurance, the most common being to experience a 'third man syndrome' and to get into conversation with this presence at one's side. It is never anyone recognizable but nevertheless it gives comfort and confidence and can be a life-saver providing the advice offered is taken. It would seem by doing this sort of thing areas of our being which are normally hidden are revealed, as is the hidden help within.

At 6pm we finally walked up onto the summit together to watch the sun go down. Our headlamps failed descending the Hillary Step, wind had blown snow into our steps, our oxygen had run out and so we thought it prudent to bivouac at the south summit where we already had a small hollow from our brew stop which we enlarged into a cave. Strange things happened in that cave, sitting there on our rucksacks for nine hours in temperatures of around minus 40. Dougal had a long and very involved conversation with Dave Clark, our equipment officer, just as if Dave was there with him. 'They' were discussing the relative merits of various sleeping bags. Not having a sleeping bag was obviously very much on Dougal's mind. I began to think he was losing it, succumbing to cerebral odema until I realized I was in and out of conversations with my feet that had now become like two separate entities in the cave. I asked the right foot what could we do with the left and the left replied, complaining that I never used it, always kicking a

RIGHT: Doug Scott snoozes in the sunshine after his major attempt on Makalu in 1980. 'It was far more satisfying than after Everest', he describes. 'On Makalu the media was absent. Only our three Sherpas were in attendance and they were in the same headspace as ourselves'.

rugby ball with my right foot. In this dreamlike way it was getting through to my consciousness that I must pay the left foot more attention so it was off with the boot and sock to rub and pummel life back into a foot wooden with cold. The fact that we did survive then the highest bivouac ever, just 100m below the summit, without sleeping bags or oxygen, and as it turned out without frostbite, was to be the most significant part of the climb for me. I realized I could now risk an unplanned bivouac anywhere – that is, where there is snow enough to dig a cave to get out of the wind. That night at 8,750m feet widened the range of what and how I would climb in the future.

Despite what I and others have written and said about fixed ropes and all the support of men and materials on these big expeditions, widening the margin of safety so much as to leave one unsatisfied, and having pointed out that the fixed rope in particular takes out of climbing the main ingredient, which is to face up to uncertainty of outcome, nevertheless on the subsequent ascent our great friend and climber, Mick Burke, did not come back from the summit. The weather had changed and we think Mick, in the storm and whiteout, walked through the cornice hanging over the Kangshung Face. His companions, Peter Boardman and Pertemba Sherpa only just made Camp 6 by the skin of their teeth, having lost their way in the storm on the upper snowfield stumbling about in a complete whiteout, unable to distinguish snow in the air from snow on the ground. No one climbing Everest is ever quite the same thereafter. We all come back a wiser man and in most cases more humble knowing we were one of the lucky ones to survive.

It is there then at the *edge* of things where nothing else exists except rock, ice and snow that we come alive. Out of necessity we are more awakened to the moment and joy of being human when we are risking our lives. There is always the conundrum, however, that when again safe back home, we yearn to be back in the mountains to recharge our batteries, to lose ourselves, to know oneself at the frontiers of existence. We return home with renewed enthusiasm for all that has to be done, tackling problems more objectively for having stepped out of the usual, habitual routine, and now, even, more tolerant and generous towards others. In my case this state of affairs doesn't always last long and so I've had to seek regular journeys back to the mountains – because 'it' is there. The mountains around us help lift the spirit once again and bring 'it' all back home, a finer man for that just as it was in the beginning.

Cumbria, 2011

FURTHER READING

There have been a number of useful books detailing the innovation and adventure of photography's early years. From the moment that photographs are created they travel widely and take many paths. The ways that people now use and describe images is equal to this variety. This deliberately eclectic list is just a snapshot of this literature. The development of photography in the mountainous regions of the world deserves greater study.

• William Adams, *Mountains and Mountain Climbing: Records of Adventure and Enterprise Among The Famous Mountains of the World* (London: T. Nelson and Sons, 1883)

• George Band, *Summit: 150 Years of the Alpine Club* (London: Collins, 2006)

• Cecil Beaton and Gail Buckland, *The Magic Image: The Genius of Photography from 1839 to the Present Day* (London: Weidenfeld and Nicolson, 1975)

• Joe Bensen, *Souvenirs from High Places: A Visual Record of Mountaineering* (London: Mitchell Beazley, 1998)

• Chris Bonington, *Quest for Adventure* (London: Hodder and Stoughton, 1981)

• Graham Clarke, *The Portrait in Photography* (London: Reaktion, 1992)

• Carus Cunningham and Captain William Abney, *The Pioneers of the Alps* (London: Sampson Low, 1887)

• Glen Denny, *Yosemite in the Sixties* (Santa Barbara: Patagonia, 2007)

• Kurt Diemberger, *Enigma Himalaya* (Milan: Mondadori Electa, 2010)

• *Everest: Summit of Achievement* (London: Bloomsbury, 2003)

• Ranier Fabian and Hans-Christian Adam, *Masters of Early Travel Photography, 1839-1919* (London: Thames and Hudson, 1983)

• Fergus Fleming, *Killing Dragons: The Conquest of the Alps* (London: Granta Books, 2000)

• James Forbes, *Travels through the Alps of Savoy* (Edinburgh: Black, 1843)

• Roger Frison-Roche and Sylvain Jouty, *A History of Mountain Climbing* (Paris: Flammarion, 1996)

• Hereford George, *The Oberland and its Glaciers: Explored and Illustrated with Ice-Axe and Camera* (London: A.W. Bennett, 1866)

• Helmut Gernsheim, *The History of Photography: From the Camera Obscura to the Beginning of the Modern Era* (London: Thames and Hudson, 1969)

• Alfred Gregory, *Photographs from Everest to Africa* (London: Viking, 2008)

• Todd Gustavson, *Camera: A History of Photography from Daguerreotype to Digital* (New York: Sterling, 2009)

• Alan Hankinson, *Camera on the Crags: A Portfolio of Early Rock Climbing Photographs* (London: Heinemann, 1975)

• John Hannavy, *Masters of Victorian Photography* (Newton Abbot: David and Charles, 1976)

• Elizabeth Hawkins-Whitshed, *Hints on Snow Photography* (London: Sampson Low, 1895)

• Maurice Herzog, *Annapurna* (Paris: Arthaud, 1952)

• Steve House, *Beyond the Mountain* (Santa Barbara: Patagonia, 2009)

• John Hunt, *The Ascent of Everest* (London: Hodder and Stoughton, 1953)

• Maurice Isserman, *Fallen Giants: A History of Himalayan Mountaineering from the Age of Empire to the Age of Extremes* (New Haven: Yale University Press, 2008)

• Jack D. Ives and Bruno Messerli, *The Himalayan Dilemma: Reconciling Development and Conservation* (London: Routledge, 1989)

• Francis Keenlyside, *Peaks and Pioneers: The Story of Mountaineering* (London: Elek, 1975)

• Anthony Kenny, ed., *Mountains: An Anthology* (London: John Murray, 1991)

• Stefan Kruckenhauser, *Snow Canvas: Ski, Men and Mountains with the Leica* (Berlin: Elsner, 1937)

• Robert Macfarlane, *Mountains of the Mind* (London: Granta, 2003)

• Hamish MacInnes, *Climb to the Lost World* (London: Hodder and Stoughton, 1974)

• Giulio Malfer, *Sguardi Dall'Alto* (Rovereto: Nicolodi, 2002)

• Mary Warner Marien, *Photography: A Cultural History* (London: Laurence King, 2010)

• Bernadette McDonald and John Amatt, ed., *Voices from the Summit: The World's Great Mountaineers on the Future of Climbing* (Washington: National Geographic, 2000)

• Reinhold Messner, *Free Spirit: A Climber's Life* (London: Hodder and Stoughton, 1991)

• Douglas Milner, *Mountain Photography: Its Art and Technique in Britain and Abroad* (London: Focal Press, 1945)

• Colin Monteath, *Climb Every Mountain* (London: Francis Lincoln, 2006)

• W.H. Murray, *Mountaineering in Scotland* (London: J.M. Dent, 1947)

• Beaumont Newhall, *The History of Photography from 1839 to the Present Day* (London: Secker and Warburg, 1982)

• Sandra Noel, *Everest Pioneer: The Photographs of Captain John Noel* (Stroud: Sutton, 2003)

• Wilfrid Noyce, *Scholar Mountaineers: Pioneers of Parnassus* (London: Dennis Dobson, 1950)

• Jim Perrin, *The Climbing Essays* (Glasgow: The In Pinn, 2007)

• Paul Pritchard, *Deep Play: A Climber's Odyssey* (London: Baton Wicks)

• Galen Rowell, *The Art of Adventure Photography* (San Francisco: Sierra Club Books, 1995)

• Doug Scott, *Himalayan Climber* (London: Diadem, 1992)

• Joe Simpson, *Dark Shadows Falling* (London: Jonathan Cape, 1997)

• Christoffer Sjöström, *The Book of Candide* (Sweden: Fälth and Hässler, 2009)

• Francis Sydney Smythe, *The Mountain Scene* (London: Black, 1937)

• Ira Spring, *High Rocks and Ice: The Classic Mountain Photographs of Bob and Ira Spring* (Guildford: Falcon, 2004)

• *Summit: Vittoria Sella, Mountaineer and Photographer, the Years 1879-1909* (New York: Aperture, 1999)

• John Szarkowski, *The Photographer's Eye* (New York: Museum of Modern Art, 1966)

• Lionel Terray, *Conquistadors of the Useless* (London: Victor Gollancz, 1963)

• Stephen Venables, *First Ascent* (London: Cassell, 2008)

• Stephen Venables, *Painted Mountains* (London: Hodder and Stoughton, 1986)

• Bradford Washburn, *Mountain Photography* (Seattle: Mountaineers Books, 2000)

• Mike Weaver, ed., *The Art of Photography, 1839-1989* (New Haven: Yale University Press, 1989)

• Colin Wells, *Who's Who in British Climbing* (Buxton: The Climbing Company, 2008)

• Edward Whymper, *Scrambles Amongst the Alps in the Years 1860-69* (London: John Murray, 1871)

• Gordon Wiltsie, *To the Ends of the Earth: Adventures of an Expedition Photographer* (New York: Norton, 2006)

• Heinz Zak, *Rock Stars: The World's Best Free Climbers* (Munich: Rother, 1995)

ABOVE: Warren Harding on the last pitch of the North Face of the Rostrum, on the first ascent, 1962.

RIGHT: Nico Favresse and Sean Villanueva 'big-wall jamming' on their free repeat of the *South African Route*, East Face of Central Tower, Torres del Paine, by Ben Ditto, 2009.

INDEX 100 PORTRAITS

PICTURE CREDITS

Cory Richards: 2, 7, 24, 130-31, 152-53, 188-89, 222-23, 258-59, 260, 286, 287. **Nigel Millard:** front cover, 6, 7, 46-47, 62-63, 82-83, 142-43, 146-47, 164-65, 180, 199, 244-45, 286. **Royal Geographical Society:** 6, 16, 28-29, 30, 32, 38, 74, 182, 185, 242. **Doug Scott:** 6, 134-35, 272-73, 278, 279, 281. **Claudia Lopez:** 6, 7, 25, 50-51, 78-79, 240-41, 287, 288. **Private Collections:** 6, 7, 34, 39, 104, 140, 159, 192, 197, 268, 286, 287. **Kurt Diemberger:** 6, 54-55, 287. **Bogdan Jankowski:** 6, 94. **Gordon Wiltsie:** 7, 93, 208, 246-47, 248, 250, 255, 256, 262, 263. **Tom Frost:** 7, 132. **Chris Jones:** 7. **Jamling Tenzing:** 7. **John Norris:** 8-9. **Marko Prezelj:** 10-11, 22, 210, 235, 264-65. **The Alpine Club:** 12, 17, 18, 35, 37, 42-43, 52-53, 56, 69, 81, 89, 120, 136, 144-45, 148, 163, 179, 195, 224, 277. **Glen Denny:** 14-15, 48, 169, 175, 252-53, 254, 276, 282, 286. **Sir Chris Bonington:** 19, 67, 91, 138, 171. **Alexandre Buisse:** 20-21. **Thomas Senf:** 24, 26-27, 59, 287. **Hans-Ludwig Blohm:** 24. **Whyte Museum of the Canadian Rockies:** 41, 216-17. **Jimmy Marshall:** 61. **National Portrait Gallery:** 64, 73, 96. **Ed Luke:** 70, 166-67, 186-87, 214, 233, 236-37, 239. **Corbis:** 5, 76-77, 126-27, 129, 172-73, 204-05. **German Alpine Association:** 228-29. **Reinhold Messner:** 86-87. **Jimmy Chin:** 99, 206-07. **Nick Sinclair:** 100. **Ed Cooper:** 103, 286. **Rick Ridgeway:** 106-07. **Craig Richards:** 108-09. **Huberbuam:** 110-11. **Camerapress:** 112-13. **Martin Hartley:** 115. **Andy Anderson:** 116. **Greg Von Doersten:** 118-19. **Press Association:** 122-23. **Alastair Lee:** 124-25, 287. **Fondazione Riccardo Cassin:** 150-51. **Getty:** 154. **Pat Morrow:** 156. **Jim Whittaker:** 160. **Rex:** 176, 284-85. **Leo Houlding:** 191. **Eastern California Museum:** 200. **Christoffer Sjöström:** 202-03. **Klaus Fengler:** 212-13. **James Bowden:** 218. **Bruno Engler Archive:** 220, 286. **Corey Rich:** 227, 286. **Fredrik Schenholm:** 230-31, 287. **Jeff Curtes:** 266. **Ben Ditto:** 269, 283. **Christian Pondella:** 270. **Ed Webster:** 32, 271, 274. **Stephen Venables:** 286.

Wherever possible, when there is any doubt, effort has been made to identify the current copyright holders of imagery.

ACKNOWLEDGEMENTS

Huw Lewis-Jones: Thanks again to everyone who made this third book possible, in particular the super team at Conway, Liz House our dedicated and understanding designer, generous individuals, private collectors, exciting alpinists, a great number of talented photographers, and my friends and family. To John McCarthy, mentor and friend, who over many years has taught me to ask new questions, developing both a healthy level of disrespect for authority and a genuine respect for the mountains. And to Kari and little Nell, for your patience, love, and smiles, making a mad year nonetheless a wonderful one.

LEFT: Porters make steady progress up the Baltoro Glacier towards K2, 'through the inner sanctum of the Karakoram Himalaya, a hundred miles from the nearest road', by Galen Rowell, 1975. 'In 1989 I walked for ten days,' he lamented, 'only to find the same spot destroyed by the influence of man – a mess of military phone wires and other trash. A similar photograph can never again be taken as so many of our wilderness areas have become marred by human activity, by gross development, even war. Is there an end to all this?'